The
Welfare State Crisis
and the
Transformation of Social Service Work

The
Welfare State Crisis
and the
Transformation of Social Service Work

Michael B. Fabricant
Steve Burghardt

M.E. Sharpe Inc.
Armonk, New York • London, England

Library of Congress Cataloging-in-Publication Data

Fabricant, Michael.
The Welfare state crisis and the transformation of social service work /
by Michael Fabricant & Steve Burghardt.
p. cm.
Includes bibliographical references and index.
ISBN 0-87332-642-3 (cloth)
—ISBN 0-87332-643-1 (paper)
1. Social service—United States.
2. Public welfare—United States.
3. Poor—United States.
4. Welfare state.
I. Burghardt, Stephen.
II. Title.
HV91.F3   1992
361.973—dc20
91–21549
CIP

Printed in the United States of America

The paper used in this publication meets the minimum requirements of
American National Standard for Information Sciences—
Permanence of Paper for Printed Library Materials,
ANSI Z39.48–1984.

MV   10   9   8   7   6   5   4   3   2   1

With love, to
Betsy, Niki, and Matt
and
Lila and Josh

Contents

Foreword

As state and city governments everywhere confront the fiscal and political consequences of recession and federal abandonment, bureaucratically based professionals such as social workers, school teachers, and nurses must attend to the social and physical wreckage. They do so with fewer resources and less public sympathy. "Accountability" is now the watchword, and public mistrust has shifted from the fear of "welfare chiselers" to concern about overly indulgent service workers. Universally, one hears that clients, students, patients, are more psychologically damaged, less educationally prepared, sicker. Despite claims about the "thousand points of light," community resources are flickering and families are disintegrating under the weight of the "caregiver burden."

Our society *is* in crisis and social service workers are strategically and painfully positioned to see it. But do they? And, if they do, how do they explain it? What is their response? Indeed, how should they respond? Some of these questions are addressed indirectly, quantitatively, and, in many respects, atheoretically in Linda Cherry Reeser's and my recent book *Professionalization and Activism in Social Work: the 60's, the 80's and the Future* (Columbia University Press, 1990).

In the present work, Michael Fabricant and Steve Burghardt face these difficult questions directly. In so doing, they employ a neo-Marxist theoretical perspective and a qualitative research methodology. More specifically, their study represents a courageous attempt to describe and explain the crisis of the welfare state to those who are the inadvertent carriers of the "bad news."

Told from the alternating perspectives of political theorists and front-line workers, the book is doubly "courageous" because the former are generally loath to test their theories against the daily experience of those in the trenches and because the latter are generally unaware of, uninterested in, and curiously insulated from the broader political and economic significance of their work. Possibly, they would prefer not to know.

Their lack of political consciousness (or some would say "false consciousness") is a consequence of bureaucratic as well as psychological compartmentalization, myopic education and agency-tailored training, the preoccupation with professionalism, and the romance of technology. These forces allow people in public agencies to work for low pay, under the most alienating conditions, and with enormous resource deficits with the hopelessly deprived and downtrodden. That is, until "burnout" sets in. Then comes client-bashing, self-blame, substance abuse, psychosomatic illness, and/or the flight to private practice. Recently even this escape has proven illusory. Although these patterns preserve the bureaucratic machinery, they grind down the workers in the process. As a result, clients can only suffer more.

Moreover, as Fabricant and Burghardt effectively and powerfully demonstrate, these destructive and dysfunctional patterns are no longer confined to public bureaucracies. With "privatization" and purchase of service contracting, the infection has spread to those settings that were previously seen as most innovative and reflective of the highest standards of professional practice. Through the eyes of social service workers in health care, child welfare, family service, and employment counseling agencies, the authors document the deterioration of voluntary agency services and workers alike.

The natural response is to deny this reality. However, a reading of this book will not allow it. At the same time, Fabricant and Burghardt are not messengers of doom. Instead, they offer a sober yet hopeful, "generative" model of how social service workers might respond to the crisis. This response involves recapturing our history, our craft, our progressive mission. The authors neither indict social workers for the social ills they attempt to ameliorate nor do they impose upon social workers the unrealistic task of transforming society single-handedly. That transformation awaits a more comprehensive political theory and a broader sociopolitical movement. Nonetheless, this book offers a new building block to the construction of that political theory and places a new paving stone on the road to that movement.

Irwin Epstein, Ph.D.
Professor of Social Work
Hunter College School of Social Work

Acknowledgments

There are a number of people whom we wish to thank for their help in developing this book. The first, literally, are our students who, over the years, awakened us to the changing dimensions of their daily practice and, through their commitment to their clients, challenged us to explore more thoroughly the issues found in this book. We also extend the same gratitude to the workers from three agencies, whose perceptions of their daily work form the basis of the fourth chapter. While both the agencies and the workers must remain anonymous, the effort they extended to us will not be forgotten.

Mimi Abramovitz, Joel Blau, Irwin Epstein, and Betsy Fabricant all gave careful and helpful readings to various sections of the book. Marilyn Russell of the University of Southern Maine and Peter Pecora also provided us with some of their own important work, which helped us as we developed our ideas. We also wish to pay an intellectual debt to Fred Block, Christine Cousins, Paulo Freire, Ian Gough, M. L. Larson, Pat Morgan, and James O'Connor for the influence of their work on our own.

Tom Jennings and Judith Segel of the Hunter College School of Social Work were consistently available and remarkably adept at locating often-difficult reference and bibliographic material, always handling our requests with graciousness and professionalism.

Liz Addis, professional typist and amateur hieroglyphics expert by the end of the final draft, was a great help throughout. Philip Selikoff handled our duplicating needs with promptness, efficiency, and a dash of needed humor.

Michael Weber, Alexandra Koppen, and Susanna Sharpe, our editors at M.E. Sharpe, provided thoughtful, painstaking, and helpful comments throughout our work. Our book has been strengthened through their efforts.

Finally, we wish to thank our families and friends for all they endured over the last two years. Their love, support, and tolerance were all greatly appreciated.

Introduction

Over the course of the past eleven years, we have had many conversations with students both in and outside the classroom. A recurrent focus of these conversations has been the worsening conditions associated with social service work. The points made by students have remained fairly consistent. The increasing case loads, more complex problems of clients, and contraction of resources have profoundly affected the quality and content of their work. Equally important, they suggest that the very process of delivering services is changing.

Over time we discovered that the content and tone of these conversations was not idiosyncratic. As we discussed these issues with colleagues, it became clear that this dialogue was being privately conducted throughout the field. People knew that social service work was changing, but no one seemed to want to say why or, for that matter, to publicly examine the problem. Instead, the anecdotal war stories of increasingly dissatisfying work conditions have become a part of the folklore of the service professions. We realized that the oral communication of discrete anecdotal data, however useful and at times powerful, was no substitute for more systematic analyses.

This book emerged in response to many social service workers' vivid descriptions of changes in the practice of their craft and to the scanty literature that addressed these concerns. Few works have attempted to explore the interplay between the recent broader changes affecting the welfare state (cost containment, privatization, etc.) and the restructuring of social service work. For instance, the critical dialogue throughout the 1980s on fiscal cuts experienced by the welfare state was almost exclusively focused on policy issues and their effects on various populations. Rarely, if ever, were practice concerns given equal weight or even mentioned. Yet it is clear that the fiscal decisions of the 1980s profoundly affected both the context (intensifying bureaucratization) and content (deprofessionalization) of social service practice.

These larger forces have created significant changes for the line practitioner. The new services being offered by practitioners and developed by agencies are increasingly disconnected from the circumstances of clients. The greater emphasis on volume (productivity) in the face of resource scarcity is redefining service encounters in ways that are more likely to meet the quantitative fiscal needs of the agency and less likely to meet the qualitative service needs of the client or the professional needs of the worker. The service agency is increasingly emphasizing uniform, factory-like (industrial) practices in order to address the deepening dilemma of expanding service needs and intensifying cost-containment policies. These more uniform or industrial practices are restructuring the content, timing, and rhythm of encounters between worker and client, and contributing to a process of professional deskilling. Fundamentally, these new priorities are stimulating an ever-widening gulf between the service worker and client. Equally important, these pressures are further distancing service agencies from the community. Ultimately, the disaffection of clients and communities from social services threatens the very legitimacy of workers, agencies, and the welfare state.

The increased inability of social service workers to meet many of their historic practice obligations is part of a larger shift. The budget cuts experienced by the welfare state, and consequent changes in the structure of social services, are fundamentally linked to a declining U.S. economy. These policies are further destabilizing the living situations of poor people. The emergence of new subgroups of the poor, such as the homeless, can also be directly traced to these policies.

We argue that the deepening fiscal crisis of the past two decades has placed the enterprise of social services at risk. Hospitals, child welfare settings, and employment training programs are but a few of the service agencies that are increasingly unable to carry out their basic functions. As these institutions break down, media and professional associations are blaming the decay in the quality of service on the incompetence of individual workers. This response is not unlike a range of welfare state policies that blame poor people individually and collectively for their circumstances.

Yet as we enter the 1990s, government is indicating that it is preparing to do less, not more, to help support poor communities and social service agencies. The federal government's 1990 deficit reduction package has marked both Medicare and employment training programs for deep cuts. Equally important, state and city governments are not likely to reallocate resources to make up for these federal policies as they did in the 1980s. A growing number of state and municipal governments are also faced with substantial deficits. Clearly, this is a grim and increasingly bleak period for almost all Americans, but especially for the poor and very poor.

This book is principally devoted to exploring the dynamic interplay between the implementation of cost-containment policies and the changing structure and content of social service practice. It will also be the purpose of this inquiry to richly describe the emergent industrial structure of social services. A number of the tendencies that will be discussed are not new phenomena. Many of the points that will be raised represent historic areas of tension for professional social service workers. These struggles to some extent germinated from the bureaucratization of social services. Bureaucratizing tendencies (centralization, uniform practices, paperwork) have been dramatically intensified during this most recent period of fiscal crisis. Consequently, a new balance is being struck between the needs of organization, worker, and community. As has been suggested, this reconfiguration of service priorities is increasingly emphasizing the needs of the bureaucracy or state at the expense of the service worker and client. It is within this crucible of familiar but heightened tensions and ongoing struggles between economic constraints and worker needs that the character of professional social service work is being recreated.

This book is comprised of five chapters. The first chapter briefly sketches recent shifts in the American economy and their relationship to the deepening and changing nature of poverty. More specifically, the recent redistribution of wealth, the creation of an expanded service economy, and the growing economic crisis are discussed. The relationship between these trends and the mounting problems of the elderly, young women on AFDC (Aid to Families with Dependent Children), and men of color are also discussed.

The second chapter explains recent changes in the welfare state using the theoretical frameworks of conservatives, liberals, and neo-Marxists. The deficiencies embedded in each of these formulations are described. This part of the discussion concludes that the neo-Marxist perspective is best able to explain the complex relationship between the private economy and the welfare state. Recent neo-Marxist analyses, however, have overly stressed broad policy changes. Chapter 2 attempts to expand this framework through its analysis of the changing, contradictory nature of the social service labor process and the struggle of workers to improve or accept the conditions.

Chapters 3 and 4 are intended to correct this imbalance. These chapters focus on the interaction between broader social forces and the role of the service worker. Chapter 3 specifically describes the impact of recent cost-containment policies on public social service work. The chapter draws on a broad literature to document the substantial effect of these policies on social service practice in public hospitals, child welfare agencies, and welfare programs. This part of the analysis suggests that the most advanced forms of industrialized and bureaucratized practice are found in public service agencies. The stages of development of these programs are a direct consequence of less control over intake, greater legal obligation(s) to serve the poorest and often most difficult populations, and a less diversified funding base than not-for-profit agencies.

Conversely, not-for-profit agencies are presumed to be relatively insulated and consequently more able to protect their work force from the debilitating consequences of cost-containment policies. In a sense, not-for-profits continue to be perceived as settings that nurture service innovation and quality. This point of view is consistent with historic beliefs regarding the special role or function of nonprofits. it is therefore reasonable to use nonprofits as a kind of baseline for practice or service change. In effect, not-for-profits represent a barometer of the minimal levels of practice change experienced by the welfare state.

Consequently, as presented in chapter 4, the particular impact of recent cost-containment policies on not-for-profits was examined, and a qualitative inquiry on their labor process was initiated. Three not-for-profit agencies in the New York City metropolitan area providing health, children's, and employment training services were investigated. We believe that the New York City experience is not idiosyncratic. On the contrary, national problems ranging from municipal fiscal crises to homelessness are often foreshadowed through events and responses that first emerge within New York. (A fuller discussion of the strengths and limits of the study's method is presented in Appendix 4–A.) The fundamental test of the study's accuracy, however, is the extent to which it resonates with the experience of a broad cross section of service workers throughout the country. We are confident that the study findings will pass this most critical test.

The final chapter identifies and summarizes the central findings of the qualitative study. New service strategies, such as intensive case management, designed to address fundamental dilemmas and deficits of the present service structure are also discussed. The particular strengths and weaknesses of these models are noted.

These relatively limited response to a fundamental institutional and community breakdown provided us with the stimulus necessary to develop an alternative formulation of social services. This alternative approach (named generative social services) emphasizes learning, experimentation, and growth. Our discussion struggles to integrate the primary but often fragmented concerns of social services with individual, organizational, communal, and social change processes into a coherent vision. We then address the dilemmas or contradictions that are a by-product of this service approach.

Ironically, as social problems expand and decay into a new order of complexity (e.g., from public housing problems to outright homelessness), there seems to be a certain resignation to these new realities. This passivity is greatly affected by economic instability and a growing sense that both government and social services as they are presently constituted cannot alter these conditions. These public concerns represent primary themes of this analysis. It is imperative that we marshal the necessary resources, resolve, and imagination to address a range of critical social problems.

This effort is essential if we are to stem the rapid decay in the quality of life for a broad cross section of communities. However, if future initiatives are to have any hope of succeeding, we must first understand the context and content of present programmatic failures. Only in this way can we develop approaches that do not unwittingly replicate the conditions that led to the present dysfunction of social service agencies. We hope that this book contributes to a widening dialogue on the critical relationships among economic crisis, fiscal policy, organizational structure, practice, and the delivery of social services.

The
Welfare State Crisis
and the
Transformation of Social Service Work

1 • The Response to the Poor by a Debtor State: The Economic and Social Crises of the 1990s

Introduction: Unanswered Questions in Unsettling Times

Judy R. graduated from social work school in 1986 with a master's degree in social work and a deep commitment to work with the homeless. She accepted a low-paying job as coordinator of social services in a North Philadelphia homeless shelter. She loved her work with the homeless women and children who crowded her facility: finding needed entitlements, working with a mothers' support group, watching joy and hope fill the faces of families as they learned they would soon be moving to permanent housing.

Judy R. loved her work until the summer of 1990, that is, for at the end of the summer the city of Philadelphia, confronted with a $206 million deficit and a bond rating so poor that it could no longer sell its municipal bonds, withdrew almost all funding for homeless shelter facilities across the city (Hinds 1990a, 1990b). Even though the homeless population of Philadelphia continued to expand, Judy R. was out of a job.

Across the nation in the rural California county of Butte, Dorothy S., a native of Oroville, works as a Department of Social Services employee, handling cases of the one in six county residents who receive some form of welfare assistance. The size of its welfare load, comprised of chronically unemployed, unskilled workers, welfare recipients, and retirees on fixed incomes, is so large that 57 percent of the county budget goes to some form of social service. However, because the 185,000-person county, nestled in the center of the state about sixty miles from Sacramento, faces a deficit of $14.1 million in the coming year and is without prospects for increased tax revenues, the county supervisors are now considering filing for bankruptcy (Bishop 1990). Recent data indicate that counties in Kentucky, Oklahoma, and West Virginia are confronting the same option (Bishop 1990). No county in the United States has ever gone bankrupt, and Dorothy S. is worried about her future. Whether the state rescues the county or not, she is thinking about leaving Oroville for Sacramento.

In New Jersey, Robert G., a medical social worker with fifteen years' experience, attends a burnout seminar sponsored by his social service department because he feels overwhelmed by the tidal wave of Medicaid and Medicare forms on his desk. This paperwork, in combination with the restrictive procedures of Diagnostic Review Groups (DRGs), has left Robert with little time to meet with his clients, many of whom seem far sicker than his patients of ten years ago. He indicates that "the hospital expects me to do more and more, especially with all their forms, and I think I'm just doing a lot less than our patients need, and they need more than ever before. . . . What's going on?"

Robert's question is echoed in the brief stories of these other social workers. They are people involved in what they know to be important and vital work. Their client populations have been expanding, not shrinking, and significant sections of those populations have problems far more chronic and complex than in the past. But just as the needs of the poor are increasing, the economic wherewithal to handle the financing of service interventions seems to be collapsing. How can it be that in this nation of ours, long assumed to be the richest and most powerful on earth, such problems are now emerging?

This unsettling question is asked more and more as people become aware that our nation is in deep economic trouble. For example, discussions of deficits and lost revenues are not simply the domain of rural California counties and beleaguered northeastern cities. Deficit discussions occur at the federal level every year, and yet annually the deficits grow larger. Counting the cost of the Savings and Loan (S & L) bailout, we now face deficits that will average $339 billion annually through 1995 (Peterson 1990). It is quite troubling indeed when the largest rate of increase in the budget is for debt financing.

Equally unsettling is the fact that revenues—the other side of every budget equation—are so much smaller. If revenues come from income, profits, savings, and wealth, does this talk of "larger deficits" not mean that our nation—not just an occasional rural county or an old eastern city—is in a deep economic crisis? Yet how could there be a drop in revenues when the number of millionaires doubled between the late 1970s and late 1980s? (Phillips 1990). By 1988, three million people were registered as millionaires, yet our national assets at the end of the decade dropped below those of Japan. (In 1985 our national assets stood at $30.6 trillion, compared to $19.6 trillion for Japan. Two years later our assets had risen to $36.2 trillion, overtaken by Japan's astounding 120 percent increase to $43.7 trillion [Phillips 1990; Shimbun 1990]). How could the United States have fallen so quickly from its position as the world's richest nation?

The problems of Judy, Dorothy, and Robert are experienced as personal work issues. However, it is increasingly clear to the American public that there are close links between the problems in Washington, where politicians on nationwide television networks discuss debt in the trillions, and the stresses of downtown Oroville, where, over coffee and donuts at the local diner, county supervisors cannot find a way out of their financial woes. Likewise, it is increasingly obvious that there is an important relationship between the closing of a North Philadelphia shelter and the ongoing inability of American firms to compete with the Japanese.

These intensifying relationships are troubling, for they foreshadow greater economic constraints and more combustible social conditions. A clearer understanding of these deepening crises, along with the development of viable responses, will only emerge if the times demand it.

The 1990s may be such times.

A Deeper Look at the Financial Problems of the 1990s

The budget impasse, now a yearly event in Washington, is probably the most powerful symbol of the deepening economic crisis. Hard-to-follow discussions of debt, as well as the annual federal debate over which taxes to raise and what services to cut in order to accommodate yearly shortfalls in revenues, are as common to the evening news in early September as the weather forecast—and about as reliable. The ominous call by various politicians to resolve the deficit crisis "so that we do not burden our children's futures" rings as a disquieting, longer-term alarm. A more immediate debacle is promised if the dreaded Gramm–Rudman law—with its draconian 10 percent across-the-board cuts of the entire budget—goes into effect on any October 1 that should dawn without a federal budget. Between the clarion calls of doom and the saber rattling, huge numbers reeled before the American public in 1990 as Washingtonians argued over an annual budget of $1.5 *trillion*. A number of the specific costs associated with this budget included: a $500 billion Savings and Loan bailout (Peterson 1990); a $108 billion expenditure on Medicare (10.9 percent higher than the year before) (Freudenheim 1990); an $18.1 billion allocation for Food Stamps (an increase of 22 percent from 1989) (Pear 1990c); and $216 billion in interest payments on debt in 1988 (an astounding 150 percent increase in only five years) (Phillips 1990). The numbers are substantial, and growing.

Equally important, Americans continue to hear unsettling news about our country's ability to pay. For example, weekly *per worker* income, adjusted for inflation, dropped from $366 in 1972 to $312 in 1987, a 15 percent decline that represents a part of the government's shrinking tax base (Phillips 1990, p. 15). Likewise, within a three-year period (1984–87), the United States' overall wealth, which includes savings, real estate, insurance, stocks, and income, dropped far behind Japan's ($36.9 trillion compared to $43 trillion) (Shimbun 1990). Why are the incomes of American workers in rapid decline? Why is Japan's wealth increasing so much more rapidly than America's? Can the disturbing tension between the federal government's ballooning expenses and diminished revenues be explained adequately?

Politicians and pundits in Washington have provided little guidance. More adequate explanations for this deepening crisis lie not within the budgetary process itself, but within the broader economy that frames the legislative decision-making process.

The Decline of the American Economy:
Deindustrialization and the Restratification of the Labor Force

It is no accident that economists often compare the real wages of American workers in the 1990s to those in early 1970s. For it was during this period that the profitability of American manufacturing firms rapidly declined (Bluestone and Harrison 1982, 1988). Blaming their problems on high wages, high taxes, aging manufacturing plants, inflation, and the declining infrastructure of the American manufacturing heartland (Sale 1981), the leaders of American capitalism intensified a process of industrial "restructuring."

The three basic prongs of this industrial policy have had a direct impact on the jobs people hold and their per capita real income. The first prong of this tripartite strategy was the globalization of American-owned industry. Within this context, American firms relocated large sectors of their business apparatus to countries with far less costly labor forces and negligible corporate taxes. This process has contributed to plant shutdowns and a loss of 39 percent of the U.S. jobs that existed in 1969 (Bluestone and Harrison 1982).

Indeed, the 1990 census reveals a precipitous drop in manufacturing jobs; in 1950, manufacturing accounted for 38.9 percent of all employees in private industry, compared to only 21.6 percent in 1990 (Phillips 1990). In short, the American economy is no longer a manufacturing-based economy, and the relatively high-paying jobs common to manufacturing industries ($22,000 annually, on average, according to Bluestone and Harrison) are an endangered species.

The second prong is the shift of private industry into the service and finance sectors of the economy. In the 1950s, only 17.5 percent of all workers could be found in these industries, compared to 37.1 percent today. In effect, the proportion of American workers laboring in service industries during the past forty years has doubled. Indeed, over 70 percent of all the new jobs created during the last twenty years are located within these sectors (Rothschild 1981; Harrison 1987).

Finally, the average service job wage is little more than half the average manufacturing wage—$12,500 a year (Rothschild 1981; Levy 1987; Thurow 1988). Furthermore, the structure of the workplace is different. The average service sector income of $12,500 is based on a thirty-five-hour week. However, the trend within the service sector is toward a reduced workweek. Part-time has replaced overtime as the new jobs in insurance, real estate, and other service industries average 15 percent fewer work hours per week (Harrison 1987; Thurow 1988). The result is that weekly wages are substantially lower in service industries than in manufacturing: 46.5 percent in retail trade and 75.3 percent in insurance, real estate, and finance (Bureau of Labor Statistics 1984).

The implications of this restructuring are obvious for workers. Their real incomes have diminished. As has already been noted, the economy is increasingly producing jobs that pay less and offer a reduced workweek, thus necessitating an increase in the number of dual and triple wage earners in each household. Such "doubling up" is necessary if the family is to approximate a middle-class life style. Particularly critical to this discussion is the relationship between shrinking wages and a contracting tax base.

Increased Wealth in the 1980s

As was mentioned earlier, the number of millionaires doubled between the late 1970s and the end of the 1980s (*Forbes* 1987). Between 1980 and 1988, the top 1 percent of Americans increased their income share from 9 to 11 percent, the highest ratio since the Census Bureau began collecting income statistics in the late 1940s (Phillips 1990). In 1981, Americans with the largest incomes (the top 1 percent) received 8.1 percent of the country's total reported income; by 1986, their share had risen to 14.7 percent. How can this rapid expansion of wealth be explained in the midst of the concurrent decline in Middle America's real income?

Unlike the robber barons of the industrial revolution, who, despite their ruthlessness, were "wresting a semblance of industrial stability out of the chaos left by the Civil War" (Burt 1987, p. 50), today's financial titans did not create their wealth through *investment leading to productive industrial growth and widespread job creation*. As Harvard economist Benjamin Friedman reports, the net business investment even during the halcyon Reagan years of 1983–86 ran *below* the thirty-year average of the fifties, sixties, and seventies (Friedman 1988, pp. 198–201; also Phillips 1990). As Phillips indicates, "corporations were simply buying other companies, merging, taking on debt to go private, or otherwise reshuffling structures and assets. In the wake of the 1981 tax cuts, American business enjoyed rising profits and cash flow, but much of what they were spending it on was an ersatz enterprise—*paper entrepreneurialism.*" (Phillips 1990, p. 70).

More concretely, before 1981 American business invested about 12.2 percent of its total income in new plants and machinery (a clear measure of industrial expansion and job creation). Since then, the percentages have fluctuated wildly—on an essentially downward spiral culminating in 11.3 percent in 1989, one of the lowest levels since World War II (*Los Angeles Times* 1987; Phillips 1990). This trend at least partially explains the drop in America's share of world GNP from about 40 percent in the 1950s to an expected approximate level of 25 percent in the 1990s (Phillips 1990, p. 115).

Part of the puzzle falls into place with these figures. The poor and middle-income sectors of the population are earning less because of the diminished job opportunities available to them in an economy that is investing less and less in job creation. But how did the entrepreneurs of the eighties grow so rich?

The Use of Debt

Quite simply, the rich made their wealth through new debt instruments, not the expansion of productive capacity. According to Grieder (1987, p. 501):

> As the percentage of national income by wages and income shrank in the early 1980s, the relative contribution of interest soared—a record 14 percent by 1982. By 1984, interest payments and stock dividends combined would total 20 percent of national income, up from 11 percent in 1979—almost a hundred percent increase!

Kevin Phillips's discussion on the rise of debt in the 1980s is illuminating. (See Phillips 1990, esp. ch. 4.) He summarizes the panoply of debt structures that emerged in the Reagan years:

> household debt climbed to over $3 trillion, while U.S. nonfinancial corporate indebtedness grew to $2 trillion (with 25 percent of cash flow being used for debt service). . . . And just as they had done sixty years ago (in the pre-Depression 1920s) new forms of debt became an art form. The financial community pioneered hundreds . . . Wall Street even turned car loans, boat loans, credit-card bills and recreational-vehicle loans into "asset-backed securities." . . . Federal government deficit strategies were equally loose . . . they allowed federal credit programs to balloon from $300 billion in 1984 to $500 billion in 1989. (Phillips 1990, p. 114)

And this was before the scope of the Savings and Loan crisis became clear.

At some point debt must be paid. If the S & Ls go under, insured deposits must be protected; bearer bonds mature and must be borne; stockholders look over their portfolios and expect their rates of return to keep rising. However, the debt of the 1980s has proved to be the house of cards that economists like Reich, Bluestone, Harrison, and

Thurow always feared. The payments that fall due, *because they have not been invested in productive growth*, can only be paid through the creation of more debt. Like the overstretched credit card holder who takes an even higher-interest loan to pay his or her bills, the financial windfall of the 1980s can only be maintained if someone pays more dearly than they did in the past. At a certain point this upward cycle of debt is no longer viable for either the individual or the economy. The recent breakdown and withdrawal from this process of rapid debt accumulation has resulted in the loss of jobs in the boom sector of the 1980s; for instance, financial services were down 27,500 jobs nationwide in 1990, with the bottom nowhere in sight (Phillips 1990). Chase Manhattan alone has announced a reduction of 5,000 employees (*New York Times*, September 22, 1990, p. 1). In short, the debt crisis in the private sector has come full circle. It is presently contributing to the rapid destabilization of various sectors of the economy.

The implications of these recent trends in the private sector are ominous: The manufacturing base is smaller, and the service economy is built on a disproportionately high percentage of debt. For the public sector, this means that the ability either to create more revenues or to increase expenditures is less possible. The pain of increased public debt is becoming more evident, as people are taxed at higher levels on lower real income.

A Closer Look at the Fiscal Crisis of the State

The previous discussion helps to explain the smaller and more debt-ridden private sector of capitalist America in the 1990s. It also clarifies the revenue crises of cities, counties, and states. But what about Washington? Given its traditional roles since the 1930s of aiding American business while supporting (at least in part) its most desperate populations, we must ask whether it is in a financial position to aid the private sector and/or various populations whose needs are increasing.

The answers here are equally unsettling. There was substantial debt creation under Reagan. The 1981 tax revisions, combined with other adjustments over the decade, have led to a greatly diminished burden on the wealthiest Americans—those most able to pay. After looking at shifts in Social Security taxes, federal income taxes, and other tax changes (from capital gains to bracket shifts), Kevin Phillips sums up the outcome of Reagan's tax policies succinctly:

Under Reagan, as under Coolidge, the clear evidence is that the net tax burden on rich Americans as a percentage of their total income *shrank* substantially because of the sweeping tax cuts. The surge in actual tax payments was the result of higher upper-bracket incomes. To measure the benefits, imagine a businessman who had made $333,000 in salary, dividends, and capital gains in 1980, and paid $120,000 in federal income taxes. As prosperity returned in 1983, his income climbed to $500,000. Yet with the applicable tax rates reduced, he might well have paid, say, $150,000 in taxes, *more actual payment,* of course, but *less relative burden.* That many blue-collar and middle-class Americans have lost their jobs in 1981–82 . . . also helps explain why the top 1 percent of all taxpayers—disproportionate beneficiaries of a surging stock market—wound up shouldering a higher percentage of the overall federal income tax burden. They were gaining while the bottom half of the population was losing. "Soaked" is hardly the term to describe what happened to millionaires paying out lower percentages of sharply rising incomes. (Phillips 1990, p. 82)

Phillips further notes that because increased Social Security taxes reduced the modest benefits of those income tax changes for middle-income groups, the "upper echelon alone was projected to benefit from a large net reduction in effective overall tax rates for the entire 1977–1988 period" (Phillips 1990, p. 83; see also Congressional Budget Office 1987, Table 8, p. 48). Clearly, the amount of potential revenues forgone by the federal government soared in the 1980s.

That the Reagan administration returned between $40 billion and $80 billion a year to the wealthy (through forgone taxes) was only one aspect of the budgetary problem. In order to continue paying for entitlements, defense expenditures, and an already huge debt, new resources had to be located. Additional public debt was therefore incurred. According to Phillips (1990, p. 90), "Under Reagan, annual federal expenditures on interest would climb from $96 billion in 1981 to . . . $216 billion in 1988." No other expense, including defense (which did rise from 23 to 28 percent of the budget between 1980 and 87) or human resources (down from 28 to 22 percent in the same time period) rose so sharply (Center on Budget and Policy Priorities 1990).

In order to finance this rapidly expanding debt structure and to attract investors, the interest rate on federal bonds increased to 12 percent. Some of the buyers were Americans—that wealthy top half of 1 percent who could afford them (Grieder 1987, p. 401). But many of the largest investors in U.S. bonds were from Germany and Japan. These investors were understandably attracted to federal bonds that promised interest rates twice their own countries' 5 to 6 percent rates of return.

 The results of these policies were more startling than perhaps even the staunchest American entrepreneurs had anticipated. As Lester Thurow put it, "When Ronald Reagan became President, the United States was the world's largest creditor nation. When he left the presidency, we were the world's largest debtor nation. In 1980, we had a trade account surplus of $166 billion; by 1987, we had an indebtedness to foreigners of $340 billion" (Thurow 1988, p. 14).

 The combination of a federal government ridden with financial crises and an economically weakened private sector, bloated on debt and experiencing diminished productive growth, largely explains why America no longer has the world's strongest economy. It is evident in the 1990s that America has diminished resources. At the local level, where programs are implemented, there is a dynamic interplay between the troubles in the larger political economy (the federal government and the private economy) and the breakdown in the delivery of social services. Homeless shelters, hospital programs, and other social services are being affected by the economic priorities created in the debt-ridden eighties. Given present political alignments, such programs have suffered the lash of cutback and the sting of financial retrenchment. Not unlike middle-income workers in the United States, service programs must make do with less. These programs, however, are distinguished by their work with the most desperate sectors of the American population—the chronically ill homeless person, the pregnant teenager on crack, or the unskilled entry-level worker earning minimum wage who cannot feed her family.

By looking at these exploding populations of the poor, the dilemmas of the economic crisis (and resultant financial constraints placed on social programs) are ground in terms every social worker can understand. The economic decisions of the last ten years have contributed to a rising tide of social problems (homelessness, hunger, etc.). Poverty and its consequent social dislocations do not disappear simply because the programs to serve the poor are cut back. As we will see later in this chapter, problems simply reappear in more intensified form, as witnessed, for example, by the explosive growth in the need for foster care rather than preventive family services.

In the 1990s, American policymakers may have to engage social problems differently than they have in the past, because today, for the first time in American history, the problems of the poor must be approached from the weakened position of a debtor state.

Beyond the "Intensification of Poverty": The Response to the Poor by a Debtor State

It is important to reiterate that as the real income of the American worker is dropping, the incidence of poverty is increasing. The extent of this correlation is hotly debated in part because a tenth of a percentage point of new poor adds millions of dollars to various entitlement programs such as Food Stamps and Medicaid.

Budget Cuts and the Expansion of Poverty

The Census Bureau determined that in 1989 only 9 percent of the population was poor. This percentage is relatively low because various government benefits were factored into the calculations. The "official" poverty-level income of $12,092 for a family of four places the number at 31 million, or 13 percent of the population. A more liberal formula, which substitutes escalating housing expenses for food as a more reliable measure, places the numbers at 44.6 million and 18 percent, respectively (U.S. Census Bureau 1990; Center on Budget and Policy Priorities 1990; Families USA Foundation 1990).

Despite the debate on the precise dimensions of poverty, there is a general emergent consensus that an increasing number of Americans are falling into poverty. The middle-range figure of 13 percent places more Americans below the poverty line now than at any other time in the post–World War II era, except the early 1980s (Bluestone and Harrison 1988; Levitan 1985; Burghardt and Fabricant 1987, p. 17).

American poverty has recently expanded after a period of unprecedented growth in the welfare state. For approximately a fifty-year period, entitlements and benefits available to the aged, the unemployed, poor single parents, and the disabled (while lower than those of any other industrialized nation) consistently expanded. (For an extended discussion of these populations and the entitlements they have received, see Burt and Pittmann 1985; Danziger 1989; Burghardt and Fabricant 1987.) More recently, however, with the emergence of the economic crisis and the rise of the debtor state, access to and benefit levels of entitlement programs have diminished. Overall, cash welfare benefits (including Food Stamps and AFDC) declined by 17 percent in the early 1980s (Hopper and Hamberg 1984). By 1989, the maximum AFDC benefit had declined by 37 percent (Blum 1990). "In 1988, the maximum AFDC cash benefit for a three-person family was one-eighth of the median income of three-person families in the United States ($33,614)," lower than at any time since the 1950s (Blum 1990, p. 42).

As for unemployment insurance, in 1988, "only 31.5 percent of all unemployed workers received unemployment insurance in an average month . . . the lowest rate ever recorded in the program's history . . . and the fifth consecutive year that . . . coverage either set or tied a new record low. The [unemployment insurance] coverage rate now is well below the levels of the late 1970s" (Center on Budget and Policy Priorities, p. 50). Ninety percent of all working families on welfare had their benefits reduced or eliminated, while Social Security Disability Insurance (SSDI) cuts affected 450,000 disability recipients (Rich 1989). The results were clear: federal outlays for all human services between 1980 and 1987 had dropped from 28 percent to 22 percent (Center on Budget and Policy Priorities 1990).

The Varying Effects of Age, Race, and Gender on the Intensification of Poverty

The Impact of Age

Government cutbacks have affected all poor and near-poor citizens. However, specific social groups have experienced the effects differently. For example, the effect on the elderly is less pronounced. In 1960, 25 percent of the elderly were classified as poor, compared to 12.6 percent of the entire population. By the early 1980s, 14 percent of the total population and 15 percent of the elderly lived in poverty. By the mid-1980s, the percentages were reversed. For the first time, older Americans were marginally less poor than other Americans (Burt and Pittmann 1985, p. 117).

The reasons for this economic shift relate to the increased size and political power of older Americans as a group. Recently, the elderly have pushed to strengthen certain sectors of the welfare state, especially Social Security and Medicare. Attacks leveled against Social Security by the Reagan administration and others have consistently failed because of the rapid and effective responses of organizations of the elderly.

Other key entitlements, such as Medicare, have not been as immune to cost-cutting policies (see Olson 1982). Medicare has been under attack because of the escalating costs of health care. Between 1947 and 1987, expenditures for health care grew 2.5 percent faster annually than expenditures for other goods and services (Fuchs 1990, p. 534). In 1989, the United States spent a colossal $600 billion on health services, a sum that was more than 11 percent of the Gross National Product (GNP). The annual spending on Medicare represents one of the largest rates of increase in health care costs. Medicare cost $108.2 billion in 1990, over a fifth of all health care expenses. Consequently, this entitlement has been targeted by public officials desperately attempting to cut costs.

These attacks have occurred despite the solvency of Medicare (the *Social Security Bulletin* projects a surplus in Medicare until 1998 [*New York Times*, March 29, 1990, p. 1]) and have most affected the poor elderly and those with long-term illness. The deductible for the first sixty days of care in 1990 was $420, a 100 percent increase since 1980. This represents at least 18 percent of the yearly income for recipients receiving minimal benefits. In 1990 at least $15,000 was borne by a private individual or an insurance carrier for serious, long-term illness, an expense twice that of 1981. For the poor, of course, these trends are all the more frightening because Medicaid has been cut by 10.1 percent since 1981. The total dollar value of these cuts is over $20 billion (Brand 1985, pp. 15–17).

The trends are obvious—costs are skyrocketing and benefits eroding, especially for the poorest older Americans. Politically constrained from making wholesale cuts or passing on more expenses to the entire elderly population, the health care system has devised other programmatic responses that specifically target the poor. For example, Diagnostic Review Groups (DRGs) have been designed to limit the length of hospital stays and possible duplication of costly services. This system assigns a fixed value for every health procedure diagnosis and a maximum period of treatment for each Medicare patient. In effect, the more rapidly the hospital discharges the patient, the more profitable the reimbursement. If the patient stays longer than the allotted time period, the hospital pays the difference. The elderly poor, who have been found to have more complicated illnesses that require longer periods of hospitalization, are less likely to receive the care they need, thus increasing the likelihood of repeated hospitalizations and the emergence of even more serious illnesses (cf. Kotelchuk 1984; Olson 1982).

The impact of DRGs on the quality and availability of health care services to poor Americans is easily derived from the following data. A study released by the District of Columbia Hospital Association indicates that the overall cost per case rises dramatically as a hospital's volume of poor patients increases. After comparing 257 hospitals in five major metropolitan areas, investigators discovered that *Medicare* costs averaged $568 more per case among hospitals when 10 percent (compared to 0 percent) of a hospital's total volume of cases were *Medicaid* patients. Even more dramatically, the costs were $1,118 higher per case when the percentages of Medicaid patients reached 30 percent of the hospital's total case load (Ashby 1984).

The implications are obvious. First, public hospitals will have far more costly poor elderly patients—those who are the most likely to go beyond DRG maximum limits. This means that public hospitals are much more likely to be in the red as they are forced to pay for these cost overrides. Second, private hospitals are "dumping" their poor patients at the doors of the financially overstretched public hospitals, which can least afford to respond to the poor, but under law must provide health care (Kotelchuk 1985). The result is that more and more public hospitals are being forced to close their doors to populations who need them the most. More public hospitals have closed during the 1980s than in any other decade (Koplin 1990). Finally, the quality of care for the elderly and others at the remaining facilities, already short-staffed and overburdened, has deteriorated (Fergin 1985).

The Impact of Race and Gender

While the elderly as a social group have had a varied experience during the 1980s, there has also been a rapid intensification of poverty among poor people of color. It is important to underscore that this discussion, while centering on poor African-Americans, is not about the entire African-American community. As Billingsley (1990, p. 91) recently pointed out, the family income of intact, two-parent African-

American families actually rose during the 1980s. However, the differences within the African-American community are becoming more pronounced. For example, the number of two-parent African-American families dropped from 48 percent in 1980 to 37 percent in 1990, while the number of female-headed, single-parent African-American households rose from 49 percent to 57 percent in the same time period (Billingsley 1990, p. 91).

The percentage of nonpoor working-class African-American families dropped from 44 percent in 1980 to 36 percent by 1986. During the same period, the underclass expanded from slightly less than 10 percent to over 14 percent—an expansion Billingsley traces directly to the families who were once part of the working class but have been hardest hit by the economic crisis.

We can see how devastating these shifts are by focusing on two groups that at present are the subject of much social welfare policy analysis: young African-American men and women living in poverty. For poor, young African-American males, the economic crisis and the budget cuts under Reagan have led to spiraling rates of unemployment, violent crime, and entry into the criminal justice system; for their female counterparts, the results have been a lack of job opportunity, increased teen pregnancy, and an entrenched presence within the child welfare system.

In 1980, the employment rate for black teenagers fell to 27 percent, compared to 53 percent for whites. While overall employment levels for both teen populations improved during the 1980s (in part because of the shrinking size of the overall youth population), the employment ratio worsened, growing from slightly less than 2 to 1 to 2.5 white teens employed for every 1 African-American teenager (National Urban League 1990). As Freeman and Holzer (1989) noted, "In many respects, the urban employment characteristics of Third World countries appear to have taken root among Black youths in the United States."

At the same time that young African-Americans were unable to find employment, the federal government was severely restricting job training and work incentive programs. For example, the budgets of the Summer Youth Assistance programs were cut from $1.1 billion in 1981 to $696 million by 1989; the Work Incentive Program was cut from $527 million to $97 million during the same time period; Job Corps funding was cut from $747 million to $698 million. The combined employment and training outlays between 1981 and 1987 went from $13.2 billion to $5.6 billion, a precipitous 58 percent drop (Center on Budget and Policy Priorities 1990).

Young, poor African-Americans have not been immune to the currents and social trends of wealth expansion and conspicuous consumption that marked the 1980s. After all, the average American child watches four hours of television *per day*. The images and trends of current fashion are part of its standard fare. Faced with economic dead ends and crumbling family structure where overstressed parents (mostly single mothers) are less available for parenting responsibilities due to job demands, more and more angry and alienated teenagers have responded to the splendors of the 1980s by turning to the sole fast track on which they can travel: drugs and crime.

The social costs have been staggering. Homicide is the leading cause of death among young African-American males and females between the ages of fifteen and thirty-four (*Secretary's Task Force on Black and Minority Health* 1985). In 1986, the last year such statistics were available, African-Americans accounted for 44 percent of all murder victims, even though they comprised only 12 percent of the population. Homicide arrests of youths between the ages of ten and seventeen is 10 per 100,000—the highest in the history of the arrest-reporting system. One out of every five African-American men between the ages of fifteen and twenty-four is likely to come into contact with the criminal justice system—a larger percentage than the numbers attending college (National Urban League 1989). The links among poverty, race, drugs, and crime come full circle as the ten largest cities currently report that a significant majority of arrested males (disproportionately young African-American men) test positive for drug use (*New York Times*, February 20, 1989, p. A–18).

The rise in youth violence, drugs, and crime has had an intense impact on social service programs. Instead of addressing youth unemployment through a package of job training programs and economic development, the overwhelming emphasis in the 1980s has been on control measures—tougher sentencing, faster adjudication, more prisons. There are more people in prisons now than at any other time in American history, and the majority are people of color (Kolbert 1990, p. B–1).

However, the programmatic and financial impact on the state seems more and more problematic. Twenty-nine states, confronted with fiscal red ink in the midst of their intensifying "get tough" campaigns, have established mandatory prison population caps. These new policies have resulted in the paradoxical outcome of early release for populations that each of these states originally intended to control. In New York, 30,000 new prison beds have been added during Governor Mario Cuomo's administration. No cap exists, even though each bed costs approximately $20,000 a year to maintain (see Kolbert 1990, p. B–1). However, the number of prisoners added to the system has doubled to 55,000, with no end in sight. Despite the surge in prisoners and an annual budget of over $2.7 billion, the crime rate has grown worse.

Poor, young African-American women confront an equally troubling future for themselves and their children. The minimum-wage jobs they qualify for now offer a progressively smaller fraction of the income needed to stay out of poverty. By 1987, a minimum-wage job paid only 77 percent of the poverty line income for a family of three, the smallest percentage in over two decades (Blum 1990). Similarly, between 1979 and 1989, African-American families with incomes of less than half the poverty line amount ($4,942 for a family of three) grew substantially—from 32 percent to 38 percent of all African-American families below the poverty line (Center on Budget and Policy Priorities 1990, p. 9).

At the same time, young African-American women who had children were increasingly unlikely to be married. Eighty-six percent of all African-American mothers under age twenty were single parents (Billingsley 1990). Overall, 46.3 percent of all African-American families were headed by single women, an increase of over 30 percent since 1970 (Billingsley 1990). When we factor in the 37 percent decline in AFDC benefits during the 1980s (Blum et al. 1990), we can see how poverty has intensified within this population.

This is most graphically understood when we look at the increased numbers of poor children in our society. Between 1966 and 1979, the proportion of children who were poor remained stable at 17 percent. After 1979, the figures rose dramatically. By 1987, the rate was 23 percent. The actual proportion of poor children grew by about 50 percent (3.5 million to 5.3 million). Fifty-eight percent of those poor children were youngsters of color. Within the African-American community, the percentage of poor children grew from 41 percent in 1981 to 48 percent in 1987. (The percentages are only slightly smaller for Hispanic children.) These figures, upon closer inspection, reveal an intensifying poverty among the poorest African-American families. In

1979, 38 percent of all African-American children who were poor lived in families with incomes that were minimally 50 percent below the poverty line. By 1989, *half* of all poor African-American children were among the very poor (Center on Budget and Policy Priorities 1990).

Thus, at the very time when the fiscally troubled state is cutting back social services to meet its debt obligations, and the private sector is continuing to contract in its process of "restructuring," there has been a dynamic expansion of poverty and attendant need among the poorest sectors of our society, especially poor children of color and their mothers. The consequences are increasingly disturbing.

In 1974, for example, the health index of the 1.8 million children in New York City stood at 67 (on a scale of 1 to 100). By 1988, the figure had dropped to 33 (Miringoff 1990). Forty percent of these children now live in poverty, compared to 20 percent in 1974. In 1987 and 1988, infant mortality increased in New York City for the first time in decades. Things are hardly better nationwide. The overall U.S. infant mortality rate of 9.7 deaths per 1,000 births is the highest of eighteen developed nations.

Equally frightening, the rate of child abuse is spiraling out of control. While child abuse cuts across all income groups, in 1986 it was found that there was seven times more abuse reported in families with incomes below $10,000 than in those with higher incomes (Blum 1990, p. 45). *Time* magazine sought to capture this horror with a graphic use of statistics: "Every 47 seconds, a child is abused or neglected" (*Time*, Oct. 8, 1990, p. 42). Equally dramatic is the increase of abuse cases in New York, from 27,207 cases in 1974 to 62,492 in 1988. Nationally, the numbers have gone from 600,000 reports of abuse to 2.4 million during the same time period. According to Miringoff (1990), "Even though the reporting has increased, it still increased every year, without exception. And, most importantly, there are far more cases than are reported."

Programmatic responses to these problems reflect the fiscal and social contradictions of the 1980s. For instance, foster care, that part of the child welfare system responsible for children deemed at too great a risk to remain with their biological families, was targeted for federal budget reduction in the early 1980s. However, foster care has grown approximately 50 percent, from 270,000 children in 1985 to 360,000 by January 1990 (Pelton 1990). The result is that overall costs in foster care have risen from $327.2 million in 1980 to approximately $1.2 billion in

1990, a 300 percent jump. This increased use of foster care represents only a modest fraction of the swelling social costs associated with the recent intensification of poverty (Pelton 1990).

All of these groups—foster children and their overwhelmed mothers, elderly Americans frightened by skyrocketing health costs, the unemployed adolescent making fast, dangerous money in the drug trade—are increasingly being defined as expendable. However, as each group is marginalized, the social costs that are associated with such neglect begin to expand, be it through foster care, prisons, or health care for the poor. The tension between tightened social spending and expensive, increasingly problem-ridden social groups represents an ominous contradiction as we approach the twenty-first century.

An Ominous Future: The Inability of States and Local Communities to Do More

The problems of intensifying poverty and heightened economic vulnerability are frightening, in part because it is unrealistic to think that local communities and states can easily increase their levels of support. As Neil Gilbert notes, the great expansion of federal social service grants that occurred in the 1970s represented a transfer of service costs from municipalities and states to the federal government (Gilbert 1983, p. 50). This occurred because the initial effects of restructuring the economy were felt in older northeastern and midwestern cities as local businesses and firms moved to the South and Southwest to take advantage of cheaper labor pools and lower taxes (Sale 1981). The shrinking local tax bases of these communities in turn intensified their requests for federal aid. The more recent globalization of industrial firms only heightens the fiscal vulnerability of every region of the country. We may have reached the point where no locality or state will be able to sustain service levels without federal assistance. This possibility is consistently underscored by recent events.

For instance, "despite an overall 12.8 percent budget increase, California faced a $3.6 billion budget shortage in 1990, an increase of 200,000 new students, a 14 percent annual increase in its prison population and welfare rolls that are growing three times as fast as that in the general population" (Applebone 1990, p. 7). In Miami, 150 Food Stamps positions have been lost in the state despite a 15 percent increase in applicants. In Georgia, 40,000 additional cases of child abuse were reported between 1983 and 1988, yet only 131 additional case-workers were hired during the same period. An attempt to recruit 150 more workers was halted when the state froze all hiring because of budget deficits. Intensifying financial strains in the state have forced a $29 million reduction in the program's budget (Applebone 1990, p. 7).

The 1990 Federal Budget Impasse: The State's Fiscal Crisis Intensifies

The intense budgetary struggle between Congress and the Bush administration suggests that the situation is no better at the federal level. While the 1990 federal budget impasse was short-lived, political experts identified it as a "watershed event" in our legislative budget process (Rosenbaum 1990, p. 1). For the first time since 1974, the tax/services debate had to be conducted as a "line-by-line," openly partisan debate. This occurred because of the breakdown of the previous sixteen-year practice of voting up or down on an entire package, developed in closeted deliberations by less visible legislative leaders.

There were three primary reasons for this shift. First, the original revenue package emphasized "user" taxes—straight levies on consumption items such as gas and beer that were disproportionately shouldered by citizens of moderate means. Those in the income range of $30,000 to $50,000 would pay an average of 3.3 percent more under the plan; those between $75,000 and $100,000 would pay 2 percent more; while those over $200,000 would pay less than three-tenths of 1 percent (Hershey 1990, p. 1). The rage of the lower-income taxpayers, already reeling from drops in real income and aware of the debt-based windfalls of the wealthy accumulated in the 1980s, forced legislators to more openly reconsider the regressive tax package. Middle-income people in the 1990s are increasingly unwilling to bear any more of the tax burden.

Second, the organized responses to potential cuts in services affected legislators concerned with reelection. The proposed cuts in Medicare caused an uproar; senior citizens and their allies rallied against increased copayments and other charges that would have decreased their ability to afford health care. Furthermore, there was anger over proposed losses for other services now viewed by larger and larger segments of the public as critical—education, drug prevention, law enforcement. They were less politically organized and effective than the elderly, but people were clearly not in a mood for higher taxes, and opposed cuts in programs they viewed as concretely improving their lives.

Finally, there was resistance to the more general call for public support of a deficit reduction package that would increase the tax burden of the middle class. In general, American taxpayers refused to accept greater taxation to pay off the public debt—the great creator of nonproductive wealth discussed earlier in the chapter. It therefore proved to be politically difficult for legislators to sell increased taxes to their constituents. Consequently, the federal government was closed for a weekend as politicians were forced to grapple with an upsurge in political protest and anger (Pear 1990b).

The social and economic implications of this political protest are obvious. People are less willing to accept either greater tax burdens or a loss of services. In turn, they are less receptive to the supply-side argument which suggests that diminished tax rates for the wealthy will lead to increased investment or a more robust and productive economy. The yawning deficit, the drop in industrial production, and the S & L crisis have combined to illustrate the emptiness of that promise. The American citizenry may be starting to pay closer attention to who really benefits from the economic package of tax benefits and incentives offered by the state.

The Increasing Struggle over Essential Social Services

Equally important, there may be an intensifying struggle to preserve (and extend) services offered by the state. In the 1980s, political leaders led an attack against Social Security, only to be soundly rebuked. They have attempted to do the same to Medicare, but once again have been forced to look toward other service cuts to reduce the budget. The outcome will depend to some extent on the willingness of other constituent groups to protect their services.

Yet policymakers must make cuts if they are to take care of the deficit, protect Social Security and Medicare, and reduce defense cuts to a modest crawl. The watchword—echoed by policymakers in the City Hall corridors of New York City, Philadelphia, Atlanta, Los Angeles, and Chicago—is that only "essential services" will be spared.

But the determination of what is essential will grow more, not less, difficult, given the intensification of poverty and the social and personal dislocations that it creates. The federal drug program proposed in 1990 for the turn of the decade cost $5.1 billion—a 40 percent increase over previous years' requests, even though it de-emphasizes prevention efforts. Federal funding for prevention services was $246 million for fiscal year 1990, an increase of 50 percent over the past ten years. However, foster care costs have quadrupled in the same time period to over $1.2 billion. It is obvious that expenses in all areas of social service are moving upward due to increased need. But which expenses will the American public bear? Hard choices, clearly articulated in terms of financial costs and social outcomes, are going to have to be made during this decade by political leaders who are less certain as to what direction they should take.

The question of "essential services" will continue to be highly politicized. The policy choices will affect the dollars available to respond to the entire range of economic and social forces pressing against the state. Measures for determining essential service outcomes (in the short or long run) are presently crude or undeveloped. This is an especially critical dilemma that will be more fully discussed in the final chapter. However, it is clear that different service structures and work processes either minimize or maximize opportunities for effecting such change. To a great extent, a program's opportunity to succeed will depend upon its service structure.

Recent budget decisions have not only altered the scope and quantity of available services, but also the nature of services delivered by particular agencies and their workers. As resources have diminished there have been visible consequences for fields of service and groups of clients, many of which have been cited. Less visible, yet equally powerful, is the impact of these cuts on the line level worker and the social service work process. Cost-containment and budget-cutting policies (in combination with the ongoing bureaucratization of social services) are profoundly altering the very content of social service work. The shifting nature of practice in service work raises a number of questions that include but are not limited to the following:

• Are job employment programs organized to train their clients for skill-based jobs?
• Are hospital workers structurally able to develop the professional skills or establish the autonomy necessary to deliver critical services to their chronically ill patients?

• Are services for troubled families designed to nurture effective problem-solving tools that the family can use on its own?

Answers to these and other questions are critical because they help to explain how services can be structured either to fail or to succeed. This point becomes more pivotal now that budget decisions may be rapidly reinforcing the conditions for programmatic failure. Left unchecked, the restructuring of services over time may affect the very legitimacy and survival of social services.

As the fiscal crisis intensifies during the 1990s, budgetary debate and decision making will be conducted more along social and economic lines. Consistent with this point, it is clear that the reactionary camps are increasingly relying on the use of racist myth, xenophobia, and sexism as they demand a greater dismantling of the welfare state in favor of the police state—that is, more prisons, faster sentencing, and the "temporary" suspension of civil liberties. As the 1990s begin, this is clearly one major direction for change in our society.

Proponents of an expanded welfare state can only counter conservative myths with facts that reassure and services that work. But do social services work? Equally important, is it really necessary for social services to be thought of in such political terms?

We address the second question in the next chapter. In particular, we suggest that the welfare state is an inevitable arena for class and social struggle over the coming decade—indeed, to suggest otherwise would be to devise strategies for change and expanded social services that are doomed to fail. Furthermore, we show how and why the structure of social programs and the practice of workers are organically part of this struggle.

After placing social service programs and practice within this context, we shall look at the changes in the structure of social services provoked by cost-containment policies. Identifying these changes and determining their impact on social service workers is the primary focus of this book. These themes are explored in the last three chapters.

As this chapter suggests, our exploration is not an academic exercise. Given the economic crisis of American capitalism and the fiscal crisis of the debtor state, it is essential that the daily practice of welfare state workers be explored within a broader context if the breakdowns—and the potential—of social services are to be better understood and acted upon.

References

Applebone, Peter. "Growing Fiscal Problems Put Squeeze on Social Programs in Many States." *New York Times*, September 4, 1990.

Ashby, John. "The Inequality of Medicare Prospective Payment in Large Urban Areas." Washington, DC: District of Columbia Hospital Association, September 1984.

Barden, J.C. "Foster Care System Reeling, Despite Law Meant to Help." *New York Times*, September 21, 1990.

Bell, Carl, and Esther Jenkins. "Preventing Black Homicide." In Janet Dewart, ed., *The State of Black America, 1990*, Washington, DC: The National Urban League, 1990.

Billingsley, Andrew. "Understanding African-American Family Diversity." In Janet Dewart, ed., *The State of Black America, 1990*, Washington, DC: The National Urban League, 1990.

Bishop, Katherine. "County vs. State on Bankruptcy Issue." *New York Times*, September 10, 1990.

Bluestone, Barry, and Bennett Harrison. *The Deindustrializing of America*. New York: Basic Books, 1982.

———. *The Great U-Turn: Corporate Re-Structuring, Laissez-Faire, and the Challenge to America's Wage Society*. New York: Basic Books, 1988.

Blum, Barbara. *Five Million Children: A Statistical Profile of Our Poorest Young Children*. New York: Columbia University School of Public Health, 1990.

Brand, R. "Into the Bone: The 1986 Reagan Health Budget." *Health-Pac Bulletin*, (January 1985), p. 389.

Burghardt, Stephen, and Michael Fabricant. *Working under the Safety Net: Policy and Practice with the New American Poor*. Beverly Hills, CA: Sage, 1987.

Bureau of Labor Statistics. "Economic Projections to 1990." Bulletin 2121, p. 37 Washington, DC, 1984.

Burt, M., and K. Pittmann. *Testing the Social Safety Net*. Washington, DC: The Urban Institute, 1985.

Burt, W. "A New View of a Legendary Robber Baron." *Reason* (April 1987).

Center on Budget and Policy Priorities. *Laboring for Less: Working but Poor in Rural America*. Washington, DC: Spring 1990.

Congressional Budget Office. *The Changing Distribution of Federal Taxes, 1975–1990*. Washington, DC: October 1987.

Danziger, Sheldon. "America's Income Gap." *Business Week*, April 17, 1989.

DeParle, Jason. "In Rising Debate on Poverty, the Question: Who Is Poor?" *New York Times*, September 2, 1990.

Families USA Foundation. *What Are the Real Numbers?* Washington, DC: 1990.

Fergin, Sylvia. "Sicker and Quicker." *Village Voice*, August 14, 1985.

Forbes. "The Four Hundred Richest People in America." October 26, 1987.

———. "A Wealth of Billionaires." July 24, 1989.

Freudenheim, G. "Medicare's Economic Troubles Growing Worse." *New York Times*, September 6, 1990.

Freeman, R., and H. J. Holzer. "Young Blacks and Jobs: What We Now Know." In Janet Dewart, ed., *The State of Black America, 1989*. Washington, DC: National Urban League, 1989.

Friedman, Benjamin. *Day of Reckoning.* New York: Random House, 1988.

Fuchs, Victor. "The Health Sector's Share of the Gross National Product." *Science*, February 2, 1990.

Gilbert, Neil. *Capitalism and Social Welfare.* New Haven, CT: Yale University Press, 1983.

Glaberson, William. "One in 4 Young Black Men Are in Custody, Study Says." *New York Times*, October 4, 1990.

Grieder, William. *Secrets of the Temple.* New York: Simon and Schuster, 1987.

Harrison, Bennett. "The Impact of Corporate Restructuring on Labor Income." *Social Policy* (Fall 1987).

Hershey, Robert, Jr. "Tax Burden Expected to Fall on People of Moderate Means." *New York Times*, October 1, 1990.

Hevesi, Dennis. "Health Conditions Worsen for the Young." *New York Times*, November 3, 1990.

Hinds, deCourcy Michael. "Without Money or Choices, Philadelphia Plans Big Cuts." *New York Times*, September 14, 1990a.

————. "Governors Say Budget Plan Shifts More Burdens to States." *New York Times*, October 2, 1990b.

Hilts, Philip J. "U.S. Returns to 1820's in Care of Mentally Ill, Study Asserts." *New York Times*, September 12, 1990a.

————. "U.S. Health Care Costs Soar, but Not as Much as in New York." *New York Times*, November 1, 1990b.

Hopper, K., and J. Hamberg. *The Making of America's Homeless: From Skid Row to New Poor.* New York: County Service Society, 1984.

Kolbert, Elizabeth. "Criminal Justice: Priority Proves Elusive for Cuomo." *Newsday*, October 2, 1990.

Koplin, A. "The Future of Public Health: A Local Health Department View." *Journal of Public Health* 11, 14 (1990).

Kotelchuk, R. "The Effect of DRGs on Health Care." *Health-Pac Bulletin* (January 1984).

Kotelchuk, Rhoda. "The Effects of DRGs on Health Care." *Health-Pac Bulletin* (January 1985).

Levitan, Sar, *Beyond the Safety Net.* Cambridge, MA: Ballinger, 1985.

Levy, Frank. *Dollars and Dreams: The Changing American Income Distribution.* New York: Russell Sage Foundation, 1987.

Los Angeles Times. "Supply-Side Tax Tonic Has Been a Fantasy." December 21, 1987.

Miringoff, Marc. "The Index of the Social Health of the Children of New York." New York: Fordham University, Institute for Innovation in Social Policy, Fall 1990.

Mydans, Stan. "Homicide Rate Up for Young Blacks." *New York Times*, December 7, 1990.

National Urban League. *The State of Black America 1989.* Washington, DC: National Urban League, 1989.

————. *The State of Black America 1990.* Washington, DC: National Urban League, 1990.

New York Times. "Drug Use High among Arrested Males." February 20, 1989.

————. "Surplus Predicted in Social Security." March 29, 1990.

———. "Banking Layoffs Mount." September 22, 1990.

O'Hare, William, Tayna Mann, Kathryn Porter, and Robert Greenton. "Drifting Apart: New Findings on Growing Income Disparities between the Rich, the Poor, and the Middle Class." Washington, DC: Center on Budget and Policy Priorities, 1990.

Olson, Laura K. *The Political Economy of Aging.* New York: Columbia University Press, 1982.

Pear, Robert. "Focus on the Tax Package: Who Will Pay How Much?" *New York Times,* October 3, 1990a.

———. "Many States Cut Food Allowances for Poor Families." *New York Times,* May 29, 1990b.

———. "Welfare on Rise, Reflecting Slump in Economy of U.S." *New York Times,* August 19, 1990c.

Pelton, Leroy. "Resolving the Crisis of Child Welfare." *Public Welfare* (Fall 1990).

Peterson, Peter G. "The Budget, from Comedy to Tragedy." *New York Times,* October 17, 1990.

Phillips, Kevin. *The Politics of the Rich and Poor.* New York: Random House, 1990.

Rich, D. *The Economics of Welfare: A Contemporary Analysis.* New York: Praeger, 1989.

Rosen, Sumner. "The Economy and the Welfare State." *Social Policy* (Fall 1988).

Rosenbaum, D. "1990 Budget Impasse Sets Ominous Trend." *New York Times,* June 1, 1990.

Rothschild, Emma. "Reagan and the Real Economy." *New York Review of Books,* February 5, 1981.

Sale, K. *Power Shift.* New York: Random House, 1981.

Secretary's Task Force on Black and Minority Health: Washington, DC: Department of Health and Welfare, 1985.

Shapiro, Isaac, and Miriam Nichols. "Unprotected: Unemployment Insurance and Jobless Workers." Washington, DC: Center on Budget and Policy Priorities, August 1989.

Shimbun, N. *Nomura Medium-Term Outlook for Japan and the World,* 1990.

Smith, Rex. "New York's Prison Boom." *Newsday,* October 8, 1990.

Suro, Robert. "Behind the Census Numbers, Swirling Tides of Movement." *New York Times,* October 7, 1990.

Thurow, Lester. "The Great Wall." *Alexander and Alexander World,* First Quarter, 1989.

———. "Pound GOP on Jobs Issue." *Atlanta Constitution,* July 17, 1988.

Time. "Suffer the Little Children." October 8, 1990.

U.S. Census Bureau. *Mean Incomes of Population Quintiles, 1954–86.* Washington, DC, 1988.

———. *Mean Incomes of Population Quintiles, 1989.* Washington, DC, 1990.

2 • The Political Economic Framework of the Welfare State Crisis

Introduction

The previous chapter identified how serious the United States economic crisis is today. It also made clear the fact that the state is integral to the development of solutions to this crisis. It is equally apparent that the overwhelming majority of social service employees are employed directly or indirectly as welfare state employees, either as public workers or through public contracts and grants administered by not-for-profit agencies. Given these late-twentieth-century developments, social workers and other welfare state professionals need to understand how the state functions in relation to the broader economy so they can act more effectively to advance both their own interests and those of clients.

In order to frame the content in which agency practice dynamics emerge, this chapter addresses two central issues of the welfare state debate. First, we believe it is important to situate the agency within the broader framework of the welfare state and its relationship to the political economy. This larger framework is necessary if the changes in agency functioning that we describe in chapter 3 are to be fully understood. In that chapter, for example, we illustrate how social workers in health settings are constrained in their practice decision making by Diagnostic Review Groups (DRGs), introduced in the early 1980s. The emergence of DRGs, however, occurred while the welfare state engaged in across-the-board cost cutting in response to a crisis of profitability in the capitalist economy that had begun a decade earlier. Despite the pressures for cost cutting, Medicare entitlements won by senior citizens from the state in the 1960s have for the most part been spared. To a great extent, the preservation of Medicare can be traced to the political activism and influence of numerous senior groups (Olson 1982). If social workers are to effectively utilize their agencies' financial decision making, they need to understand the reasons for the pushes and pulls within this broader system. Where should they push hardest to maintain services and entitlements? Where must they compromise? Understanding the dynamics of the state and its relationship to the political economy can help answer these questions.

As we will show later in this chapter, the two most powerful arguments in the current literature on the relationship between the political economy and the welfare state are in sharp opposition to each other. One position, presented by conservatives George Gilder and Charles Murray, envisions a deadening, all-pervasive interference of the welfare state into the economy and the lives of its workers, especially the poor. Gilder and Murray argue that progressive state expansion of welfare and liberal intellectual indifference to normative standards have undermined the black family (Gilder 1979; Murray 1984).

The opposing position, taken first by James O'Connor, Ian Gough, and Fred Block (and since modified by others), describes a more contradictory relationship of welfare state expansion and contraction. As neo-Marxists, they view the welfare state's functions as twofold, primarily supportive of capitalist accumulation, but also intervening at critical junctures to provide life-sustaining aid to the working class, the elderly, and the poor. Social Security and unemployment insurance are examples of the latter; liberal tax deductions for high-income taxpayers are an example of the former.

We will more fully delineate these two positions later. Our other objective in this chapter, however, is to suggest an important omission in both theories. *In our view, both theories ignore the active roles, in policy or program, that social service workers can play as employees of the state or of state-contracted services. In some respects, these roles are not predetermined by the larger social and economic forces affecting the state.* For Gilder and Murray, this gap is not surprising, for theirs is the view of *A Thousand Clowns* and popular culture: the social worker as unthinking bureaucrat and unwitting agent of social control, complete with bleeding heart and condescending indifference to the "real" plight of the poor.

For the neo-Marxists, the failure to delineate a clear role for social workers as active change agents in the process of welfare state development is more problematic. O'Connor and Gough, for example, have argued that the welfare state's functions are contradictory, sometimes aiding capital, sometimes, but less often, improving the "social wage" of the working population (O'Connor 1973, 1984; Gough 1979). But *how? In what ways* does the improvement emerge? *Who* is involved in that improvement? (Skocpol 1979; Block 1977; Hirschorn 1984). Neo-Marxist analyses tend to ignore the political and actual effect that state workers have both in developing services and entitlements and, equally important, in influencing the relationship of the state and the political economy. Instead they tend to locate their discussion at a level of abstraction involving primarily capitalists, political leaders of various branches of government, and the recipients of various services: the elderly, the industrial working class, etc. While recent work by Pat Morgan (1982), Ann Markusen (1985), and O'Connor himself (1984) (among others) suggests that the state is an arena for "class struggle," this struggle, in terms of social service worker activity, has a decidedly deterministic cast.

Christine Cousins (1987) claims that professionals inevitably capitulate to and benefit from the processes of bureaucratization used by the state to limit social reforms such as welfare. By seeing professionalization as integral to the processes of co-opting social movements, the neo-Marxists situate their otherwise seminal analysis of the professional social worker within the far less rich radical critiques of the 1960s.

Our modification of the neo-Marxist analysis highlights the role of social service workers as active agents in their work place and through their profession. In our view, social workers are fully capable of influencing the direction and intensity of reforms emerging within and outside the welfare state in ways that are not predetermined forms of co-optation. For just as Block and others argue that the state has a degree of independence from the political economy in its decision making, so social service workers have a degree of independence in the implementation of larger state functions—*if* they are conscious of their role within the welfare state. (One can see this, for example, in the different ways in which social service workers run senior centers—some quite progressive and empowering with seniors, others as bureaucratic and stultifying as any welfare office.) The latter part of this chapter will delineate the dilemmas and tensions in the development of this active role.

Three Theories of the Welfare State:
Conservative, Liberal, and Neo-Marxist

Any theory of the welfare state must answer two critical questions posed by Claus Offe (1984, p. 152):

> First, what is the desirable form of organization of society and state and how can we demonstrate that it is at all workable, i.e., consistent with our basic normative and factual assumptions about social life? This is the problem of defining a consistent *model* or goal of transformation . . . [e.g., what type of work force will we have in 2020?]. Second, how do we get there? This is the problem of identifying the dynamic forces and *strategies* that could bring about that transformation.

Offe goes on to point out that only by answering the second question can validity be established for the answers provided to the first. In other words, *the theory is tenable only if it provides real answers about how people actually live.*

George Gilder, the social theorist of the Reagan administration, answered Offe's first question with a stirring vision of a free market economy. For conservatives like Gilder, the desirable form of state and society was pristine and simple:

> Capitalism consists of providing first and getting later. The demand is implicit in the supply. . . . Capitalist production entails faith—in one's neighbors, in one's society, and in the contemporary logic of the cosmos. Search and you shall find . . . supply creates its own demand. It is this cosmology, this sequential, that essentially distinguishes the free from the socialist economy.
>
> Under capitalism, the ventures of reason are launched into a world ruled by morality and Providence. The gifts will succeed only to the extent that they are altruistic and spring from an understanding of the needs of others. They depend on faith in an essentially fair and responsive humanity. (Gilder 1979, p. 24)

We await Gilder's philosophical interpretation of the Savings and Loan bailout of the early 1990s. Nonetheless, his view of the welfare state for the poor is clear and emphatic:

> Originating in a liberal effort to respond to the popular will and relieve

the pressures of poverty, demand-oriented politics (of the welfare state) end in promoting unemployment and dependency and creating a less open and accessible economy and a more stratified and hierarchical political order. Government bureaucracies proliferate to furnish the services that overtaxed businesses can no longer provide. . . . As bureaucracy grows, moreover, industrial progress declines. . . . (Ibid., pp. 39–40)

Not only does the state overtax businesses, stem the tide of industrial progress, and heighten personal dependency. It also creates a kind of mind-set that deadens life as well: . . . It is impossible to create a system of collective regulation and safety that does not finally deaden the moral sources of the willingness to face danger and fight, that does not dampen the spontaneous flow of gifts and experiments which extend the dimensions of the world and the circles of human sympathy. . . . (Ibid., p. 27)

Gilder's Social Darwinist argument, complete with quasi-religious overtones and hint of *machismo,* is obvious: capitalism, as *opposed* to the state (and "collectivism" in general), is what creates economic prosperity and social harmony. Government, by shackling initiative and stultifying creativity, does the opposite—it "dampens the spontaneous gifts" of what capitalism has to offer.

We can see that Gilder answers Offe's first question by indicating that the mode of production (capitalism) is the only mechanism capable of organizing or structuring the "good society." Indeed, he and Charles Murray agree that the state otherwise has a deleterious effect on human behavior. For example, Gilder states:

real poverty is less a state of income than a state of mind and . . . the government dole blights most of the people who depend on it. The lesson of the period since 1964 [caused by the War on Poverty] is [that] the moral blight of dependency has been compounded and extended to future generations by a virtual plague of family dissolution. . . . (Ibid., p. 12)

Likewise, Murray contends that:

what [the welfare state] did for the mediocre [in providing welfare] hurt many others who were *not* of average abilities and (originally) average industriousness . . . [and] diminished their quality of life in ways that the added dollars could not compensate. (Murray 1984, p. 177)

Both Gilder and Murray suggest that these harmful effects of welfare state interference lead to dependency and indifference on the part of the poor. Embedded in their analyses is the presumption that the workers of the welfare state are indifferent to the real plight of the poor as well:

> The welfare prone always prefer fake jobs supervised by social workers to the necessarily unpleasant demands of actual employment. Far from learning the harsh disciplines required for productive work, recipients learn that you can have a job without really working—the most crippling illusion both of the poor and of the academic and government students of poverty. (Gilder 1987, p. 22)

To conservatives like Gilder, social workers are the personification of collectivist indifference and beneficent sloth: they provide easy jobs, demand no supervision, and support the illusion that paid work should only require showing up on the job. While it is obvious that Gilder has never visited a welfare office nor spoken with a welfare worker, he offers an image of the social worker as a dupe who should in all likelihood not have a job. If the welfare state were to wither away as he and Murray prescribe, this would be a distinct possibility.

However, before accepting their views of capitalism and the state, we need to see what answers their theories provide to Offe's second question: How do we create "the good society"? Does their theory of the state and its relationship to the economy contain a strategy that considers how particular objectives are to be achieved?

Gilder and Murray advocate a return to the free market (or the supply side). They wish to remove all taxation from businesses so that the fundamental logic of capitalist enterprise can flourish:

> To overcome [the social and economic crisis of the age] it is necessary to have faith, to recover the belief in chance and providence, in the ingenuity of free and God-fearing men.
>
> This belief will allow us to see the best way of helping the poor, the way to understand the truths of equality before God that can only come from freedom and diversity on earth. It will lead us to abandon, above all, the idea that the human race can become self-sufficient, can separate itself from chance and fortune in a hubristic surge of rational resource management, income distribution, and futuristic planning. Our greatest and only resource is the miracle of human creativity in a relation of openness to the divine. (Gilder 1979, p. 227)

In less theological words, men (women do not seem to play an active role in Gilder's world view), unshackled by government planning and callous management, through their own creative effort and a spiritual closeness to a transcendent being, can and will save the world. One appreciates the goal, but Gilder's means, while perhaps spiritually moving, only vaguely indicate *what to do* concretely to achieve such universal harmony. The only jobs one can see emerging from his conception are venture capitalist and entrepreneurial minister. But what will happen to the poor and unskilled young people whom he and Murray find nestled within the welfare state's overly comfortable doorway?

Having strategically dismantled AFDC, Murray describes the economic and social trajectory of the young poor as follows:

> Adolescents who were not job-ready find they are job-ready after all. It turns out they can work for low wages and accept the discipline of the work place if the alternative is grim enough. After a few years, many—not all, but many—find that they have acquired salable skills, or that they are at the right place at the right time, or otherwise find that the original entry-level job has gradually been transformed into a secure job paying a decent wage. A few—not a lot, but a few—find that the process leads to affluence. (Murray 1984, p. 236)

As our first chapter's analysis of the fiscal crisis makes clear, Gilder's religious rhetoric has come full circle in Murray's socioeconomic predictions for unemployed youth. Their reification of notions of effort, creativity, and transcendent outcomes collide against the rock-hard reality of an economy already lacking jobs, mobility, and national investment in job creation (Bluestone and Harrison 1982; Phillips 1990).

For example, chapter 1 describes how the shift from a manufacturing to a service-based economy lowers both weekly and hourly wages of almost all entry-level workers. Consequently, the same type of economic opportunity that was available to Gilder and Murray as young white men entering the labor force for the first time in the 1950s and early 1960s no longer exists. Furthermore, these findings of lowered real income more fully capture the dynamic interplay between poor people and welfare than simplistic "dependency" arguments. The results of the University of Michigan Panel Study on Income Dynamics do not reveal a pattern of long-term dependency: "Only 8.3% received welfare for five or more years, and only 4.4% were on welfare for eight or more years. A very large majority of those who used AFDC did so temporarily, during periods of difficulty, and then became self-sufficient" (Patti et al. 1987).

Indeed, the single largest state subsidy of the 1990s has been directed not toward poor, seemingly dependent, minority youth, but rather the Savings and Loan associations. The $500 billion bailout of the S & Ls, in combination with the documented greed and callousness of the associations' directors, represent fatal flaws in Gilder's and Murray's analyses.

More importantly, this kind of state subsidy again suggests that the relationship between the state and the capitalist economy is more complex than conservatives are willing to admit. We therefore must turn elsewhere for a more plausible and dynamic theory that both (a) explains how the welfare state operates in relationship to the economy; and (b) provides the outline of a strategy for how to make our society—including social work—operate more effectively in the future.

The Limitations of Liberal Theory

Despite its limitations, the conservative analysis has obvious appeal and enjoys substantial influence within dominant economic groups. Its ideas, while empirically flawed, lend credence and support to the economic and social activity of large numbers of wealthy corporate raiders, investment bankers, and entrepreneurs threatened by the growth of world competition and the shrinking economic power of the U.S. dollar (Phillips 1990). It "explains the world" in *their terms,* even if its rationality cannot withstand other, more objective forms of scrutiny.

Liberal theory, on the other hand, has always posed a middle ground between conservative and more leftist analyses of the role of the state in relation to the economy. From economists such as Schumpeter to political scientists such as Easton, liberals have argued since the 1940s that the state played a "mediating" function between social and economic groups in the larger society. By posing a model of the state that was "above" these contending forces, they were able to argue for an incrementalist, slowly evolving, reformist state. State expansion was an outgrowth of its attempts to modify economic conflicts and maintain social harmony (see Schumpeter 1962; Easton 1965; Dahl 1982).

However, the contentiousness within both the state and the larger political economy over the last twenty years has revealed the underlying weaknesses of traditional liberal theory. In general, liberalism has had no answers for either the increased bureaucratization of services—the conservatives' most telling point—or the interpenetration of the state into the economy. Instead, liberal theorists suggest that the welfare state and its managers operate with a voluntaristic sense of free will common to most theories of charitable enterprise. For example, in an updated version of liberal theory, Neil Gilbert argues that the "social market" of the welfare state operates on its own in performing the twin functions of social integration and social control:

> security and equality are viewed as cardinal objectives of the social market. In order to hold the course, these objectives must be pursued with restraint. . . . The purpose is not to achieve perfect equality of material conditions and total security but to achieve a social balance amid the play of opposing values. From this perspective the central puzzle is to determine the size of the safety net and the extent of the redistribution through the social market that are necessary to sustain a dynamic equilibrium among the competing forces of the mixed economy. (Gilbert 1984, p. 172)

Gilbert's normative assumptions about the "equal degree" of independence between the state and the economy lead him to propose that the state and its agents have primary responsibility for social integration and control. He suggests that they are the actors who determine both the extent of redistribution and the size of the safety net. This presumption of extraordinary autonomy and discretionary authority implies that social welfare professions have the power to create, define, and maintain the safety net. Clearly, Gilbert's analysis does not consider how the decision making of agencies and workers is significantly constrained by other state mandates and financial considerations.

Gilbert's language socializes practitioners into accepting responsibility and culpability for matters that are well beyond a worker's professional capacity, such as redistribution of services or the size of the safety net. As chapter 1 makes clear, simultaneous to the expansion and intensification of poverty during the past decade there has been a reduction in the authority of social workers to ameliorate the worsening circumstances of their clients. These trends suggest that social workers, instead of striking a "fine balance" between social and political forces, are themselves confronting a diminished level of control over the workplace and the decisions they can make to effect either social integration or social control. Gilbert's assumption of a highly independent state fails to explain increasing poverty and the simultaneous weakening of social workers' control over their organizations. These are critical omissions. Earlier, we documented the increase in poverty in this country. Later, in chapters 3 and 4, we will describe how the social worker's autonomy at the workplace has declined significantly in the 1980s and 1990s.

The Neo-Marxist Alternative

The weakness of liberal social or political theory is evident by now. In general, liberalism has few answers to either the interpenetration of the state into the economy or the dominant influence of capitalism on state functioning. Alternatively, conservative theory is unable to account for the necessity of state intervention in economic and social affairs. Neither of these theories adequately addresses Offe's questions; both are unable to develop an adequate model of the state during late-twentieth-century capitalism.

However, an important conceptual breakthrough occurred with James O'Connor's *Fiscal Crisis of the State* (1973), which was further developed by Gough (1979) and Block (1977). (See also Miliband 1982; Poulantzas 1973; and Piven and Cloward 1971.) We explore this model in great detail because we believe its basic paradigm provides answers to Offe's questions through its analysis of the state and the economy. Furthermore, through its analysis, the theory provides clear directions on how "the good society" can be developed for all its citizens.

A Basic Outline of the Neo-Marxist Theory

The neo-Marxist theory is a complex and multilayered analysis encompassing a variety of concepts that can intimidate a reader unfamiliar with the classical European terminology of political economy. We will provide a brief outline of these concepts, drawing examples from the first chapter to describe their most central terms. We will then look at the framework in greater detail as we develop our own contribution to this body of work by locating welfare state programs, and worker activities and roles within this theory.

O'Connor's conceptual breakthrough began with his departure from the already widely held functionalist belief that the state, rather than standing above the economic and social landscape, is integrated into and responsive to the economic needs of the capitalist system. Rather than developing a simple functionalist analysis, whereby the state simply does capitalism's bidding, O'Connor argued that the state performs two contradictory functions: *accumulation* and *legitimation.* The *accumulation function* aids in the processes of capital investment and economic development. The *legitimation function,* on the other hand, develops from the social fallout caused by the investment decisions of the capitalist economy. For example, as we saw in chapter 1, the federal budgetary process has been a protracted fight over how much investment credit (such as capital gains taxes) to provide for the owners of capital while simultaneously trying to determine how much money to set aside for crime fighting, drug programs, and prisons— programs that the state must develop in its legitimation function, as it attempts to regulate the social and political consequences of economic decision making. The federal budget debate suggests the concrete pushes and pulls of competing interests to which the state responds through its accumulation and legitimation functions.

These contradictory functions are expressed through various state *activities* that require *social capital* or *social expenses.* While Gough, O'Connor, and Block apply various definitions to these terms, state activities requiring social capital are seen as either directly aiding investment (tax credits), or indirectly aiding business by helping to prepare and/or maintain the working populations at skill levels consonant with the job demands they will have in the workplace (educational services, health care). In addition, state activities support the maintenance of traditional notions of a patriarchal family (Abramovitz 1989). Activities requiring social expense allocations (such as welfare), on the other hand, are seen as providing no benefit to the larger economy other than their maintenance of social harmony. These expenditures are *quantitative* expressions of social expenses and social capital.

These activities also occur through *qualitative processes* of *social reproduction.* Social reproduction activities take place within services and programs that socialize and educate people to standards of behavior, expectations of performance and payment, or skills, etc. For example, job training programs that are structured in a way that is detached and indifferent to the full range of needs of their student populations, such as by emphasizing only basic skills, socially reproduce a set of expectations for these students, preparing them for a market that is quite distinct from, say, that of a New England prep school.

What O'Connor and others go on to argue is that the welfare state, with its contradictory accumulation and legitimation functions, will develop programs that are reflective of the same dynamic tensions associated with larger, macrolevel issues seen in the budget battle of 1990. By seeing the welfare state and its programs as engaged in processes that are connected to the larger accumulation and legitimation functions of the state, they thus situate these programs within the core dynamic of *class struggle*. To them, class struggle is not a simplistic "war" between workers and owners, but an ongoing, complex, and contentious relationship among actors in the state, in the economy, and in other social groups struggling over the direction and extent of state intervention. Ultimately, this struggle will either enhance the legitimacy of social services through a combination of expansion and restructuring (the generative model of services that we present in the last chapter would effect such an outcome), or encourage greater accumulation and unfettered private investment—with the resultant industrialization of social services that we outline in the next two chapters.

It is through this paradigm that O'Connor and others describe the state and society. Furthermore, they identify a strategy for improving society by looking at the role of class struggle among groups contending for the direction of the state's accumulation–legitimation functions. We will look more carefully at the strengths and limitations of the neo-Marxist analysis to see whether or not its strategy for interpreting and developing the welfare state is valid. Equally important, if it is valid, we need to analyze the role of the welfare state worker within this paradigm.

The Contradictions between the Democratic State and Capitalist Society

O'Connor, Gough, and Block begin by clarifying the relationship between state and society. Block argues that there is a basic "division of labor" between those who accumulate capital in the private sector and those who manage the state and its institutions (1977, p. 10):

> Those who accumulate capital are not conscious of their interests as capitalists and, in general, they are not conscious of what is necessary to

reproduce the social order in changing circumstances. Those who manage the state apparatus, however, are forced to concern themselves . . .
with the reproduction of the social order because their continued power
rests on the maintenance of political and economic order.

This point, however, raises another question: What keeps the state
managers from becoming more and more independent of the economic
sphere? Would it not be possible to "throw the rascals out," place a
number of highly progressive, pro–welfare state leaders in office or
throughout state institutions, and make major reforms? Block indicates
that this cannot occur because certain "structural mechanisms" require
the state to serve capitalist ends regardless of whether or not capitalists
intervene directly and consciously.

The most important brake on reform activity, he suggests, relates to
"the fact that those who manage the state apparatus—regardless of
their own political ideology—are dependent on the maintenance of
some reasonable level of economic activity" (Block 1977, p. 15). This
is true for two reasons: First, the capacity of the state to finance itself
through taxation and borrowing depends on the health of the economy.
The state will have difficulty maintaining revenues if the economy in
general is in decline—one can look at Argentina to understand this
point. Second, public support for state leadership declines rapidly if
there is a serious drop in the level of economic activity, a parallel rise
in unemployment, or a shortage of goods and services. The Carter
administration learned this in 1980, when both double-digit inflation
and unemployment gripped the nation. George Bush's slump in popu-
larity over the 1990 budget impasse reflects the same set of forces at
play.

Block avoids the trap of far-left instrumentalism (which argues a
more conspiratorial, highly planned approach to all forms of state decision making) through a careful analysis of investment decisions. To
him, the most valuable concept is that of "business confidence." Investment decisions are based not only on variables such as price and
market share but on the capitalist's evaluation of the general politi-
cal/economic climate: "Is the society stable; is the working class mili-
tant; are taxes likely to rise; do government agencies interfere with
business freedom?" These questions, asked and answered across the
business strata of every capitalist nation, create a gauge of business
confidence that is distinct from "class consciousness."

A brief look at the Mitterrand socialist government of France in the early 1980s underscores the political significance of "business confidence." Elected on a sweeping platform of economic and social reform, including increased corporate taxes and greater state ownership of business, the Mitterrand regime was met by a dramatic flight of capital and a staggering withdrawal of investment (Petras 1983). This sent inflation and unemployment skyrocketing while tax revenues dropped precipitously. Within two years, most plans for reform were scrapped. Business confidence was so undermined that the state, lacking a countervailing class force to protect it, could no longer function. A brake on reform was effectively applied, for the state operates within the context of dominant economic relations, not outside of it.

However, if a brake can be applied to progressive reform, why has there not been a rapid dismantling of historic working-class gains? The answer to this question can be traced to another structural mechanism only hinted at by Miliband and Poulantzas but fully developed by Block, Gough, and O'Connor: *the advancement of the working population's ability to articulate and fight for its needs, which the economic sector was either no longer capable of or no longer willing to fulfill on its own* (Thompson 1969). The historic fight between workers and owners in the private sector was over wages, working conditions, and the right to organize. As the welfare state has expanded in the United States after the New Deal, working people have also fought for health care, housing, education, and employment training (Schlesinger 1959; Levitan 1985; Trattner 1984; Ehrenreich 1985).

The evolution of the capitalist system created not only higher levels of production, but also a more organized, educated, articulate, differentiated, and conflictual working class than had existed in previous historical epochs (Thompson 1969). For example, during the 1930s, trade unions organized and channeled parts of their working-class agenda into demands upon the state for unemployment insurance and Social Security. Their political strength, which over the last fifty years extended to civil rights groups and older Americans, has translated into a countervailing mechanism to that of "business confidence" that state leaders must reckon with if they are to stay in power. The inability of popular state leaders like Ronald Reagan and George Bush to radically dismantle either Social Security or Medicare speaks to this influence. As Block states, "In its struggles to protect itself from the ravages of a market economy, the working class has played a key role in the steady expansion of the state's role in capitalist societies . . . both in the regulating of the economy and in the provision of services" (Block 1977, p. 22).

In other words, shifts in the nature and direction of capitalism over the years have in turn affected corresponding pressure from the working class for expansion of the welfare state. Just as capitalists came to see the need for greater state intervention in the maintenance of their own industries (because of the increasingly complex interrelationship of the national and world economies, cf. Bluestone and Harrison 1982; Reich 1983), the working class has looked to the state for the resolution of its maintenance concerns. Consequently, in the early 1990s we see private industries pushing for the state to intervene in everything from trade protectionism to job training for unskilled, entry-level workers, while working groups are demanding subsidies for child care to support working mothers and job training for the new unemployed.

Why Groups under Capitalism Must Turn to the State: The Development of the State's Accumulation–Legitimation Functions

In answering his first theoretical question, Offe notes how capitalism "paralyzes itself" by the very nature of its functioning. Put simply, Offe suggests that the cyclical dynamics of the capitalist system are as follows: investing resources in new markets; producing for those markets; diminishing profitability as the market is saturated with the product or service; and then searching to reinvest in newer markets elsewhere. The cycle creates a spiral of long-term economic and social problems that constantly threaten capitalism's ability to invest in the first place (Offe 1984). For example, capital flight from older cities and metropolitan areas toward investment in other parts of the nation (and the world) where labor markets are cheaper has led to burned out central cities and diminished economic vitality in many regions of the country. These problems in turn diminish the domestic consumer market for the firms that have left. By leaving, these firms lose a large number of well-paid workers who can buy their goods and services. This dilemma places a concomitantly larger burden on the public sector to resolve these new municipal or regionwide employment–consumer problems through some form of economic redistribution, job retraining, or both.

In short, individual decisions of capitalists to search for more profitable areas in which to work have bred problems that later necessitate more rationalized, systemwide responses. These policies, because they now affect so many displaced workers and economically strapped regions (e.g., the farm belt, the Northeast), by definition cannot be developed or implemented through individual, private firms. (For example, no one firm or industry can respond to the greenhouse effect or deal with the number of ghost towns that are springing up throughout the farm belt.) The need for the state to intervene becomes axiomatic in such a dynamic. Business confidence may suffer, "but the nature of the problem no longer lends itself to actions by individual units of capital" (Keane 1984, p. xiii).

There are also simultaneous shifts among working groups of people. Child care, the extension of Social Security to all working groups, job retraining, and the like are collectivist interests recently advanced by working- and middle-class citizens who are no longer able to independently maintain their own family units. The proliferation of single-parent households, dual wage-earner families, and isolated elderly are social issues emerging due in great part to the demands of the changing economy discussed in chapter 1. The response of these groups is based on a collective recognition that their needs can no longer be resolved through voluntary or private efforts. Consequently, the state, with its array of social welfare institutions, huge revenues, and authority to respond to social needs, becomes a primary target for collective public pressure.

In short, the social and economic dynamics of late capitalism have bred the inexorable push toward greater and greater state intervention, even when individualized political sentiments may hope for an entirely different scenario. For example, though one may want to return to a society of traditional nuclear families, the conditions to create and sustain such family units no longer exist (Abramovitz 1989). At the same time, these economic and social pressures occur within a political economy that necessarily places primacy on both maintaining business confidence and resolving working people's increasing personal needs.

The Contradictory Functions of Accumulation–Legitimation

The ongoing tension between economic and social dilemmas, as O'Connor and others suggest, is played out through the twin functions of accumulation and legitimation. As has already been noted, certain state expenditures are functionally designed to help in the process of capital accumulation. Legitimation, on the other hand, relates to expenditures for nonworking and other financially marginal sectors of the society—expenditures that are necessary if the state is to maintain the political consensus and harmony demanded for widespread economic confidence.

Yet legitimation does not exist only on this plane of ideological justification. "The social integration [necessary for business confidence to be maintained and accumulation functions of the state to be uninterrupted] requires not only certain belief systems and normative actions but also material resources" (O'Connor 1973, p. 46). Thus, the expansion of entitlements is necessary "for those class groupings which do not participate in, or which suffer from, economic growth and development. This is especially true in periods of crisis" (Ibid.). This financial dimension of legitimation explains why, in the 1980s and early 1990s, severe "deindustrialization" and "capital flight" caused a simultaneous pull toward the maintenance of Social Security, a broadening of health programs, and new educational initiatives—all of which increased the very costs that the economic restructuring had been trying to avoid. We have seen the same processes at work in the 1990 budget imbroglio, one of the longest in modern times, where legislators wrangled with both a demand for tax cuts (to further the push for investment) and a "pent-up demand" for social spending.

In short, the functions of the modern state are contradictory. They involve pulls toward maintaining business confidence that justify increasing subsidies to capitalist firms at the expense of other social groups. At the same time, the process of subsidization and justification so destabilizes other populations that the state is pushed toward legitimating new forms of activity.

Importantly, the state cannot provide a service or good just as the private sector might. It must do so in ways so distinctive from capitalist firms that noncompetitiveness with the private sector is guaranteed. In this way, the state creates legitimacy for the service within the broader system. Yet, as O'Connor points out, the state " 'pollutes' capitalist relations insofar as transport, education, health services, and so on are organized by the state and hence are not based exclusively on capitalist criteria of profitability."

For example, public hospitals do not operate on profit-making criteria in terms of their admittance and reimbursement procedures. Instead, they are open to both working and nonworking populations alike for health care. These services must be maintained if workers are to be healthy enough to be employed consistently and reliably. At the same time, many workers have not been able to afford such care. There has been consequent pressure on the state to create eligibility requirements so that the poorest citizens would have at least minimal free services, even though the creation of this right becomes a threat to the assumption of profitability that is the norm within the private health care system.

Obviously, entitlement issues and rights to service are not a part of a private hospital's structure, but their creation within the public sector spills over into the public assessment of all medical facilities. For example, if the poor receive free services, why shouldn't other hospitals and insurers provide low-cost coverage for all working populations? To raise the question of low-cost coverage—now posed in every debate on health care across the nation—is to place the profitability of private corporations at greater risk. *Thus, state intervention both advances capitalist development and threatens it at the same time.*

The Quantitative Processes of State Functioning: Social Capital and Social Expenses

As has already been noted, the contradictory state functions of legitimation and accumulation can be seen in two important dimensions. The first dimension, discussed in terms of state activities calling for either "social capital" or "social expenses" by O'Connor and others, relates to the more directly quantitative processes of state expenditure.

One aspect of social capital has already been discussed: the direct tax credits and forms of state expenditure (e.g., the building of roads) used to bolster business confidence for investment purposes. Another aspect of this quantitative dimension of social capital maintains the consumption needs of the working population (e.g., unemployment insurance). By providing a modest subsistence income to temporarily unemployed workers, such insurance stabilizes the social positions of these workers so that they can readily return to work once an economic upswing begins. The insurance money also allows them to continue as active consumers whose purchasing power remains valuable for other sectors of the economy.

These activities of the state directly help private firms maintain their profitability in ways that are financially clear and thus quantifiable as "social capital." Not unlike private capital, such state activities can be seen as helpful for firms in planning their investment decisions.

Social expenses, on the other hand, have no *direct* benefits for private investment, but are used for the maintenance of nonworking groups—prisoners, welfare recipients, and the like. In fact, social expenses essentially are a drain on funds that could otherwise be used for social capital but need to be spent in order to assure widespread social harmony. For example, income maintenance for unemployable drug addicts neither stabilizes a working sector of the population nor aids firms in their investment decisions. The funds do, however, decrease the likelihood of a community's being perceived as excessively "crime-ridden" or "dangerous." These are quality-of-life dimensions in which the state must invest, yet they have no direct business payoff. Nonetheless, they are necessary for the long-term stability of a society.

The Qualitative Activities of State Functioning: The Dynamics of Social Reproduction

Given the push–pull between the social and economic groups in society on the one hand and the state on the other, it is inevitable that the overarching accumulation–legitimation functions of the state are laden with conflict. This conflict expresses itself both in economic terms (social capital versus social expenses) and through the processes of ongoing state operations. The state's involvement in mediating the demands of various contending social groups while maintaining business confidence requires that it develop *processes* that are not defined through financial means. The simple "quantitative" approach of totaling up two ledgers, one marked "social capital" and the other "social expenses," would imply a fiscal determinism that leaves out the variability that occurs in the legislative process and in the implementation of social policy (cf. Skocpol 1984).

Furthermore, the dynamic interplay among the state, the economy, and its social groups is also expressed through the way in which welfare state institutions socialize and support working populations (Gough 1979, pp. 44–54; see also Gorz 1969). These processes are known as "social reproduction." As developed here, Gough states that social reproduction refers to "state action to modify the nature, extent, and distribution of services," that is, the maintenance of and caring for the working population. Such qualitative processes—the "how" of policy implementation—complement the quantitative activities of social capital and the broader accumulation functions of the state.

On the other hand, the social reproduction of nonworking populations considers how welfare state institutions socialize and maintain nonworking groups that are not expected to contribute to the labor force. The social reproduction processes used to maintain these groups complement quantitative social expenses and the broader legitimation functions of the state.

Put simply, socializing groups of pregnant teens, monitoring first-time offenders, imprisonment, and the development of residential group homes for developmentally disabled adults are *socially reproductive processes that do not aid in the process of accumulation*. The current structure and delivery of services to these populations therefore socially reproduces behaviors, skills, and attitudes among these groups that are unlikely to prepare them for entry into or upward movement in the labor market. Neo-Marxists argue that this type of social reproduction complements state social expenses by keeping significant segments of the population from becoming either too troublesome (e.g., criminals) or too troubling (developmentally disabled adults) within society.

However, the neo-Marxists indicate that state activities directed at young people who are expected to be entry-level, skilled workers (to cite one example) will socially reproduce relations that are distinct from those developed for nonworking populations. The structure and delivery of services that lead to genuine skill development and relatively flexible behavioral change among young, skilled working populations is preparing them more adequately for the future requirements of the labor market. A comparative tour of a workfare program, an inner-city junior high school, and an upper-middle-class suburban high school could give one a quick sketch of how differently these organizations are structured—and the distinct effects the varying forms of service delivery have on the behaviors, attitudes, and expectations of the populations they each serve.

Conflict-Laden Activities and Processes of the Welfare State: The Role of Class Struggle

As we can see from the above discussion, the activities and processes of the state and its institutions take place on three levels: direct social expenditure on a material level that supports capital investment; training, maintenance, and support programs that the labor force needs in order to meet the demands from new forms of capitalist enterprise; and less costly support for the working and nonworking populations that stabilizes the population at large, either by maintaining consumption power (among temporarily laid-off workers) or by maintaining social harmony (among the nonworking).

Gough argues that these state activities (and the way in which they are delivered) in turn create social welfare policies that are conflict-laden. How, for example, is it possible in a democratic state with universal suffrage to both educate and prepare the young for future careers while simultaneously socializing large sectors of that population to accept entry-level jobs that have little future? How can an income policy be developed for targeted social groups (e.g., poor women, second-generation welfare families) without raising the job market expectations of these targeted groups to a higher level? As Gough mildly puts it, "An education system geared to the productive requirement of the economy may not serve the purpose of integrating and socializing the young" (Gough 1979, p. 53).

The most important contribution of the neo-Marxists is that their framework addresses the above questions by linking policy outcomes to a *continuum of class struggle between different social and economic groups affected by the state.* For them, class struggle is not simply a confrontation between dominant and subordinate groups (which would reinforce a false economic determinism), but rather a push–pull over the mix of accumulation–legitimation functions found in every state policy. As an ongoing process, the neo-Marxists argue, class struggle is an integral part of "push[ing] forward the development of capitalism—speeding the process by which capitalism advances the development of the productive forces" (Block 1977, p. 21).

Such struggle is not only part of a macrolevel legislative process. It is contained both in the push and pull of state activities that determines the mix between social expenses and social capital and, equally importantly, in the structure of social welfare institutions that socially reproduce relationships among the working and nonworking populations whom they serve. Additionally, neo-Marxists argue that the conflict-laden nature of the broader accumulation–legitimation functions makes change and development a more dynamic process that interacts with and influences the various dimensions of the welfare state.

To illustrate, if the state supports accumulation functions by reproducing a less skilled work force that lowers future labor costs, it may sacrifice the maintenance of social harmony and its own legitimacy. On the contrary, if the state concentrates on maintaining social harmony by increasing its social expense allocations, the process of accumulation may be stymied. For example, the growing trillion-dollar deficit created by Ronald Reagan and sustained by George Bush has contributed to the intensification of poverty. On the other hand, escalating health care costs and their attendant fiscal pressures on the public purse reduce resources for more direct subsidies to the private sector. Finally, the emphasis on expensive prison programs and social control measures for the increasing number of criminals has siphoned funds from educational programs. These choices limit the capacity of schools to train and socialize students adequately for emergent entry-level jobs. Thus, the circle is drawn, as decisions by welfare state agencies on how to deliver services and reproduce relationships among clients affect the investment capacity and the decision making of private firms. It is a model of ongoing change that shows how welfare state workers and their programs are linked to the larger dynamics within the state and society.

The Neo-Marxist Deterministic Analysis of Welfare State Programs

Early neo-Marxist writings have a curiously deterministic cast in the way they analyze not social policy but social welfare *programs*. As Elizabeth Wilson writes,

> In attempting to escape 'overpoliticization' Gough has denuded his work of any real . . . detailed discussion of the relationship of welfare state, cuts, and crisis, and has lapsed into economic determinism. . . . Since [he] explicitly seeks to reach workers in the social services and other areas of the welfare state . . . [the lack] of political argument will certainly discourage [them]. (1980, p. 88)

Gough's analysis implies that agency functions are collapsed into a predetermined process of aiding capital accumulation. This is accomplished by reproducing a less costly labor force, such as by lowering wages, deskilling workers, and diminishing the expectations and demands of the work force. Furthermore, his analysis suggests that programs that engage in primarily social expense activities play a consciously co-optive or controlling role with society's nonworking populations.

We must reiterate that neo-Marxists have developed a far more dynamic and conflict-laden framework to explain what occurred within the crisis of the state itself. "Tensions," "dilemmas," "unresolved con-tradictions within welfare state policies"—the terms themselves are dynamic and open-ended in terms of potential change. The use of such language suggests another, equally compelling reality regarding the modern state. Rather than being overly deterministic, the welfare state, because of its crucial role in the reproduction and maintenance of society's various populations, is also an arena of great struggle and ideological debate.

In her analysis of the New Deal, for example, Skocpol suggests that "state organizations have their own structures, their own histories and their own patterns of conflict that impact upon class relations and economic development" (1984, p. 200). Cousins also notes that "state management is embedded in a political apparatus with its own mode of rationality" (1987, p. 54; see also Offe 1973). In short, there is ongoing debate and conflict among actors within the state over the roles, re-sponsibilities, and functions of the welfare state and its representatives.

Consequently, in their more recent writings, neo-Marxists have begun to consider the state as an important arena for class struggle. Writers such as O'Connor (1984), Skocpol (1979, 1984), and Offe (1973) have analyzed the parliamentary and judicial policy-making dimensions of legitimation. Pat Morgan (1982, 1985), Marc Renaud (1975), and others were principally interested in the relationship be-tween class struggle and welfare state *programs*. These authors argue that the state has become a critical arena for worker and client-group efforts to advance a range of social policies. They also note, however, that processes *within the state apparatus* (e.g., welfare state programs) undermine social movements' pursuit of greater social and economic equality.

These authors emphasize the ways in which social welfare programs *individuate needs over collective social concerns*:

> *Individuation* is the process of narrowing structural issues into single ones, or fragmenting class relationships into atomized segments of the social order. *Bureaucratization* offers a method whereby "individuals" can be removed from their class relationships in production . . . and

reinstituted as a "mass of individuals." . . . *Professionalization* further insures that these individuals are kept from recognizing their own class position and needs. (Morgan 1982, p. 198).

O'Connor suggests that in the health field, "the first and easiest path is to put the blame for bad health on the individual. . . . Health policies focus on individual at-risk behaviors and all have in common the importation of responsibility on the individual" (O'Connor 1984, p. 176; see also Renaud 1975). According to Pat Morgan (1985), the definitions, policies, and programs designed to address alcohol abuse originally emphasized overall prevention. "However, it was reoriented [through the processes of individuation, bureaucratization, and professionalization] to 'individuated treatment' and the onus of the problem changed from the 'substance' itself to the 'individual's pathology.' " The resultant programmatic emphasis was on private, individualized forms of treatment controlled by private practitioners and profit-making clinics. Simultaneously, a proliferation of voluntaristic self-help groups concerned with supporting and responding to ongoing needs of members emerged (Peel 1989). "The result was an epidemic of self-blame and scapegoating and widespread personality disintegration" (O'Connor 1984; Lasch 1979).

Morgan's rich insights provide at least part of a preliminary framework for analyzing social programs of the welfare state. She argues that through individuation, bureaucratization, and professionalization, social expenditures are lowered in the short run. For example, despite the spread of Employee Assistance Programs (EAPs), alcohol and drug treatment continue to be the primary responsibility of the individual rather than the place of employment or the state. Social problems are reproduced within the welfare state, becoming problems of individuals (albeit masses of them) that each person is expected to solve independently. When that is not possible, the individual's problem can only be ameliorated through professionally controlled programs. The continuum becomes clear. Alcoholism and drug abuse, as an employee's problem, are dealt with primarily outside the workplace, thus lowering the costs incurred by the employer. Productivity of the firm is thus increased. However, if an individual drops out of the work force because of chronic substance abuse problems, he or she confronts onerous one- and two-year waiting lists and limited public treatment programs. These conditions often intensify criminal behavior to maintain an addiction and/or lead to distinct social isolation, only modestly ameliorated through programs of marginal assistance, such as congregate shelters for the homeless. Equally important, these programs often fail to recognize or address the complex social context that is rapidly reproducing substance abuse. Limited access to help and the inability of some programs to identify and address the nature of problems are but two of the factors that can transform social breakdown into more discrete, individuated—and crisis-ridden—concerns.

Locating the Class Struggle within Social Welfare Programs

This focus on programmatic dynamics makes clear that class struggle is inescapable *within* the organizations of the welfare state. Workers and managers of these organizations are involved in decisions concerning client problems. These decisions either prefigure or reinforce the processes of individuation, bureaucratization, and professionalization. The options chosen by social welfare programs in turn will affect how different client groups are socialized, their behaviors supported, and their aspirations raised or lowered—in short, these decisions affect the nature of social reproduction within social welfare organizations.

However, the process of social reproduction within social welfare programs is perhaps more fluid and tension-filled than Morgan and others might suggest. To begin with, there may only be surface validity to the compelling picture of bureaucratization, professionalization, and individuation working together to isolate and depoliticize social problems. There is little question that bureaucratization as an organizational process does seek to routinize and standardize the response to societal issues and needs, as Weber pointed out (Weber 1981; Mills 1959). Furthermore, bureaucratization has been found to permeate the response of the welfare state to social problems (Blau 1960). However, Cousins points out that most models of bureaucratization have "an over-emphasis on unilinear management strategies and [an] underestima[tion] of worker resistance" (Cousins 1987, p. 42).

Likewise, Reeser and Epstein have found that social workers' allegiance to professionalism is a more variable and less organizationally predetermined process than the neo-Marxists would suggest. For example, they found that among four distinct professional groups, social workers were the group "in which the demands of profession, organization, and client are more integrated and less conflictual than in other professions" (Reeser and Epstein 1989, p. 86). Indeed, their profile paralleled other empirical findings that suggest that "bureaucratic and professional orientations are independent dimensions" (Reeser and Epstein 1989; Wilson, Voth, and Hudson 1980, p. 28). If their findings are accurate, the interplay between professionalization and bureaucratization is as open to struggle as other welfare state processes.

Reeser and Epstein also found that a significantly *smaller* percentage of social workers interviewed in the 1980s, as compared to the 1960s, believed that their own definitions of problems were superior to those of their clients (22 percent from 34 percent) (see Reeser and Epstein 1989, pp. 88–89). Their findings undermine the neo-Marxist assumption that professionalization leads to minimal acceptance of the problem definitions offered by the poor themselves. This premise underpins the neo-Marxist belief that client–worker relationships are at best distant and highly proscribed. We therefore need to ask why it is inevitable that program professionals will individuate and bureaucratize in ways that place blame and heightened responsibility on their clients. For it is only through such aspects of professionalized distancing that neo-Marxists *ensure* a lowering of labor costs, as clients are removed from or become marginalized in the workplace.

There are other examples, however, drawn directly from daily human service work, that suggest a different expectation—and potentially different outcomes. For example, a child welfare worker makes innumerable decisions about her clientele (on referral, assessment of family strengths and problems, etc.). While these decisions do not have an apparent systemwide impact at any one moment in time, they frequently reflect ideological and material tensions associated with a significant sector of the population. Does the social worker have time to use an assessment strategy that will note an unemployed, unskilled young mother's concern for her children's health and hygiene as an important strength to build upon? There are supervisors and managers who struggle to allow such a worker both the time and skill to ferret out strengths in the midst of trying family problems. They recognize that this methodological emphasis on building upon strengths, while seemingly minor, contains ideas and beliefs that can help strengthen the client's self-esteem as she approaches a General Equivalency Diploma (G.E.D.) or job training program. With an increased sense of personal competence, the client begins to approach her work with higher expectations about her future, a greater interest in skill development, and, concurrently, greater demands that those skills and expectations be utilized. *These human service workers' decisions can socially reproduce expectations and reinforce personal competencies for skill development that increase workplace demands, in turn raising productivity or consumption.*

Likewise, the professional social worker involved with hospital discharge planning is struggling to balance her fiscal responsibilities to the hospital against the impact specific decisions will have upon the health of clients. The more effort made to improve the health and stability of patients, the greater the likelihood that these patients will come to expect similar service in other areas of their lives. Although social workers may not be thinking about either "business confidence" or "lowering social expenses," the thoughtful, planned decisions they make, when aggregated as part of the sum of many such decisions made by human service workers across the welfare state, are inextricably linked to the development and change of the legitimation–accumulation functions of the state.

These types of practice tensions and choices more accurately reflect the actual behavior and decision making of line social service workers (Lipsky 1983). This decision-making process contradicts the presumption by Morgan and others that state (or state-contracted) programs *will* succumb to the negative processes and outcomes they associate with individualization, bureaucratization, and professionalization. As has been suggested, decisions that professionals make about their methods of intervention or the manner of program implementation are open to class struggle in the same way larger accumulation–legitimation functions of the state experience such tension.

As Cousins argues, "the ambiguous and contradictory nature of state work does have consequences for both managers and workers . . . many of the government's policies with respect to welfare work have had contradictory and unintended effects, have generated resistance and oppositions and produced further problems and tensions for state managers which have to be resolved" (Cousins 1987, p. 63).

It is a mistake to analyze the structure and functioning of social programs as if the ideological processes that are associated with those programs will seek to socially reproduce behaviors and skills that only lower labor costs. Furthermore, it is incorrect to assume that professionalization inevitably reproduces a deferential, cheaper labor force.

The neo-Marxist analysis implies that the search for social harmony, while expensive, is designed consciously to control and permanently co-opt the nonworking populations whom the welfare state and its workers serve. It is instead more reasonable to assume that the struggle over the scope of one's program and level of fiscal costs carries the same contradictory tensions that O'Connor identifies at the level of the state. For example, many shelters for the homeless, while originally little more than barracks-style facilities, have been developed into far more service-driven and empowering organizations for their clients. *This has occurred in part because of the utilization of discretion, thought, and struggle by the workers and clients within those shelters to develop and expand new forms of service.* Such results emerged out of the clients' and workers' analyses of problems and tensions in their daily programs. When they were successful, their demands over time *increased* social expenses and, as some of the formerly homeless from these facilities reentered the labor force, produced less deferential, less marginalized workers, who in no way guaranteed a less costly work force.

We can avoid the trap of assuming *only* lowered costs and a pre-planned, consciously co-optive role for workers by using the same dynamic framework to explain the social service work experience in relation to state functions. Business confidence and the dominant accumulation functions of the state will seek in the long run to lower costs and maintain social harmony. This does put a limit on unendingly expansive reform under present social and economic conditions. Social workers will thus continue to confront fiscal pressures and constraints in the running of their programs. However, it cannot be predetermined that social service workers and the programs they implement will operate in a controlling manner. By examining the decisions and choices workers make to socially reproduce a less deferential and more skilled clientele (among both their working and nonworking clients), we can see that their actions connect to the same dynamic opportunities of class struggle that O'Connor and others identify at the level of the state itself.

Erik Olin Wright's analysis of "the contradictory class location" of professional social workers (1978) further helps to explain the tensions and dilemmas within the human service workplace. While individual service workers have little control over their wages and working conditions, they must have a degree of autonomy to apply their skills and perform certain functions on a daily basis. For example, the child welfare worker must have the time and discretion to note strengths and problems within the family situations he has been asked to investigate.

This contradictory role—having little control over general working conditions but needing professional discretion to implement service—creates ongoing tensions for human service workers and their supervisors. These tensions in turn influence the workers' daily decisions.

Such tensions could be easily resolved if there were a predetermined, primary commitment to maintaining business confidence. However, as Reeser and Epstein's comparative study of social workers across two decades makes clear, the training, socialization, and belief systems of social workers and others throughout the human service professions are not based on this single premise (Reeser and Epstein 1989). This accumulation obligation (experienced as "fiscal constraints necessary to maintain high bond ratings") is counterbalanced by the complexity and persistence of client problems. As occurs daily in homeless services, job training programs, health care settings, etc., the pressure to respond effectively to complex client needs is the countervailing dynamic that consistently reconnects workers and programs to processes of change that cannot be predetermined in a mechanistic fashion.

Summary and Conclusions

The active role of state workers in the processes of social reproduction with their clients enriches the neo-Marxist analysis of the state and better enables it to answer the two primary questions asked by Offe of any theory of the state. First, in capturing the contradictory functions of accumulation and legitimation in aiding capitalist development while responding to the needs of the population at large, the neo-Marxist analysis describes the economic and social relations of our society more accurately than other, more popular theories.

Equally important, elucidation of how these contradictory functions affect and are affected by the activities of the state develops a clear strategic direction by which change can emerge. Perhaps most critically, such strategic clarification explains how class struggle can develop through welfare state programs.

Because welfare state programs contain a mix of activities requiring both social capital and social expenses, there will be an ongoing struggle over the mix of those costs. Some of the outlays will be directly quantifiable as outlays for construction or as transfer payments that maintain working and nonworking populations' levels of consumption. These costs—fought over in budget talks on capital gains write-offs, tax credits for working parents, welfare, and the like—are the broad-scale measures of class struggle that emerge within the state and have been discussed by O'Connor, Skocpol, and others.

At the programmatic level, this struggle continues along two dimensions. The first, of course, relates to the amount of funding provided to programs (which service workers experience in terms of fiscal constraints or opportunities). The second level relates to the processes of individualization, bureaucratization, and professionalization and their interaction with social issues. It is within this context that professionals, clients, and others contend over the structure and delivery of programs. *We argue that in such programmatic situations, how workers choose to act, and the degree to which they seek to socially reproduce behaviors, skills, and expectations that raise labor costs and improve conditions for nonworking populations, are elements of class struggle. This conflict is embedded in ongoing decisions and practice debates made by the worker, the agency, and the profession.* As with any strategic debate, it is not a foregone conclusion that outcomes are predetermined to reproduce lowered costs and a more deferential, acquiescent, and less skilled population. Instead, the programmatic decisions that daily affect worker–client interactions reverberate with the same contradictory tensions that affect broader state strategies for allocating society's goods and services. Only by seeing the links between daily programmatic practice and these larger systemwide dynamics can human service workers, supervisors, and managers affect policy as well as program.

Such an understanding demands that social workers take on a more active responsibility to affect their programs and the conditions that shape them. While social service workers are neither primary determinants of the social safety net (the traditional liberal interpretation) nor willing agents of social largesse (the conservative assumption), they also are not well-meaning bystanders in these processes of class struggle. Service workers must understand the dynamic interplay between their roles and those of larger social forces. In effect, they perform on their jobs either as conscious actors in the struggle to improve the scope and direction of services that affect their clients (and their own lives), *or* as passive recipients in a process that is defined by others. To understand the modest but very real role they play in these processes is both humbling *and* liberating, for there is one other strategic implication: no one who engages in human service work stands outside of this struggle.

Chapter 5 identifies an important new direction for human services.

This approach, which we describe as generative social services, structurally encourages a more active, experimental role for social workers. The social worker is defined as a primary participant in a process intended to improve the scope and direction of social services. We also examine the dilemmas and contradictions associated with this activist/learning/teaching role and generative structure.

However, it is clear, with the ascent of cost-containment mechanisms to decrease social welfare expenses, that social welfare organizations and professionals are increasingly less prepared to encourage such experimentation or struggle. More likely, the leadership of social welfare organizations is passively accepting and/or actively enforcing policies and programs that threaten the field's survival.

Indeed, as the next two chapters make clear, bureaucratization and individualization are now being used as cost-containment mechanisms to erode rather than expand the professionalization of service. Workers today are being assaulted with an increasingly narrow, less autonomous, and mechanistic form of work. These conditions diminish the line worker's professional expectations of the craft while heightening managerial demands for productivity. Presently, managers are developing a more proletarianized work force to insulate themselves and their organizations from the increased demands of the poor.

To some extent, the tacit embrace of these shifts on the part of social welfare organization managers can be traced to their minimal understanding of the dynamic interplay among the political economy, the welfare state, and its programs. As the next chapter explains and the fourth chapter documents empirically, by ignoring the structural shifts and tensions within the service workplace, administrators and line staff may have acceded to the decay of areas of practice that could have been preserved, including prevention, outreach, society–family relations, and appropriate discharge planning (to name but a few areas within traditional social service work that have been affected by recent changes). If these core areas of social work practice continue to erode and are replaced by increasingly mechanistic and bureaucratic forms of service, the result will be a diminished legitimacy for the entire field.

The erosion is real, as the data in the fourth chapter make clear. The next chapter examines in greater relief the ominous trends in the field that have developed with startling clarity during the crisis of the American political economy: the loss of agency autonomy and the decline of professional skill.

References

Abramovitz, M. *Regulating the Lives of Women.* Boston: South End Press, 1989.

Blau, P. "Orientation toward Clients in a Welfare Organization." *Administration Science Quarterly* 5 (1960).

Block, Fred. *The Origins of International Economic Disorder: A Study of the United States.* Berkeley, CA: University of California Press, 1977.

———. *Revising State Theory: Essays in Politics and Post-Industrialism.* Philadelphia: Temple University Press, 1987.

Bluestone, Barry, and Bennett Harrison. *The Deindustrialization of America.* New York: Basic Books, 1982.

Bowles, Samuel, and Herbert Gintis. "The Crisis of Liberal Democratic Capitalism: The Case of the United States." *Politics and Society* 11, 1 (1982).

Cousins, Christine. *Controlling Social Welfare: A Sociology of State Welfare Work and Organizations.* Brighton, Sussex: Wheatsheaf Books, 1987.

Dahl, Robert. *Dilemmas of Pluralist Democracy: Autonomy vs. Control.* New Haven, CT: Yale University Press, 1982.

Easton, David. *A Framework for Political Analysis.* Englewood Cliffs, NJ: Prentice-Hall, 1965.

Ehrenreich, J. *The Altruistic Imagination: A History of Social Work and Social Policy in the United States.* Ithaca, NY: Cornell University Press, 1985.

Gilbert, Neil. *Capitalism and Social Welfare.* New Haven, CT: Yale University Press, 1984.

Gilder, George. *Wealth and Poverty.* New York: Bantam Books, 1979.

———. "The Collapse of the American Family." *Public Interest* (Fall 1987).

Gorz, Andre. *Strategy for Labor.* Boston: Beacon Press, 1969.

Gough, Ian. *The Political Economy of the Welfare State.* London: Macmillan, 1979.

Hirschorn, Larry. *Beyond Mechanization.* Cambridge, MA: MIT Press, 1984.

Keane, John. Introduction. In Claus Offe, *Contradictions of the Welfare State.* Cambridge, MA: MIT Press, 1984.

Lasch, Christopher. *The Culture of Narcissism.* New York: Vintage Books, 1979.

Levitan, S. *Programs in Aid of the Poor.* Baltimore, MD: Johns Hopkins, 1985.

Lipsky, Michael. *Street-Level Bureaucracy: Dilemmas of the Individual in Public Service.* New York: Russell Sage, 1983.

Markusen, Ann. "Class and Urban Social Expenditure: A Local Theory of the State." *Kapitalistate* 4–5 (1985).

Miliband, Ralph. *The State in Capitalist Society.* New York: Basic Books, 1982.

Mills, C. W. *White Collar.* New York: Oxford University Press, 1953.

———. *The Sociological Imagination.* New York: Oxford University Press, 1959.

Morgan, Pat. "From Battered Wife to Program Client." *Kapitalistate* 9 (1982).

———. "The State as Mediator: Alcohol Problem Management in the Post-War Period." Unpublished manuscript, 1985.

Murray, Charles. *Losing Ground: American Social Policy 1950–1980.* New York: Basic Books, 1984.

O'Connor, James. *The Fiscal Crisis of the State.* New York: St. Martin's Press, 1973.

———. *Accumulation Crisis.* New York: Basil Blackwell, 1984.

Offe, Claus. "Political Authority and Class Structure: An Analysis of Late-Capitalist Societies." *International Journal of Sociology* 2, 7 (1972).

————. "The Abolition of Market Control and the Problem of Legitimacy." Parts I and II. *Kapitalistate* 1–2 (1973).

————. *Contradictions of the Welfare State.* Cambridge, MA: MIT Press, 1984.

Olson, Laura K. *The Political Economy of Aging: The State, Private Power, and Social Welfare.* New York: Columbia University Press, 1982.

Patti, Rino, Mimi Abramowitz, Steve Burghardt, Michael Fabricant, Martha Haffey, Elizabeth Dane, and Rose Starr. *Gaining Perspective on "Losing Ground."* New York: A Saul Horowitz, Jr., Memorial Series of the Hunter College School of Social Work, 1987.

Peel, Stanton. *The Myths of Drug Addiction.* New York: Doubleday, 1989.

Petras, James. "The Impasse of Euro-Socialism." *New Left Review* 146 (November/December 1983).

Phillips, Kevin. *The Politics of the Rich and Poor.* New York: W. W. Norton, 1990.

Piven, Frances Fox, and Richard Cloward. *Regulating the Poor.* New York: Pantheon, 1971.

————. *The New Class War.* New York: Pantheon, 1982.

Poulantzas, Nicos. *Political Power and Social Classes.* London: New Left Books, 1973.

Reeser, Linda C., and Irwin Epstein. *Professionalization and Activism in Social Work.* New York: Columbia University Press, 1989.

Reich, Robert. *The Next American Frontier.* New York: Times Books, 1983.

Renaud, Marc. "On the Structural Constraints to State Intervention in Health." *International Journal of Health Services* 5, 4 (1975).

Schlesinger, A., Jr., *The Age of Roosevelt: The Coming of the New Deal.* New York: Houghton Mifflin, 1959.

Schumpeter, Joseph. *The Theory of Economic Development.* Cambridge, MA: Harvard University Press, 1962.

Shimbun, N. K. *Nomura Medium-Term Outlook for Japan and the World,* 1990.

Skocpol, Theda. *States and Social Revolutions.* Cambridge: Cambridge University Press, 1979.

————. *Vision and Method in Historical Sociology.* Cambridge: Cambridge University Press, 1984.

Thompson, E. P. *Making of the English Working Class.* New York: Random House, 1969.

Trattner, W. *From Poor Law to Welfare State.* New York: Free Press, 1984.

Weber, M. *The Theory of Social and Economic Organizations.* New York: Free Press, 1981.

Wilson, E. "The Political Economy of Welfare." *New Left Review* 122 (July-August 1980).

Wilson, P., V. Voth, and W. Hudson. "Professionals and the Bureaucracy: Measuring the Orientation of Social Workers." *Journal of Social Service Research* 4(1980):15–30.

Wright, Erik Olin. *Class, Crisis and the State.* London: New Left Books, 1978.

3 • The Crisis and Transformation of Public Social Services

Introduction

Christine L. is a black woman who has been working in a public New York City child welfare organization for twenty years. She now views her job as little more than a paycheck, finding almost no hope of effecting even modest positive change in the lives of the children with whom she comes into contact daily. Her efforts to get an advanced degree beyond the B.S.W. have been stymied by the heavy caseload and stress associated with agency work. Ms. L. now engages her work in an increasingly mechanical manner. In dealing with uniform case record forms, for instance, which structure encounters with agency clients, she tends more and more to see the completion of the forms as the focal point of her work.

Ms. L.'s work was not always so devoid of hope and narrowly focused. She entered the field of children's services with the intention of working imaginatively and passionately to assist troubled and poor youngsters. She also understood that such work would depend on the development of skill and maintenance of commitment. Her idealism was tempered by the realization that she could not help every youngster in need. Despite these tensions, she maintained that modest, even slow progress in some children's functioning was the foundation for the development of practice and what she enjoyed most about social work. Many years later, Ms. L. no longer talks about the joys or frustrations associated with her work. Her singular preoccupation is surviving the five years before she is eligible for retirement.

What happened to Ms. L.? Why is she so estranged from her work? How does Ms. L.'s approach toward her work affect clients? Can we generalize her experience to other child welfare workers? Finally, are social service workers in other types of agencies experiencing their work similarly? Before we can even begin to address these questions, we must look briefly at a professional social worker who is struggling to provide quality social services to clients in a health care setting.

Bryn M. is a white M.S.W. worker who has been employed by a public hospital in Boston for seven years. She has specialized in the delivery of a range of services to patients in an oncology unit. She has counseled patients, developed support groups for "critical others," and participated in discharge planning.

Ms. M.'s time is now primarily devoted to discharge planning functions. At the same time, the delivery and creation of quality services has been deemphasized in favor of moving people through the unit in increasingly shorter, more proscribed periods of time. This shift in emphasis has caused Ms. M. to raise questions and objections at departmental and interdepartmental meetings. The consistent response of administrators is that financial considerations have forced a restructuring of priorities. They have also noted that the only alternative to present policies would be to shut down the hospital. The tension between hospital or administrative directives and the patients' needs has consequently been intensified. Ms. M. finds that professionals within this social work unit are being required to discharge terminally ill patients to facilities and private homes that do not meet minimal standards of medical care. Additionally, more and more of her time is being claimed by the mounting demands of discharge planning. Bryn M.'s work is rapidly being redefined. She does not fully understand the reasons. She does understand, however, that her daily work has become less meaningful and more stressful. She has also been concerned that the social work department's "turf" is being increasingly narrowed and marginalized. She has come to the conclusion that agency-based social work offers diminished opportunities for skill development or career advancement. Ms. M. is consequently preparing to leave the hospital and develop a private practice.

These illustrations concretely highlight a number of the changes that are transforming social service work. As chapter 1 makes clear, public agencies were especially hard hit in the 1980s by a combination of deep budget cuts and a steeply rising demand for services from eligible citizens. This tension was experienced initially and most intensely by public agencies because of their entitlement obligations. The accumulation–legitimation tensions of the state brought about the critical agency dilemma of diminished financial capacity, and hence the growing inability of agencies to meet the escalating costs of a more troubled client population. These conditions caused fundamental shifts in the delivery and structure of public social services. This chapter will explore the content and impact of these changes. Illustrative material will be drawn from the experiences of hospitals, child welfare agencies, and income maintenance centers.

Public social service agencies are presently faced with a number of very serious dilemmas. For instance, public hospitals must be more fiscally conservative yet simultaneously maintain and serve more impoverished populations, including the homeless, AIDS patients, and crack-addicted newborns (Cousins 1987; George 1985; Wilding 1982). Efforts to resolve these dilemmas through heightened bureaucratic control are experienced by social service workers in many ways. Perhaps most importantly, new forms of accountability or daily social service tasks are contributing to increased worker frustration and burnout while undermining long-term organizational effectiveness.

These emergent frameworks for social service practice threaten the viability or legitimacy of workers (with clients) and more generally, the welfare state (with the polity) (Cousins 1987). The state may very well be engaged in a form of institutional delegitimation by implementing policies that in the short run contain costs only by shattering the community's most basic beliefs regarding the obligation and capacities of service agencies. This contradiction is increasingly defining every facet of welfare state work.

It will be the purpose of this chapter to explain the rapid and profound changes in public-sector social service work. We will first explore the relationships among the fiscal crisis, bureaucratization, and changes in the organization and structure of social service work. Consequently, we will also examine the reduced capacity of welfare state workers to structure autonomously their encounters with clients and to develop the skills necessary for effective intervention. This process of reducing the workers' skill level and control over their work is described as *proletarianization* (Wilkins 1981; Cousins 1987; Derber 1982; Larson 1980; Braverman 1974). These changes are profoundly altering the structure, process, and outcomes of social service work. The loss of autonomy and control in the utilization of skill may well be the most powerful force redefining encounters between social service workers and clients in late-twentieth-century America.

This chapter will conclude with a discussion of the deepening social and class divisions among welfare state workers. The segmentation of this labor force divides workers by a number of variables including, but not limited to, income, race, gender, and expertise. There is a dynamic interplay between the segmentation of the labor force on the one hand and the proletarianization of social service work on the other. The divisions within the welfare state work force will be examined through the conceptual frameworks developed by Gordon, Edwards, and Reich (Gordon et al. 1982; Edwards 1979). Thus, we expect that this chapter will provide a framework for explaining the difficult dilemmas and contradictions faced by social service workers in the 1980s as the push toward accumulation, social capital, and lowered labor costs continues.

Cost Containment and the Restructuring of
Social Service Practice

Is a set of forces specific to the 1980s altering the nature and conditions of work in the welfare state? Bryn M.'s concerns about narrowed job definition and the ethical dilemmas of releasing terminally ill patients into the streets are traced by some simply to the internal dynamics of social service bureaucracies. This argument suggests that welfare state organizations that host medical, legal, educational, and social work practice have historically attempted to redefine professional practice to meet the competing needs of the public bureaucracy. The dilemmas may be as straightforward as determining how long a professional such as Ms. L. or Ms. M. can spend with a client, or as complex as choosing a primary interventive strategy for addressing client need, such as crisis intervention or long-term counseling. However, it is the contention of this analysis that the changes presently affecting welfare state professional practice are substantively different from the historic demands that bureaucracy has made upon human service workers laboring within the welfare state.

Clearly, the process of bureaucratization is an independent phenomenon that predates recent transformation(s) of welfare state work caused by the fiscal crisis (Stinchcombe 1959; Dressel 1984; Lipsky

1980). Bureaucratic attempts to control the service process did not begin with the fiscal crisis. However, the recent intensification and direction of these bureaucratic tendencies represents the context for today's profound changes. Recent cost-containment policies have heightened the bureaucracy's need to control the labor force and redefine the content of its work (Lipsky 1980), Dressel 1984).

These cost-containment policies have affected agencies in a variety of ways. Many professionals within public agencies have witnessed a deterioration in their working conditions, salaries, opportunities for advancement, and job satisfaction. These experiences are the result of policies that have been tailored to limit the costs associated with social services. Whether the policy is the use of Diagnostic Review Groups (DRGs) or quality control for Income Maintenance Centers in Texas and Georgia, the objectives are similar (Palmer and Eisenstadt 1984; Patry 1980; Joe 1985). Policymakers are primarily concerned with heightening worker and agency efficiency within the established boundaries of accountability in order to reduce the costs of social services. However, almost without exception, cost-containment policies tend to favor fiscal austerity over the delivery of quality services. The following quotations illustrate this point:

> This emphasis [for P.R.O. (Peer Review Organization)] would appear to entail significant risks of restricting the availability of desirable health care services for the elderly. . . . For example, one P.R.O. is required to reduce total Medicare hospital admissions by 13.25%, admissions for procedures safely performed on an outpatient basis by 25% and admission under the ten most common D.R.G.'s by 6.8%. (Palmer and Eisenstadt 1985, p. 8)

> In 1981 the Reagan administration proposed and Congress enacted a set of policy changes in [AFDC] designed to pare down the welfare roles and save money. The Reagan administration argued that . . . changes would make the system more efficient.

> Regardless of the intent of the 1981 changes (A.F.D.C.), one effect is clear. The policy changes reduced benefits to the poor while vastly increasing the complexity of the system. . . . (Joe 1985, p. 5)

> The major new and serious problems that have emerged in the 1980s also have placed new burdens on child and family services—once again

without any increase in resources. . . . The inadequacy of federal funding for social services, as contrasted with expectations generated by legislation, (i.e., paperwork, standards, etc.) . . . have created major problems everywhere. (Kammerman and Kahn 1989, p. 1)

The Effect of the Fiscal Crisis

As has already been noted, welfare state programs experienced unprecedented cutbacks in their funding levels beginning in the late 1970s and continuing through the Reagan presidency. These cuts have not spared any part of the welfare state. In 1981, over 400,000 disabled citizens were cut from the SSI rolls (Burghardt and Fabricant 1987). Between 1980 and 1984, AFDC and child welfare programs were cut by 13 percent and Food Stamps experienced a reduction of 14 percent (Hopper and Hamberg 1984). It is estimated that overall cash welfare benefits declined by 17 percent. Additionally, the operating budgets of public social service agencies were cut. Many expenses associated with the delivery of services (particularly labor costs, which represent by far the largest part of an agency's budget) were considered exorbitant. Consequently, specific administrative and budgetary mechanisms were created to reduce these costs (Kotelchuck 1985; Turem and Born 1983; and Gruber 1974).

Ironically, at the time that the budget of the welfare state was being reduced, demands upon its work force increased substantially. These new demands can be traced in part to the exportation of manufacturing jobs from the Northeast and Midwest of the United States to the Sun Belt and to Third World countries (Bluestone and Bennett 1982). This job dislocation clearly placed certain immediate demands upon the welfare state. For instance, unemployed workers might be expected to apply for specific entitlements and avail themselves of other services such as rental subsidies.

Over time these short-term economic services were invariably supplemented by more discrete concrete services (Burghardt and Fabricant 1987). Unemployed workers, however, were not the only population placing increased and more intensified demands upon welfare state workers. As the state began to disengage from its programmatic commitments to the poor and working class by cutting its budget allocation to public housing, medical services entitlement programs, and the like, it heightened the stress experienced by vulnerable individuals and communities. These populations, already in need, did not disappear but rather returned with even more complicated problems that required immediate attention. For instance, AFDC mothers who had previously been able to compete, albeit marginally, for urban housing, quickly discovered that the combination of low and declining grant levels and the halt in low-income housing creation effectively denied them access to the rental market. (Hopper and Hamberg [1984] indicate that AFDC grant levels were anywhere from 40 percent to 60 percent below prevailing urban rent levels.) Over time, many of these families became homeless.

The intensification of these social problems has left welfare state workers in the middle of a fundamental contradiction. The economic crisis demands the state's emphasis on accumulation. At the same time, the welfare state cannot be cut without creating new and greater needs in both the short and long run, thus undermining the state's legitimacy (Mishra 1984). The only constant in this dilemma is that welfare state workers will be expected to function as the state's legitimating representatives and respond to these mounting demands with fewer resources and increased work loads. This transformation of one set of social problems (produced by the policies of budget cutting) into even more urgent personal and collective crises is most dramatically illustrated by the rise of homelessness.

Certain academics and policymakers have indicated that the central issue for agency line staff and administrators will be how to do more with less (Terrell 1981; Turem and Born 1983). It has already been suggested that one of the more subtle costs of fiscal austerity is that agency caseloads will be increasingly populated with clients whose problems are more urgent and complex (Fabricant 1988). On the other hand, perhaps the most visible outcome of such budget cutting is that the caseloads of individual workers and agencies will balloon. This point is illustrated below:

> The H.E.W. study also confirms that high caseloads are a considerable problem in the field. It cited as an example the fact that in public assistance, 44 states were violating a federally imposed law that caseloads should not exceed sixty. That this condition is not limited to public assistance or child welfare is confirmed by Ullman's study which indicated that 75% of all M.S.W.'s felt overwhelmed by heavy caseloads. (Wagner and Cohen 1978, p. 34)

It is important to note that these findings emerged prior to the massive cutbacks undertaken by the Reagan administration. As chapter 2 makes clear, the origins of this problem are not, then, with the policies of any particular president, but a result of the economic crisis in the early 1970s. These matters have been exacerbated by the dramatic budget cutting experienced by most sectors of the welfare state during the Reagan presidency. The 1980s offer a context for explaining the policies of austerity or cost containment that have in recent years cut very deeply into the body of the welfare state. These ever greater cuts have contributed both singularly and cumulatively to increased responsibilities and deteriorating conditions of welfare state workers.

Budget cutting, which was the hallmark of state welfare policies in the 1970s and 1980s, has not been without cost to the social order. To use the previous chapter's terms, the state's need to reduce financially the level of entitlement and service (thus contributing to the accumulation process by reducing the "burden" of "unproductive" welfare state costs on the private sector) has undermined its capacity to legitimate itself through either the maintenance of services to the neediest citizens or the reproduction of the labor force (Cousins 1987). For the purpose of clarity, it is important to distinguish among these matters.

The erosion of the state's legitimacy is powerfully illustrated through the present policies of hospitals (Baker and Vischi 1989; Kotelchuck 1985; Pear 1983; and Vladeck 1986). To what extent can hospitals in general, or social health workers more specifically, retain their legitimacy with the broader community when they are required as a matter of policy to discharge patients whom they know to be still in need of residential medical attention? As the choice between meeting real medical needs or budget targets becomes ever starker, the reputation of hospitals will suffer. How can a community invest any faith in a hospital (or the professionals associated with it) when time and again friends and relatives receive inadequate medical treatment because of apparent budget priorities? The increasing visibility of these choices adds yet another dimension to the heightened tension between the community and the welfare state agency. The inadequacy of the medical system can no longer simply be explained by technological failure, skill limitations, or patient noncompliance; instead, breakdowns in patient care are ever more clearly a consequence of economic decisions that place the highest priority upon meeting DRG or PRO standards. The increased clarity of these choices can only serve to further estrange the community from the various welfare state agencies that offer medical services, thus further undermining their legitimacy. The caseload stress being experienced by hospitals is illustrated by the following statements:

> Reports from New York City, Glens Falls, Syracuse, Buffalo and the Capital District show a system strained to the point of collapse. . . . The most striking symptom is the chronic . . . overloading of hospitals . . . that has grown into what officials call medical gridlock.

> Daniel Sisto, president of the Hospital Association which represents 280 hospitals and nursing homes, said: "Hospital people worry privately about what we should be saying. We don't want to scare the public, saying we're not giving the best care. Yet, we're in such a state of stress there are situations where there could be jeopardy. . . ."

> Health experts trace today's crises to problems past and present. . . . "We're still paying the price of fiscal crises, not only municipal hospitals, but also the private sector," said Mr. Vladeck of the hospital fund. "The municipal system was shrunk," he said, "and the state froze medicaid rates. Then came the Reagan Administration's cuts of Federal Aid." (Lambert 1988)

Welfare state agencies are also expected to reproduce the present (through housing, food, etc.) and future (through socialization and training) labor force. However, as the fiscal budgets of various state agencies are cut, it becomes increasingly difficult to offer the discrete services necessary to reproduce the labor force (Bowles and Gintis 1976; Cousins 1987). For instance, as Ms. L.'s caseload doubles, she will be less able to monitor instances of child abuse in foster homes or offer the kind of support necessary to maintain children in their homes. Equally important, the children being referred to Ms. L. today are in all probability even more troubled than youngsters referred to her ten years ago. Her caseload may increasingly be comprised of homeless children who have been living in shelters with their parent(s). The degenerative process associated with becoming homeless and the many destructive influences of shelter life in all probability have only compounded the emotional turmoil of these youngsters. Ms. L. then is caught in a double bind. She is expected to do *more* with *less* for a *more troubled* population. Implicitly, government policies have exacted a subtle long-term cost upon these youngsters. At the very least, Ms. L. is going to be less able to prepare these youngsters to function within familial units, school, and, perhaps most fundamentally, the job market.

More generally, child welfare agencies are less able because of budget-cutting policies to provide even the most minimal kinds of services. Consequently, inability on the part of public child welfare agencies to assure protection or socialization to children is having a corrosive effect upon their legitimacy (Pelton 1989). According to Leroy Pelton (1989),

> caseworkers in public welfare agencies have been overburdened with excessively high case loads . . . , received inadequate training and experience extremely high turnover. . . . Up to 50% per year have been reported in various parts of the country. Under these circumstances, the ability of the . . . agency to monitor, assess, plan for, and actually help troubled children may be marginal at best. (p. 77)

The Fiscal Crisis and the Renewed Emphasis on Privatization

The increased breakdowns of public agencies, largely triggered by fiscal austerity, have prompted policymakers to identify alternative ways to organize and deliver social services. For instance, cost containment in combination with "public sector gridlock" has produced a call for the increased privatization of social services (Wedell 1986). By and large, it has been assumed that social services can be both more efficiently and more effectively delivered by private firms. In our discussion, privatization will refer to the permanent transfer of services or goods from public service bureaucracies to private-sector or corporate firms. The transfer of goods or services to nonprofit or voluntary groups is another phenomenon that will be considered separately.

Privatization reflects a basic faith (not surprising, given the ideology of the larger social order) in private-sector dynamics and market criteria of effectiveness. It also represents a shift from collective (state) to individual (private) responsibility for the development and delivery of social services. The competition between individual firms bidding for public-sector contracts is expected both to reduce the cost and increase the quality of social services. The mechanism of competition is then expected to resolve the critical contradiction faced by the welfare state of having to maintain standards of service in the face of deep budget cuts. It is anticipated that this dilemma can be resolved by individual firms because they are leaner and more flexible than state government bureaucracies, which are increasingly characterized as bloated and rigid. The policy of privatization also enables the welfare state to contribute directly to the capitalization or profit of private-sector firms (Walker 1984; LeGrand and Robinson 1984). For all of these reasons, the New Right has championed privatization policies. Privatization is the only policy that potentially reinforces the New Right's full agenda to (1) reduce the size of the welfare state, or the scope of collective responsibility; (2) transfer unproductive state tax dollars back to the "productive" private sector or individual firms; and (3) support an ideology that emphasizes the purity or efficiency of private-sector dynamics.

A number of troubling issues associated with welfare state privatization have been either overlooked or ignored by policymakers. If social services are privatized, individuals who can afford to do so will purchase welfare services in the private market, while those who cannot will have to rely on a residual public sector (LeGrand and Robinson 1984). Privatization might be described as a euphemism for cuts in the total amount of public expenditure devoted to social services. At the same time, the quality of service is systematically individuated on the basis of financial or personal capacities. It is by no means certain that the private sector will provide the same level or quality of service as the public sector (LeGrand and Robinson 1984). In fact, historic evidence suggests that privatization of services in this century reduced the quality of services (Walker 1984).

The profit margins potentially available in these fields of service have not attracted many private firms. In order to maximize profits, the few firms interested in these service areas have chosen to target only the most compliant populations, such as minimum security prisoners. Private-sector firms have maintained a strong and growing influence during the past twenty years in those sectors of the welfare state that offer the greatest opportunities for profit maximization, for instance, medical services. Despite the substantial attention paid to privatization strategies of cost containment, there is little evidence suggesting that private firms have significantly penetrated *new service areas* traditionally administered by the public sector—such as child welfare and income maintenance—since the fiscal crisis. Again, medical services are not an exception because the substantial presence of the private sector in this arena predates the fiscal crisis (Ehrenreich and Ehrenreich 1970; Navarro 1977, 1982). Clearly, privatization is being selectively tested as an experimental tool in various sectors of the welfare state. Consequently, its influence in defining a broader range of social services may grow substantially during the next ten to twenty years as the state fashions new policies to meet the tests of this economic crisis. To date, however, privatization has not been the primary strategy for resolving the fiscal dilemmas of public and nonprofit agencies that are faced with ballooning caseloads and reduced budgets.

New Mechanisms of Internal Control at the Workplace

Public social service agencies are primarily managing the dilemmas associated with cost containment by developing new mechanisms of internal control. These new mechanisms are tied to the shifting content or retooling of social services (Newman and Turem 1974; Rosenberg and Brody 1974; Gruber 1974; Cousins 1987). This transformation of social services has clearly imposed new responsibilities upon and redefined the tasks of direct service workers. The social service agency (or more specifically, social service manager) must exercise greater control over the line staff to assure compliance with the new priorities of the agency.

What, then, are the new priorities of social service agencies? To begin with, they are expected to process substantially greater numbers of people in a shorter period of time. Only in this way can the agency manage its fiscal constraints and case overload. Conversely, the worker is expected to pay less attention to matters of quality if such concerns conflict (and invariably they do) with the financial priorities of the agency. In short, the new (or perhaps in some cases heightened) priority of agencies is to emphasize quantity and budget containment at the expense of quality.

Social service managers must be resocialized to value and enforce this singular objective. In the past, many social service managers have been drawn from the ranks of direct line staff. They had already internalized a perspective that at the very least gave equal weight to maximizing the quality of service to "productivity" (measured by the number of clients seen). However, over the last ten to fifteen years, concern for quality is increasingly at odds with the new business ethos of social service agencies. The business ethos demands a new set of skills that have eroded service staff's entry potential for top management positions. This point is underscored by Howard Karger (1981, p. 278):

> The knowledge of management information systems, statistical profiles and cost benefit analysis becomes a more important asset to administrators than a knowledge of casework. The need for the skilled administrative technicians, in effect, creates a new class of public welfare manager. Entry into this class is based more on credentials, specifically, masters level management degrees that emphasize quantitative analysis than on experience or direct service competence.

In order to effect a shift in the practices and policies of the agency, however, the new manager must expand her/his span of control and redefine success. Specific mechanisms have been created to accomplish both of these objectives. The scope of the manager's control in various agencies has been extended through a variety of accountability procedures, which are ultimately reduced to "paperwork." In recent years, most social service workers have experienced a rapid increase in their paperwork responsibilities in the form of uniform case records, which often measure a whole array of activities associated with the delivery of a service. The data culled from these forms provide managers with at least one measure of the workers' compliance with new agency standards. The measurement standards are most like the criterion used to calculate the quantitative output of business or the private sector. The standards may apply to the duration of a contact, volume of clients seen, or type of service encounter. Whatever the specific interest(s) of the agency, it is clear that these mechanisms tend to extend the influence of the agency or manager by reducing the autonomy of social service workers. The encounter between client and social worker is less private as a result of this paperwork and more available to managerial scrutiny (Lipsky 1980). Paperwork is the red dye with which worker compliance is traced by management. This effort at greater or total control, however, has certain hidden costs:

> The various workers' tasks as well as the time required for each task are systematically recorded. This record is used as the final barometer of the organization's productivity. In the end, increased amounts of a worker's time are required to fulfill these paperwork responsibilities. This expanding responsibility further diminishes the scope and duration of the worker's encounter with people. (Fabricant 1985, p. 392)

It would be logical to conclude that this effort to maximize and redefine the meaning of managerial control has also tended to resocialize workers. Line staff may have fewer expectations regarding (a) advancement, (b) substantial increases in salary, (c) satisfying encounters with clients, and (d) skill development on the job. Instead, direct line practitioners are likely to be increasingly accepting of their relatively low-paying, intense, and too often mechanical jobs. This resocialization is tied to the new production or practice processes that have been developed by service managers. These new processes offer perhaps the most vivid record of the transformation of social service work during the past ten to fifteen years.

Denying Access to Services

As the welfare state's new agenda of cost containment has stimulated changes in management practices and characteristics, it has forced certain shifts in the availability and structure of social services. New services, the paper that measures or tracks them, and the managers who monitor this process represent not simply a shift but rather a transformation in the structure and content of social services. These profound changes have been triggered and are reinforced consistently by the new singular agenda of the welfare state—to contain costs. These changes have affected every aspect of social services. Of particular importance to clients and direct practitioners are new policies that *restrict access to agencies, alter the content or structure of services,* and *recreate discharge practices.*

Recent reports indicate that access to a range of entitlements and other more discrete services has been restricted.

> Bureaucratic disentitlement is a mode of cutback politics that is more obscure, more indirect and less decisive as a budgeting tool than the more familiar highly publicized cutback decisions of legislatures and executives. (Lipsky 1984, p. 5)

> A repeated theme in state after state, county after county, is that the social service system has become so constricted that children can gain access to help only if they have been sexually abused or neglected, are found delinquent, or have run away. Doorways for "less serious" or differently defined problems are ceased. . . . Even for accepted cases, the needed help may not be forthcoming. (Kammerman and Kahn 1989, p. 9)

These policies do not dramatically cut substantial numbers of people off the rolls at a single point in time, as was the case with SSI recipients in 1981 (Burghardt and Fabricant 1987; Lipsky 1984). In the arsenal of tactics available to the state to reduce costs, "rationing" is perhaps the least bold and visible and does not result immediately in substantial cost savings. On the other hand, this approach is very powerful precisely because it gradually redraws the parameters of available social services and entitlements. The cumulative impact may affect cost savings as effectively as policies that dramatically dislocate substantial numbers of recipients. However, the incremental and relatively invisible nature of these cost-containment practices makes it very difficult to identify a policy that is hurting a class of people, and thus to mobilize resistance. The very power of rationing, then, is that by disentitling recipients individually and at the level of the bureaucracy, the state's more general intention to restrict access to a class of citizens is concealed or obscured.

Clearly, rationing is a very general concept that attempts to describe a number of recent developments. A variety of approaches were employed by the bureaucracy in the 1980s to limit the availability of services. To begin with, *access to benefits was rationed*. As Lipsky (1984) notes, public agencies confronting limited resources typically developed mechanisms to limit services to eligible citizens while ignoring the price paid by clients for the new administrative arrangements—waiting, dropping out, etc. Second, *benefits were rationed* when the gap between need and resources widened. For instance, the number of mental health hospital beds and public housing units clearly diminished during the past decade while demand grew. Just as critically, Income Maintenance Programs often provide more symbolic than real support to recipients. Their grant levels often did not allow recipients either to meet basic standards of nutrition or maintain their housing (Hopper and Hamberg 1984). In effect, as more people sought assistance in the 1980s, every benefit, entitlement, or service became less available. Lipsky remarks:

> Rationing not only reduces the number of people seeking services, it also transforms entitlement programs into conditionally restricted programs. The more difficult it is to pierce the bureaucratic veil, the more luck, persistence or the ability to manipulate public workers determine whether aid is forthcoming. Thus, rationing not only reduces entitlements, it also teaches political lessons contributing to future political expectations. (1984, p. 9)

When policies of bureaucratic disentitlement or rationing become apparent to the public, they are often perceived as a by-product of "natural" or economic forces, such as the deficit, that can only be controlled by the government through extreme austerity measures. This perception is most important because it tends to legitimate the activities of the bureaucracy as being in the best interests of the public. Perhaps most critically, rationing represents issues of policy implementation rather than executive or legislative decision making, and appears to involve technical and managerial rather than political matters. In effect, the very process, context, and manner in which bureaucratic disentitlement comes to the public's attention frames it as a technical problem. As Corrigan and Leonard (1988) have indicated, it is precisely this emphasis on technical problem solving that is most comfortable for the bureaucracy. Welfare state agencies and service professions are trained and organized to solve problems of this kind. As suggested in the last chapter, bureaucratization uses a veneer of technical problem solving to neutralize the social character of circumstances that are otherwise politically charged. Consequently, the labor force is asked to apply rationing standards and techniques to clients who understand only too well the implications of being denied access to critical services.

However, the political crises precipitated by such denials do not bubble immediately to the surface, and are in part diffused by the very technical and structured process of denying clients one at a time. Although these approaches may advance the cost-containment agenda of the state in the short run, they concurrently widen the gulf between welfare state workers and their clients. The impersonal, technical, and harsh messages that are conveyed to clients as they attempt to gain access to services or entitlements are further reinforced and refined once clients gain entrée to the service agency. Increased hostility and distrust further impair the ability of workers (and therefore the welfare state) to contribute to the social reproduction of clients. It is important to reiterate that rationing can leave many families with grant levels that do not meet basic survival needs. Such intensified poverty in turn produces new forms of stress that ultimately have a long-term impact upon the functioning of family members. This reduced functioning will also exact a range of costs within the social order.

Cost Containment and the Creation of Industrial Services

Cost-containment policies have brought about a dramatic restructuring of social service work. The resultant changes, which have increasingly industrialized the workplace and practices of social service work, are most apparent in the largest public bureaucracies of the welfare state. Income Maintenance Centers, hospitals, and public child welfare agencies have integrated many industrial practices into their daily work routine. The reason that large public-sector organizations have been among the first to experience this phenomenon is described below:

> in part, this is a consequence of the relationship between the greater amounts of resources consumed by public bureaucracies and the incentive to control expenditures. Just as important is that the very size and complexity of such organizations provide the material base for imposing more restrictive work principles on personnel. In effect, the new practice's primary interest in using smaller quantities of labor time to produce ever greater quantities of product (if savings are to be significant), requires an organizational base that maintains a relatively large work force to process a substantial flow of resources (client-citizens). (Fabricant 1985, p. 391)

The parallels between factory work and new forms of social service work are substantial. As was suggested earlier in the analysis, new managers are being trained to emphasize productivity and to increase their span of control within the work place. The influence of these new managers is increased, as it was for supervisors within Ford automobile plants, when elements of the work process are disassembled into their component parts and handed back to workers piecemeal. A number of authors have indicated that this process of job disassembly is well under way in public social services. Tudiver (1979, p. 39) remarks:

> One of the more distressing recent developments is that of functional job analysis which has been used extensively in industrial settings. The unit of analysis for job design and organization is the task, "the smallest unit of activity which makes an immediate contribution to the objectives of the system or subsystem." It employs the methods of scientific management by dividing jobs into the tiniest units possible. The U.S. Department of Health, Education and Welfare has a social welfare task bank containing 550 social welfare workers in eight states.

The development of more discrete and ultimately mechanistic job tasks for direct line practitioners is contributing to a factory-like atmosphere within social service agencies. The emergence of factories and assembly lines in the private sector at the turn of the century was underpinned by a set of principles that are being applied to service agencies today. These Taylorist principles specify in minute detail what is to be done, by whom, and the time allowed (Gruber 1974). The objective of the scientific manager is to create a work process that is standardized or routinized and, most important for the welfare state in this era of fiscal austerity, cost efficient. The work within large and midsized service agencies is increasingly being channeled through such structures. It is expected that in this process, habit will ultimately replace human judgment.

The parallels between private-sector assembly line work and the new production processes within public service agencies are striking.

> The analysis of the implications of factory work is as old as the factorization of production. . . .
>
> Street level bureaucrats do not work with the entire product, but only on segments. . . . The imperatives of processing people into the correct categories tends to overwhelm . . . professional obligation to treat the whole person. (Lipsky 1980, p. 76)
>
> Service agencies have also responded to the cry for accountability and cost savings by placing greater emphasis on service efficiency. The measures adopted to promote efficiency are not unlike those used to

extract greater profit from the manufacturing assembly line. (Dressel et al. 1988b, p. 119)

The assembly production of social services is but one dimension of the factory-like atmosphere that permeates the delivery of services. A lack of privacy, cramped working conditions, and noise increasingly characterize the environment in which social service work is conducted. Wagner and Cohen (1978, p. 34) observe:

> Wasserman's study showed that workers had no area to confer with colleagues and had to interview in cubicles which were open. There was also no area in which one could go to simply relax and think. He makes our point in saying, ". . . the setting is not one conceived of as professional," in fact, the environmental image is more industrial than professional.

> When workers have their desks lined up next to each other with constant noise and inadequate privacy, how different is this than a noisy assembly or typing pool? . . . There is constant noise, telephone calls, no confidentiality in communications, inadequate desk space and no waiting room for clients.

It is important to understand that these conditions are affecting the work process in a range of agencies and professions that function within the welfare state. The impact of these forces on social service work in public hospitals, child welfare agencies, and Income Maintenance Centers is illustrated below:

> The increase in paperwork imposed by child abuse legislation P.L. 96–272 and related state child welfare "reform" laws, are viewed by many as creating major obstacles to better service delivery. The process inhibits variability, freedom to experiment and willingness to accept risks . . . . As a consequence, professionals have increasingly less autonomy or flexibility in how they intervene and they feel less and less like professionals. (Kammerman and Kahn 1989, p. 17)

> A brief review of one particular trend in welfare departments over the last 20 years or so will help clarify the managerial issues we face today. . . . welfare departments in the United States were usually configured as a live operation: high volume, standardized processing that flows through a preset sequence of steps. The job of the welfare worker was increasingly standardized to accomplish the "front office" processing of income maintenance functions as efficiently as possible. (Rosenthal 1987, p. 298)

> In order to gain a further competitive edge and at the same time lower

their costs, hospitals are applying industrial concepts and methods to their operations. The hospital field is in the process of what Theodore Levitt has called the industrialization of service. (Mullner, Anderson, and Anderson 1986, p. 40)

No discussion of industrial line work and the reduction of costs would be complete without at least some reference to speed-ups and quotas. One of the primary tools used by private-sector managers to contain costs and thus increase profits is to intensify or speed up the production process. Managers in the social services are applying similar techniques to process more clients through the system. By fixing the variables of work force size and time, managers are intensifying the work production process.

Returning to the experiences of Ms. M. and Ms. L. for the moment, at the very least these workers expected that their clients' discharge or return to the community would be based on a standard of improvement. Such change might be as modest as a worker's assessment indicating that a troubled youngster was exercising greater emotional control, or as substantial as reports suggesting that a medical patient had recovered from a chronic condition. The degree or nature of the change is less important than the central (agency and professional) expectation that client improvement is a predicate to discharge. This presumption is at the heart of both the social service rationale and contract. The very existence of medical or child welfare services, for instance, can be traced to the belief that such intervention must make a difference in the lives of citizens. The increased inability of agencies to address this central purpose highlights the mounting tension between service legitimacy and cost-containment priorities. This contradiction is illustrated below:

> In some instances, egregious, qualitative problems have emerged. Some Medicare patients are being discharged "quicker and sicker" to their detriment. Some hospitals have cut back the availability of desirable clinical services.
>
> Prematurely early discharge is most important. . . . Nowhere do the official government communications state that PPS limits allowable lengths of stay for Medicare patients. Yet, many medical personnel believe that D.R.G.'s require shortening the length of stay. Thus, they are making or encouraging decisions to discharge patients earlier than they should be; how often, we don't know. (Vladeck 1986)

In effect, cases that might be characterized as situations of long term chronic neglect (but not acute danger) are offered no help, not because their problems are not recognized, but because there are no resources to provide help. Complex cases of abnormal behavior, disturbance, poor school and community adjustment, are referred to limited or inadequate resources, or simply ignored. . . . staff are so overwhelmed, trying to complete timely investigations of the increasingly large volume of reports and develop plans to protect the most endangered children, they do not have adequate resources to carry out appropriate community supervision where this has been ordered by the Court. (Kammerman and Kahn 1989, p. 13)

These changes in service access, delivery, and discharge have profoundly altered the content and mission of agency work. No longer do social service professionals or agencies point to their outcome record with clients as a basis for increasing funding. Although Ms. L. and her agency might point with pride to data on the number of youngsters who have successfully located jobs, increased their education, or returned to their families, the agency's legitimacy with funding sources is increasingly tested not by these measures, but by forms of output that purport to calculate productivity. The new measures of success or productivity include: (a) number of contacts with youngsters, (b) volume of cases managed, (c) unit cost per contact of unduplicated cases, and (d) number of cases closed.

It has been persuasively argued that these measures can potentially assure "reasonable levels" of accountability regarding the appropriateness and efficiency of services delivered by line workers. However, the application of these measures during a period of fiscal turmoil has been neither value-neutral nor benignly beneficial. Instead, the interaction between these output indices and a diminished fiscal base for the welfare state is an elemental part of the motor that daily drives the transformation of social service work.

It is important to understand that these new definitions of success are congruent with the new structure and practices of social welfare agencies. The primary focus of assembly line practice is to process as many clients as possible in the shortest period of time in order to reduce costs. These new standards only measure (through new forms and increased paperwork) what decision makers have established structurally as the highest service priority of the 1980s—quantitative *output* rather than effective *outcomes* (Lipsky 1980; Fabricant 1985;

Weatherly et al. 1980). In effect, service workers must adhere to cost-containment standards developed by various state agencies that may have little to do with actual client care (Kotelchuk 1985; Brodkin and Lipsky 1983; Kammerman and Kahn 1989).

Other elements of change previously identified also fit neatly into this configuration of social services. The tasks of social workers, physicians, and other human service professionals are increasingly tailored to maximize productivity. Within this context, the jobs of workers such as Ms. L. and Ms. M. have become circumscribed. On the service conveyor belt, Ms. M. increasingly has her range of tasks narrowed to include only specific discharge planning tasks, while Ms. L.'s role is redefined exclusively to handle specific intake paperwork tasks for her child welfare agency.

Contradictory Outcomes for Workers and Clients

The impact of the fiscal crisis and, more specifically, cost-containment policies has seeped into every part of the social service structure. Not a single aspect of social services has been insulated from the transforming influence of these forces. Worker practices, agency structure, client expectations, and perhaps most fundamentally, *definitions of service* have been altered. These changes, which were expected to address if not resolve the most quantifiable dilemma of the fiscal crisis (a lack of resources), have ironically produced a number of new qualitative contradictions for the welfare state.

To the extent that the welfare state measures its success by the standards of a rapid processing machine, certain social expenses can be effectively ignored in the short run. However, although clients may be moved more quickly through an agency, the very changes in agency structure that emphasize movement have diminished the probability that presenting problems will be resolved. Consequently, clients may return many times to the same agency with the same problem. In the present structure of social services, such clients are fed once more through the processor and added to the overall volume, and thus "success," of the agency. Over time, or after returning to the agency on numerous occasions and having similar experiences, these clients might drop out of the process. This attrition, again, might be designated by the agency as a closed or successful case. This redefinition of recidivism and attrition is entirely consistent with the new priorities and structure of service agencies. However, agencies and policymakers systematically fail to acknowledge the apparent failures of the new system embedded in these statistics.

If an increasingly industrial service structure substantially raises the probability of attrition and recidivism, then certain costs will surely follow for the social order in the short and long run. Problems that remain untended such as AIDS, homelessness, and drug addiction will only mushroom. Medical problems that may initially be minor may, over time, become more chronic and costly. Families that fail to gain access to economic or social support services may disintegrate. Immediate costs associated with this degeneration might include foster care, crime, or child abuse. Over time, this structural denial of needed services increases long-term social expenses by contributing to intergenerational problems of drug addiction, alcoholism, and child abuse.

The restructuring of social services has also required that the autonomy and discretion of workers be minimized. These structural requirements of "productivity" provoke new contradictions and dilemmas for both workers and agencies. The workers' narrowed areas of discretion make them less able to respond to rapidly expanding complex problems central to their work, which do not fit into the structured format of the agency. For instance, discharge planning may be complicated by critical shortages in housing or community supports such as foster care. Additionally, like their counterparts in the private sector, social service workers have become increasingly alienated from their own labor as management has expropriated more and more decision-making authority. In one respect, industrial or Taylorist principles have had a greater influence on the labor process in the welfare state than in the private sector. The differential impact is described below:

> Unlike the automobile industry, which produces a more discrete item—an item that can be more easily converted into the single focal point of the production process and be considered a unit of output—the social worker is engaged in a very different work process. The social worker is ideally engaged in a far more complex work dynamic, one that is expected to produce an array of explicit and subtle outcomes. The parallel of the product unit or item that by definition has to be the focus of an industrial production process simply does not exist. Consequently, when the production process for the automobile industry is disassembled and craft is reduced to rote, quality is lowered but the nature of the

output remains constant. In contrast, when you disassemble social work and reduce it to an assembly line process, both the product and the nature of the product are altered. This occurs because of the need that scientific managers have to both mechanize service work and narrow the scope or meaning of services. The application of Taylorist principles to social work, then, alters both the quality and the fundamental character of services. (Fabricant 1985, p. 392)

Proletarianization and the Alienation of the Social Service Labor Force

As the fiscal crisis has deepened for the state, social service workers have lost control over their daily labor. O'Connor (1973) has remarked in his theory of the fiscal crisis that problems associated with profit generation are exported to the state sector resulting in reduced budgets and an intensified rationalization of its labor force. Consequently, it would be expected that the intensity of state control would be less significant in 1970, when state and federal budget deficits were less significant, than in 1990, when the projected federal deficit is between 150 and 200 billion dollars. The phenomenon of intensifying management or owner control of the labor process is often referred to in the literature as proletarianization (McKinlay and Arches 1985; Derber 1982; Larson 1980; Dressel et al. 1988b).

In *Labor and Monopoly Capital* (1974), Harry Braverman brilliantly dissects various facets of the proletarianization process in the private sector. In general, he draws a very basic distinction between two equally important elements of proletarianization. Braverman notes that this process increasingly diminishes the worker's control over the *conception* and *execution* of his work. It also favors efficiency and productivity at the expense of worker alienation. For the purposes of this discussion, it is critical that the distinction between conception and execution be more fully elaborated.

Ms. M. and Ms. L. have clearly lost much of their capacity to implement an organic conception of social service work. Their vision of social services has been replaced by a distinctively management-centered agenda. As noted in the previous section, an emphasis upon quantitative measures of success has diminished any possibility for quality; fragmented tasks have replaced more generic or holistic approaches to social service delivery, and assembly line practice has been substituted for more discrete and varied encounters between workers and clients. The most concrete expression of the worker's continued loss of control over the conception of her labor are new monitoring forms that redefine the boundaries and content of social services. Ms. M., for instance, can no longer conduct extended counseling sessions with patients or their families, for the post–DRG environment of hospitals demands rapid turnover. Similarly, Ms. L. is less able to develop supports (through home visits or advocacy) to keep families intact or prevent abuse because of the quantitative and reactive, as opposed to preventive, priorities of the uniform case record system used by her agency.

As managers gain greater and greater control over the conception of work, their influence will rapidly extend to its execution, for these processes are highly interrelated. Management's attempts to penetrate areas of daily decision making that have historically been controlled by workers challenges both the vision and the discretion of skilled labor. The development of job descriptions for highly specialized and fragmented tasks resembling an assembly line has this dual impact. First, the structure or conception of work is redefined, breaking it down into ever-more discrete and measurable elements. Then, this structure limits the worker's capacity to exercise independent judgment or discretion by mandating what can or cannot be done at each stage of the process. In this way, the daily tasks of workers are proletarianized. In more industrialized work settings, workers exercise little independent judgment and are expected to respond by rote to defined situations. These mechanical responses and circumscribed situations have been both structured and defined by management. Such factors override any impulse a worker might have to contribute independently and positively to the production process.

Comparing Proletarianization in the Private and Public Sectors

Workers first experienced proletarianization in the emergence of modern capitalist economic organization. This process was associated with the historic interplay between the development of new machinery, or technology, and the need to reduce labor costs. Struggles between workers on the shop floor and owners confronted with declines in profit were central to these shifts in labor process. The manner in which new technology has contributed to reduced labor costs and proletarianization in the private sector is described by Larson (1980, p. 136):

> first and above all, modern machinery changes the nature and the composition of the collective worker. Workers who no longer need to be strong or previously trained in a craft (in concrete historical terms women and children) may now be brought into the factory, not as helpers of the skilled craftsman, but in their own right as unskilled servants of the new machines. Massive degradation of industrial skills by modern machinery creates a new labor market, one in which the supply of labor is enormously increased by the influx of unskilled and therefore interchangeable and eminently replaceable workers.

The introduction of new machinery and labor-saving devices had a significant impact upon both the nature of work and the utilization of line floor skill. As workers were subjected to more intensified forms of management and structural control, they suffered a loss of the skills historically associated with their craft. This loss of skill heightened the economic vulnerability of workers, making them even more susceptible to managerial control.

> under any conditions, the sale of labor . . . implies that a countable connection is established between time and task. . . . This countable connection contains the germ of alienation. . . . The forced cooperation deepens organizational alienation as the employer redefines work tasks and times in the direction of fractional specialization and increased standards of performance or yield. . . . This forced cooperation sets in motion the process which deindividualizes the worker's skills and qualifications by submitting them to the whole alien organization of the work setting and by controlling from above the conditions of any increase in skill. (Larson 1980, p. 137)

Professional work within the welfare state is also being proletarianized. The first step in this process—management's gaining control over the conception of work—is already firmly in place (Cousins 1987). Further, management's consolidation of control over the conception of work has intensified in recent years as fiscal austerity measures have reframed the nature of social service work. Finally, the increasingly mechanized and fragmented structure of work associated with welfare and children's and hospital social services illustrates the impact of this process upon a range of public agencies.

There is general agreement among authorities in the field that certain strains of proletarianization have been evident in the welfare state since the late 1970s (Derber 1982; Larson 1980). Equally important, this phenomenon has influenced the work of a broad spectrum of welfare state professionals including teachers, social workers, and physicians (Bowles and Gintis 1976; McKinlay and Arches 1985; Fabricant 1985).

However, certain distinctions can be drawn between the process of proletarianization in the private sector and the welfare state. To begin with, changes in welfare state labor production processes have not been significantly influenced by the development of new technology or machinery. As in the private sector, economic crisis has triggered the development of labor- or cost-saving devices. However, the welfare state product is quite different from its private-sector counterparts. Welfare state professionals are not producing automobiles, computers, or hamburgers. A service is less discrete and concrete than a product. You cannot hold it, touch it, drive it, or eat it. Consequently, what raw materials would welfare state managers place in the machine to produce what product?

Clearly, new technologies such as computers have significantly affected the daily practice at Income Maintenance Centers. The introduction of elaborate and otherwise cumbersome information systems such as DRGs would not have been possible without computers. Equally important, to the extent that new paperwork demands have changed the structure and content of social service work, computers have played a critical role. However, the introduction of machinery in this way, although important, is not comparable to the private-sector experience. Computers that perform clerical functions during intake at a social service agency are only vaguely or marginally attached to the creation of a product when compared, for instance, to computerized ovens or robots that reduce the costs associated with turning out hamburgers and cars.

Consequently, cost containment and increased productivity are not primarily affected in the welfare state by new machinery or technology. Instead, as was pointed out in the first part of the chapter, these changes can be traced to the development of proscribed forms of social service practice that are cheaper (uniform, factory-like, etc.) and more amenable to management control. The introduction of DRGs in hospitals, new federal guidelines (P.L. 96–272) in child welfare agencies, or quality control in Income Maintenance Centers consistently emphasize managerial, centralized state priorities (output/quantity) over client need (outcome/quality). Ground-breaking techniques have been used in the development of new forms of practice, accountability measures, and the like. It is in these areas that new techniques are tightly fastened to the altered production processes of the service agency. These new instruments have altered the nature of the encounter between workers (inputs) and clients (outputs). However, these instruments or tools do not bind the welfare state worker to machinery or technology in the manner experienced by private-sector laborers.

Another distinction often made by some academics between the proletarianization of private-sector factory workers and social service professionals is in the area of deskilling. There is substantial disagreement regarding the impact of proletarianization on professional skill. Some authors argue that there has been little indication of an erosion of such skills; others have suggested that indeed there has been a marked loss of independent decision making and skill for various professional groups located within the welfare state. These important differences in perspective will be more fully examined in the subsequent discussion.

Ideological and Technical Proletarianization

In their sophisticated analyses of the professional work force of the 1970s, Charles Derber (1982) and M. L. Larson (1980) argue (as did Harry Braverman earlier) that there are two distinct elements of the proletarianization process. These elements, although firmly embedded in the general industrial work formulation of "conception" and "execution" described earlier, have a richer, more particular meaning when applied to professional workers. The two dimensions (more accurately, the process of transformed labor) include *ideological (conception)* and *technical (execution) proletarianization.*

Ideological proletarianization represents the loss of control over the goals and social purposes (the ends) of one's work. The specific experience of ideological proletarianization includes a powerlessness to:

(1) choose or define the final product of one's work; (2) determine how it is used in the marketplace or larger society; and (3) affect the policy and values of the organization purchasing one's labor. The degree of ideological proletarianization clearly varies according to the worker's capacity to shape or control broad organizational policies and the specific goals or purposes of work.

Alternatively, the loss of control over the process of the work itself (the means) can be called technical proletarianization. This occurs whenever management subjects workers to: (1) a technical plan of production, and (2) a rhythm or pace of work that workers have not influenced or created. Characteristically, this form of proletarianization involves specialization, fragmentation, and/or the routinization of tasks. There is also an effort to minimize worker discretion and autonomy.

There is general agreement that any professional group working within a host state agency has experienced substantial ideological proletarianization. By definition, management has asserted its prerogative to define the goals of the organization and the distribution as well as social purpose of its product. It is within this context that Ms. M. has no influence, for instance, over the budgetary decisions, service priorities, and site location(s) of her agency. Although each of these matters directly and indirectly influence Ms. M's work, her status as an employee at the lower rungs of the organizational hierarchy leaves her little opportunity to affect directly such decision making. Every state employee shares this dilemma to one degree or another. What is important to understand, however, is that ideological proletarianization represents only a first step in the transformation of the labor process. This process has a second, more intensified stage of technical proletarianization.

Once management begins to penetrate the labor process or means of production, the daily tasks of the worker are redefined. This reorganization of the production process is frequently associated with the deskilling of workers—perhaps the most salient feature of the proletarianization process. Deskilling effectively robs workers of the single characteristic that enables one worker to separate himself from another. *Once skill is replaced by mechanical habits, perhaps best understood through the example of assembly line work, workers are placed at a marked disadvantage in the marketplace.* At that point, they become easily replaceable cogs in a single machine. Consequently, their capacity to bargain for better wages and working conditions is reduced.

Skill, then, is a linchpin by which workers assure themselves of some degree of independence, bargaining leverage, and control over working conditions. Hence, control over the service production process becomes the battleground between labor and management. The outcome of this conflict will in part determine the extent and nature of deskilling in social service agencies. Industrial workers lost this battle years ago and consequently have experienced a continuous erosion of their skill base. There is some disagreement, however, regarding the extent to which technical proletarianization and deskilling have affected professional workers.

A number of authors (most notably Larson) have suggested that ideological proletarianization has not led, and in all probability will not lead to either technical proletarianization or deskilling among professional workers. Instead, she suggests that there are significant differences between professionals and industrial workers. These differences can be traced to systems of labor control employed by management that assure professionals will "maintain their craft skills and relative autonomy over the technical aspects of their work" (Larson 1980). Larson and others have attempted to substantiate these critical differences by noting a lack of any substantial evidence of Taylorization in any major professional group. She also points to the complexity of theoretically based professional scientific work and the intrinsic limitations of existing managerial efforts to rationalize it (Larson 1980). She does, however, acknowledge that a number of factors may lead in the near future to technical proletarianization. The factors likely to facilitate such a shift include: (1) the revolution in computers and microelectronics; (2) an increased reliance on technically trained managers who are disconnected from the ethos of various professional groups; and (3) labor market shifts undermining the professional's bargaining position or strength and consequently heightening professional vulnerability to increased managerial control (Larson 1980).

Writing in the late 1970s, Larson did not believe that professionals were being marginalized in this manner. She asserted that although new, more technical tasks were being developed within specific state agencies such as hospitals, these functions were not being assumed by professional groups. Instead, she suggested that the principal consequence was not the deskilling of professionals but rather the progressive delegation of the less skilled, newly mechnized tasks to lower-paid occupational groups such as physicians' assistants or parapractitioners (Larson 1980).

It is important to note that Larson's analyses were developed before the intensified attacks upon various welfare state agencies and professional groups began. Although new groups of paraprofessionals have proliferated during the past twenty years and assumed more of the mechanical work of welfare state agencies, it is equally clear that during the past ten years the work of various professional groups has also been profoundly altered. Consequently, we would agree with Larson and others that a new, more segmented labor force is being developed within the welfare state. For instance, B.S.W.'s and paraprofessionals have absorbed many of the more onerous and less satisfying tasks associated with social service work (Kahn 1979).

The segmented structure of the welfare state labor force will be more fully examined in the next section of this chapter. *However, we would also contend that concurrent with the development of new rungs of welfare state workers, various professional groups have experienced a deskilling process and diminished opportunities to develop new skills.* This new reality has particularly important implications for professional workers. Historically, one of the primary attractions of professional work (apart from the status and financial rewards), has been the creative possibilities potentially embedded in such practice. As the worker is robbed of her capacity to maintain or build skills, she is alienated not only from the service agency, but from work itself. The various forms of this heightened alienation can only further diminish the welfare state's capacity to respond to the growing and more complex demands with which it is faced in the 1980s. There is substantial evidence suggesting that both technical deskilling and the alienation of the welfare state labor force are well under way.

Computerization and fragmentation of tasks are having a profound impact on the technical skills of health professionals (such as physicians) engaged in theoretically based scientific work. McKinlay and Arches (1985) have indicated that at least one latent function of the rapid specialization of medicine may be the breakdown of the now diffuse and generally mystical medical arena into discrete and manageable components. They further suggest that because of this specialization, the technical base of medicine is being continually narrowed and demystified, making it vulnerable to codification into a set of bureaucratic rules and procedures ripe for computerization and easily grasped by those without formal medical training. They have indicated that we are rapidly entering a postphysician era, and they cite six major tasks presently performed by physicians that can be performed more efficiently and effectively by computers.

> Computers can take more accurate and complex histories faster than physicians and can also complete a statistically more reliable physical examination. With regard to ancillary testing, the presence of a physician is for the most part not now required. . . . Concerning the latter three tasks of diagnosis, treatment and therapy, there are studies showing that computers can perform aspects of these tasks to a level of reliability better than that of even the most highly trained and up-to-date physician. (McKinlay and Arches 1985, p. 178)

These primary mechanisms (computers and segmentation of labor) associated with the deskilling of physicians require a host organization or bureaucracy. *This agency oversees technical proletarianization.* If computers and labor segmentation are contributing to the deskilling of more scientifically grounded groups of professionals, such as physicians, then technically trained managers and new market conditions have had a similar impact upon other human service professionals, such as social workers, who rely upon a softer explanatory framework to guide their work.

Skill reduction is not embodied in a particular *worker type* but rather in the *entire service process.* Larson notes that many of the new, more mechanical functions performed within the health domain are carried out not by physicians but by physician's assistants and other allied health professionals. Analogous situations could easily be developed for social workers. Larson asserts that new activities have not reduced the skill level of physicians or other professional groups but rather created new classes of service workers. Although this point is pertinent, it offers only limited insight into the very complex dynamics of the deskilling or technical proletarianization of service workers and social service work.

Larson fails to consider the historical process associated with the deskilling of workers. It is not enough to look at the impact of new labor production processes upon the present generation of workers. Although assembly line production significantly diminished the skills of craftsmen in the early decades of the twentieth century, it also robbed *future workers* of the opportunities to develop skills. These workers were not deskilled in Larson's technical sense because the new production processes foreclosed opportunities to develop the skills mastered by their fathers and grandfathers. The reduction of such opportunity is a critical part of the historical process of deskilling.

Larson and Derber do not sufficiently incorporate the client experience into their definitions of professional deskilling. Even when deskilling has not occurred within a professional group, services traditionally associated with particular professions may be robbed of their skill base. Another facet of technical proletarianization or deskilling specific to the welfare state is the *drop of skill level associated with the delivery of particular services.* For instance, job tasks that were traditionally the province of trained social workers may be delegated to paraprofessionals as they become increasingly routinized. The paraprofessional's (a) full understanding of the needs of the client, (b) insight into the workings of the entire agency, and (c) training are likely to be far more limited than the social worker's. Consequently, although the paraprofessional may, for instance, comply with the new requirements and forms that routinize intake, the relatively subtle opportunities of recognizing and meeting client needs (at this early stage of contact) will in all probability be minimized. These changes are not lost upon clients who may determine that their needs are being met less appropriately and effectively than in the past. Although in this instance professional social workers may not have been deskilled, the *social service experience from the point of view of the client has suffered from a loss of skill.* The delegation of specialized tasks to less highly trained and less expensive groups of workers is an increasingly popular and effective mechanism for skill reduction in the social services. This specific form of deskilling (and cost containment) is popularly described as "decertification." It has been suggested that over 50 percent of the NASW (National Association of Social Workers) chapters are struggling with reclassification and decertification (Karger 1983). Austin and Pecora (1983) have noted that many of these changes threaten social work as a profession because they eliminate positions that require a social work degree.

Perhaps the most vivid illustrations of declassification during the early 1970s occurred in the field of income maintenance (Wyers 1983;

Karger 1983; McDonald and Piliavian 1980; Hagan 1987).

> Virtually every preexisting notion of worker role and task, educational
> requirements, training, and supervision in respect to public assistance
> practice was nullified. Indeed, even the term "practice" is no longer
> appropriate, at least in the professional sense, there just is not any.
> Increasingly, the basic worker position is seen as eligibility determina-
> tion pure and simple. (Wyers 1983, p. 262)

In the 1980s, efforts to declassify various social work positions and
roles intensified. These efforts were particularly apparent in the areas
of health and child care. This point is more fully illustrated below. (See
also Teare 1983; Schachter 1988.)

> In March of 1986 concern with declassification and reclassification was
> expressed at a conference on "Professional Social Work Practice in
> Public Child Welfare." . . . 25 representatives from schools of social
> work, public child welfare agencies and the social work profession met
> to consider . . . the problem of declassification and what states are doing
> to recruit, train and retain professional social workers. . . . a comparison
> of degree requirements in 1975 and 1986 show that the educational
> requirements for social work practice are lower today than they were a
> decade ago. Three times as many states today fail to require any degree
> as in 1975. Half as many states require an M.S.W. today as then. (Rus-
> sell 1987, p. 3)

> The State [of New York] is proposing to eliminate standards for hospi-
> tal social work departments under a new section of the hospital health
> code that is currently undergoing extensive revision according to state
> officials. . . .

> Among the concerns are that standards and uniformity of social work
> practice will decrease; that less trained personnel will result in inade-
> quate delivery of social services and that no assurance of professional
> supervision would be guaranteed under the new code. (Winner 1988, p. 1)

Finally, deskilling can also be measured in terms of the present
losses in specific expertise or general knowledge for professional
groups. This type of loss is perhaps the most explicit form of deskilling. Many of these changes have occurred in the 1980s, subsequent to
the development of the Derber and Larson analyses of technical proletarianization. For instance, professional social workers in child care
agencies have fewer opportunities than in the past either to engage in
long-term counseling or to visit the homes of their clients. Instead,

M.S.W. workers are often restricted by their large caseloads to certain routine short-term activities (Russell 1987). A similar set of circumstances has also rapidly redefined the experience of M.S.W.'s in Income Maintenance Centers and hospitals. As the duration and nature of social workers' encounters with clients are increasingly restricted, the opportunities to maintain or develop certain kinds of skill diminish. Much skill refinement and development is also contingent upon instructive supervision and extended encounters with clients over time. These areas of opportunity, however, have been significantly limited by the new realities associated with social work.

The new emphases of management have reduced the chance to develop skills through supervision. Managerial staff are less available for case record reviews and training session dialogues, which sharpen clinical skills; instead, their attention is fixed on the accuracy and prompt submission of agency statistics. This more mechanical relationship between worker and manager leaves little opportunity for other kinds of training. In effect, as the breadth of the social work experience has been altered, so has the potential to develop a broad base of skills through training.

Clearly, the social worker's loss of discretion and skill can be traced to her narrowed role. The industrial forms of practice described earlier emphasize large caseloads, rote functions, and heightened accountability through quantitative measures. This labor process does not allow the worker to exercise specific skills that conflict with the fiscal priorities of the new agency structure. Although workers may have developed diagnostic counseling or other skills elsewhere, their opportunities to offer such services in an agency climate of heightened productivity are minimal.

This set of circumstances is contributing to the technical proletarianization, or deskilling, of social workers. The social worker's present *skill base* is being eroded by the new demands of agency practice. Equally important, opportunities to develop *new skills* have been reduced by the new structure and priorities of service agencies. Additionally, the new levels of skill associated with the practice of social work will influence future generations of social workers. Like their historical counterparts in the manufacturing industries, future generations of social workers will have much less opportunity to develop skill in the new workplace. Instead, future social workers will increasingly be resocialized in their training and on-the-job experience to a new and lower set of standards regarding the skill base of the field. Perhaps only certain forms of social work (i.e., private practice) will provide even a faint reminder of the discretion and skills that were once exercised in the profession.

The Implications of Deskilling for the Profession

This broad reduction in skill has profound implications for the range of professions that function within the welfare state. Historically, writers like Alfred Kahn (1979) staked out particular claims for the social work profession within the welfare state. In the 1960s and 1970s, for instance, Kahn labeled a mixture of services traditionally delivered by social workers as personnel social services, such as information, referral, and counseling.

It has been suggested that this amalgam of services provided agency-based social workers with a distinctive professional identity and opportunities to exercise professional judgment as well as to develop specific sets of skills. The historical conditions that allowed the profession of social work to have a certain degree of control over certain sections of the welfare state have been significantly altered. The economic expansion of the 1960s and early 1970s has given way to the economic crises and decay of the past fifteen years. This economic contraction triggered a fiscal crisis for the state, which in its push to support accumulation functions heightened demands for agency and professional accountability. It is the latter point that is of particular importance to this discussion.

In effect, new accountability and structural demands that have been imposed upon agencies have also brought about a reduction in *professional autonomy and control*. As Mishra (1984) has noted, there is an inherent conflict between professional power and privilege and what he describes as public interest or accountability. Clearly, Mishra's notion that the new accountability measures of the state represent the public's interest has been disputed in this analysis. However, his primary point that there is a tension between professional power and the new forms of service accountability is most pertinent.

Various guiding assumptions of the professions have been placed at risk by the proletarianization of work within the welfare state. The underpinning of professional practice, which legitimates its stature and expense, is expertise. If, however, expertise is being replaced increasingly within every arena of the welfare state by processes that empha-size uniformity and rote judgment, then questions must be raised re-garding the legitimacy of professional practice. In the push for cost containment, the autonomy necessary to develop or utilize professional skill is being undermined. Relatedly, Kahn's formulation of "profes-sional turf" within the welfare state becomes less tenable as tasks and functions in human services are carried out by less skilled workers with shifting job categories. These direct challenges to the autonomy, power, and skill of certain professions is not a minor blip in their fortunes; more likely, it portends major struggles for survival.

Professional Work and Class Struggle

Self-interest would seem to demand that a range of professions strug-gle against the state's policies of cost containment and proletarianiza-tion. The relatively tepid response of affected professions is problematic. In general, the new work processes being implemented within state agencies have not provided a major focal point for profes-sional activity. Health-related professional groups such as nurses and physicians have spoken out at legislative sessions on a number of the more visible expressions of the new service agenda, such as DRGs and peer review (Schachter 1988). However, even these activities have been episodic and inconsistent. Why have professionals been so un-willing or unable to respond to this crisis? The answer, in part, can be found in the historical relationship between the state and professional groups.

Paul Wilding (1982) has commented that "the great service which professionals render to government is that they both express social concern and exalt expert solutions to social problems at the expense of political solutions." In effect, professional groups have performed the very critical function of individualizing and objectifying shared or col-lective problems. For instance, the physician limits herself to the phys-iological system of her patient and does not explore environmental explanations or remedies for disease. Social workers may perceive a burgeoning number of hungry people, but their daily professional re-sponse is to treat problems individually. These activities contribute to a diffusion of the political content of problems shared by welfare state client groups. As Wilding notes, the technical expertise of professional groups legitimates such practices and the related actions of the state.

Historically, the state has accorded certain professional groups monopoly power or control over the "turf" associated with their area of "expertise" in exchange for their continued reliance upon technical, nonpolitical forms of problem solving. This contract was mutually beneficial in as much as it fueled the growth of professional power and enabled the state to further legitimate its authority by safely (individually, partially, technically) responding to social needs. In effect, bureaucratization, professionalization, and individuation combined to limit responses to escalating social needs (Morgan 1982).

However, this contract has also limited the capacity of various professions to respond to their own deepening crises. Their interventive tools, analyses, and individuated perceptions of problems are *not* appropriate for collective action. Equally important, a profession's contract with the state implicitly forbids political problem solving, in exchange for favored treatment (Wilding 1982). Thus, despite the rapid withdrawal of the state from its end of this social contract since the mid-1970s, the professions have been reluctant to engage the state in an adversarial and political manner.

As Galper (1975, p. 172) has noted:

> Solutions to problems that are seen in their more delimited aspects and are interpreted in technological terms will tend to be more isolated from solutions pursued in the arena of structural social change and mass political movements in the society at large. . . . Professionalism points away from these approaches by the nature of its problem solving.

Certain norms have also undermined the capacity of professionals to respond to the state's attack upon their practice and authority. The codes of ethics of various professions such as social work have consistently emphasized the primacy of agency authority and client need. The specific needs of professional workers within this framework are secondary. This point is illustrated in a historically important article that criticizes the "unprofessional stance" of social workers during the strike at Mount Sinai Hospital in New York. Rehr (1960, p. 26) quoted from the social work code of ethics when she stated:

> The social worker's primary obligation is the welfare of the person served . . . as related to the agency function . . . his professional responsibility takes precedence over his personal aim and views.

Ironically, a number of the factors that have contributed to the development of professional practice, such as individual definitions of problems and solutions, the assumption of partnership with the state, and an almost exclusive dependence upon technical expertise as a problem-solving tool, account for an otherwise inexplicable professional inertia in the face of serious threat. Varied professions are rapidly surrendering their control over the critical area of practice to management. The professions continue to focus on higher wages and new recruiting mechanisms as means to counter the deteriorating working conditions within service agencies. These tools, which traditionally functioned to strengthen the power of professional groups, cannot and will not affect the crises faced by welfare state professionals in the 1990s.

Equally important, the new areas of battle selected by the professions continue to reflect a preoccupation with controlling entry into particular positions and more privatized relationships between professional and client (i.e., professional licensing for private clinical practice). These defensive responses may in the short run expand the dues-paying membership of particular professional associations, for private practice is certainly one of the rapidly growing areas within social work. However, these limited concerns do not address the restructuring of work that has promoted pay reductions, decertification, flight from agency work, and reduced skill. Instead, these individuated symptoms of the proletarianization process are being treated, partially and technically, in much the same way that professionals responded to individual dysfunction or the symptoms of social breakdowns. In the long run, these approaches will not advance the collective interests of professional workers nor help to maintain the legitimacy of the field.

The Intensifying Contradictions Triggered by Proletarianization

Policies responsible for the proletarianization of the welfare state labor force have created a number of intensifying contradictions. The fundamental contradiction for line workers, agencies, and the welfare state is that *the legitimacy and effectiveness of social services in meeting the short- and long-term need of the social order to reproduce its labor force are being traded off for immediate financial savings.* These choices will ultimately widen the gulf between welfare state workers and their clients.

Reduced access to services, brief encounters, rapid movement, and lack of accountability increasingly mark the client's experience within service agencies and have a corrosive effect on the legitimacy of welfare state organizations. There are at least two legitimating aspects of the welfare state that have been affected by recent events. First, policies of fiscal austerity have undermined the justification for the existence of the welfare state by withdrawing the transformative *potential* associated with services. For instance, the capacity of hospitals to meet medical needs, public schools to educate children, HUD (Housing and Urban Development) to implement new housing initiatives, and local agencies to develop preventive services has been undermined by cost-containment policies. Second, the welfare state's capacity to legitimate its residual service structure in the midst of heightened fiscal crises (which ever more clearly require redistributional policies) will be minimized. Consequently, the capacity of welfare state agencies to meet the socialization, education, nutritional, or housing needs of various communities will be constricted. As resources are withdrawn, there will be fewer opportunities to meet the present needs (health, housing, etc.) of working and nonworking client groups. The services necessary to enhance the present and future functioning of children (health, education, counseling) are also being withdrawn. All of these issues are intensified by racial and gender differences.

In the long run, these policies are likely to contribute to a disjuncture between the needs of the marketplace (specific job demands) and the availability of labor. Housing may be too expensive or necessary health benefits unavailable to maintain needed workers in emergent employment areas. Locating workers that have the necessary skills for these new job markets may also become increasingly difficult in a climate of reduced financing for education and training programs. The long-term impact of fiscal austerity policies, then, may be the intensifying mismatch between labor and jobs. This set of circumstances will in turn contribute to the reduced productivity of the private sector. It can, therefore, be plausibly argued that cost-containment policies will have the longer-term and contradictory effect of shrinking the private sector (Ginzberg and Vojta 1981).

The new working conditions within the welfare state will create yet another set of contradictions for both service agencies and welfare state policymakers. To begin with, it will likely become increasingly difficult to attract skilled practitioners to welfare state agencies or, for that matter, to helping professions. As was noted earlier, discretion, autonomy, and skill development were a number of the incentives that attracted people to public-sector professional work. However, as these attractions fade, potential workers will seek employment opportunities in new, expansive labor markets (computers) or more privatized forms of practice (private clinical practice). Consequently, as recent reports indicate, public agencies are having a great deal of difficulty both recruiting and retaining new professionals. If these trends continue, they are likely to exacerbate the already substantial qualitative differences in services available to poor and working-class as opposed to upper-middle-class communities. Additionally, these staffing difficulties will further overload remaining workers who are already strained and exhausted.

For the remaining agency staff, the prospects appear particularly grim. They are faced with swelling caseloads, diminished support, and more mechanical roles. The job speedups, quotas, reduced options for clients, and frustration with the new structure of services will lead to heightened stress and an ever greater incidence of burnout. The phenomenon of burnout has raged as proletarianization processes have intensified (Karger 1981; Lewis 1980). Ultimately, burned-out staff choose either to leave the field or to invest minimally in their jobs. Either of these outcomes further undermines the agency's capacity to meet client needs.

This analysis has indicated that cost-containment policies have transformed the labor process within the welfare state by proletarianizing the work force and industrializing the production process. We have suggested that these processes are highly interactive. The welfare state labor force is also becoming increasingly differentiated by class, race, gender, and education. The deepening segmentation of welfare state workers is a powerful force highly intertwined with those processes that have already been identified in this discussion. The remainder of this chapter will explain how policies of cost containment are effecting a deepening segmentation of service workers.

The Segmentation of the Social Service Labor Market

Ms. L. and Ms. M. have both experienced deepening class divisions within their agencies. As a B.S.W. child welfare worker, Christine L. sees less and less opportunity to move beyond her present position within the agency. Her potential career ladder is quite short. Consequently, she is restricted to performing certain highly specific tasks that are associated with a narrow wage range and low salary level. Alternatively, although Bryn M. has an M.S.W. and earns a higher salary than B.S.W. workers, she also sees little opportunity for career or financial mobility without an M.B.A. unless she enters private practice. The few hospital positions to which she could aspire are already filled by social workers with far greater seniority and yet nowhere near retirement age. While there is some opportunity for horizontal movement both within and outside the agencies, these job opportunities do not offer higher salaries, greater status, or increased responsibilities. Opportunities for upward mobility have been severely restricted by policies of fiscal austerity (NASW 1987). Consequently, workers like Ms. L. and Ms. M. are increasingly viewing their jobs as dead ends.

During a period of approximately thirty years there was substantial expansion in the size of the welfare state. For instance, between 1950 and 1980 the number of social workers per 100,000 citizens grew from 49 to 169 (Hopps and Pinderhughs 1987). The increase in the number of welfare state workers was accompanied by new kinds of specialization and training. Areas of work that took root during this period include gerontology, manpower training, and community mental health services. Additionally, new hierarchical ladders and opportunities for career mobility emerged within each of these service streams. The new demands for social service workers contributed to the proliferation of B.S.W. programs for entry-level workers. It has been reported that between approximately 1960 and 1967, 232 new B.S.W. programs were created (Sheafer and Shank 1986). More recent data indicate that the number of undergraduate social work programs has leveled off at about 350 (Hopps and Pinderhughs 1987). As was reported in chapter 2, this expansion in the size and scope of the welfare state was propelled by economic growth (Gilbert 1983). Once this growth slowed and the private sector entered a period of economic crisis, the welfare state was confronted with the aftershocks of diminished economic capacity and escalating social need.

The policies of cost containment brought about not only a proletarianization but also an intensifying segmentation of the labor force. The new specialization and training that had germinated during the period of welfare state expansion became the basis for sharp divisions of the welfare state labor force in terms of skill and function. For instance,

B.S.W. workers are no longer limited to entry-level jobs, but rather are increasingly being used as an instrument to declassify or downgrade various social service positions. A new and cheaper labor force of B.S.W.'s is emerging as a primary point of contact between the service agency and community. Robert Teare (1983), Marilyn Russell (1987), and others have remarked that social services are provided more and more by individuals holding bachelor's and not master's degrees. Various kinds of services are also being delivered by workers without a bachelor's degree. Paraprofessional workers in hospitals and nursing homes provide an array of daily services to clients, including but not limited to emotional support, mobility, and home visits. Consistent with these trends, the function of the M.S.W. is less distinctive and central.

The role of M.S.W. workers increasingly overlaps with that of their B.S.W. counterparts. As has already been noted, both are fitted into formal service structures that have begun to resemble an assembly line. However, within this process, B.S.W. workers generally perform the narrower, more mechanical functions, such as intake, and the M.S.W.'s engage in the relatively discrete work associated with lower-level supervision and counseling (Russell 1987; Teare 1983). It is important to reiterate, however, that M.S.W. functions are also increasingly restricted to narrow bureaucratic proletarianized tasks. Atop this new hierarchy of social welfare state workers sits the scientific manager. The singular focus of this administrator is to develop delivery and accountability systems that reduce the cost of services.

The segmentation of the welfare state labor force, then, is highly associated with both training and work functions. This hierarchy is not simply a function of specialization or training but also of the cheapening and deskilling of social service workers. The new segmented structure of social work provides a context for understanding both the reorganization and the proletarianization of social service work. Scientific managers trigger this recreation of social service work, M.S.W.'s and B.S.W.'s perform many of the transformed, mechanistic functions of the welfare state, and less trained laborers (paraprofessionals, home attendants) carry out the "dirtiest" tasks requiring the least skill.

In many ways this segmentation corresponds to the conceptual framework developed by David Gordon et al. (1982) and Richard Edwards (1979). They examine the segmentation process that has reshaped the work of private-sector laborers. This framework is a useful device that also helps to explain the deepening hierarchical divisions within the welfare state (see also Drago 1984).

The Three Segments of the Private-Sector Labor Market

David Gordon et al. (1982) have divided the private-sector labor force into three segments. They identify these groups of workers as primary independent, primary subordinate, and secondary labor market workers. The distinctions among these worker types are based in part on wages, career mobility, and degree of independence.

Independent primary market work is characterized by stable employment, considerable job security, patterns of career progressions, and relatively high pay. These jobs often demand advanced or specialized schooling and are likely to have certain occupational or professional standards of performance. Finally, these positions require a degree of independent initiative and self-pacing.

The next point in this continuum of work is the primary subordinate labor market. The work tasks associated with these jobs are more repetitive, routinized, and subject to machine pacing. In general, the skills needed to perform these roles are learned rather quickly (within a few days or weeks). Quite clearly, these jobs offer workers little opportunity to control their jobs. Additionally, the path for advancement almost always depends on seniority.

Finally, the most general feature of secondary labor market work is the casual nature of the employment. Such employment also never requires previous training or education beyond basic literacy. These jobs are further typified by very low pay, virtually no job security, little if any career mobility, and little reward for seniority. Consequently, the turnover rate tends to be high.

In the private sector, specific kinds of workers can easily be associated with these job types. For instance, the qualities of primary independent work are associated with white-collar professional groups (physicians, engineers) and higher levels of management. Assembly line workers in most manufacturing industries are usually identified as primary subordinate workers. Finally, given the low wage structure, job turnover, and poor working conditions of migrant laborers and fast food franchise workers, it would be fair to characterize them as members of the secondary labor market.

Each of these labor markets or groups of workers is described as working under a distinctive system of managerial control. In effect, the segmentation of the private labor market is marked by both intensifying divisions and the employment of differential control mechanisms. Richard Edwards (1979) describes these managerial devices of control as *simple, technical,* and *bureaucratic.* Very briefly, "simple control" is most frequently applied in the secondary labor market. The essence of simple control in either its hierarchical or entrepreneurial form is the *arbitrary power* of foremen and supervisors to direct work, monitor performance, and discipline or reward workers. Alternatively, primary subordinate workers are directed by technical systems of control. These systems are incorporated into the structure of the organization. For instance, manufacturing workers are controlled, monitored, and to some degree rewarded by an assembly line structure. In this case, the arbitrary power of the foreman is replaced by the expectations and standards of the new technical control structure. Finally, independent primary workers are influenced by bureaucratic forms of control. These mechanisms depend far less on external monitors and sanctions to direct workers. Instead, they function to imbue the worker with habits of predictability and dependability. In effect, through training, orientation, and reward structures, the worker is expected to internalize the goals and values of the enterprise. Bureaucratic methods then foster indirect control or self-control.

Quite importantly, a number of economists have concluded that labor market segmentation has exacerbated certain social divisions that are deeply entrenched in the larger social order. It has been noted that the process of labor market segmentation has heightened class, racial, and gender differences in the marketplace. Class distinctions are intrinsically and visibly structured into these labor market divisions. However, the manner in which segmentation has affected gender and racial differences is far more subtle. Edwards (1979) suggests that labor market segmentation has interacted with historical patterns of racial and sexual discrimination to affect the job opportunities of minorities and women. Segmented labor markets tend to reproduce and reinforce patterns of discrimination. Consequently, Edwards has noted that women, blacks, and Hispanics are increasingly being distributed to lower-paying, less stable jobs. Thus, labor market segmentation (in combination with the discrimination of pre-employment and employment institutions) accounts for much of the racial and gender differences in income, unemployment, etc.

The Racial, Class, and Gender Divisions
within the Welfare State

The division of labor that was first detected within private-sector work is presently having a profound impact within the public sector. Since the fiscal crisis, deeper class, racial, and gender differences have become apparent within the welfare state labor force. It is clear that cost-containment policies have exacerbated and reinforced certain divisions that existed historically. These deepening cleavages closely parallel the experience of the private sector. Over time, this process has created three distinct groups of social welfare workers possessing the characteristics of primary independent, primary subordinate, and secondary workers.

The primary independent workers within the welfare state are, in general, elite professional workers such as physicians, lawyers, and managers. As was noted earlier, the nature of work for all professionals within the public sector has been profoundly altered during the past fifteen years. However, the more established professions continue to retain a greater degree of autonomy, and consequently have many more opportunities to determine the pace and content of their work than other groups of laborers. Additionally, the new public-sector manager's work offers many opportunities for discretionary decision making or professional judgment. The structure of these professional jobs also follows patterns of relatively high pay, career progression, and specialized training associated with this sector of the labor market. Finally, the mechanism of managerial control used to direct these workers can be characterized as bureaucratic. In effect, these professional and managerial groups have internalized the values of the service agency or organization. Consequently, their work is directed by an inner compass that is usually consonant with the priorities of the agency.

The second level of welfare state workers—the primary subordinate group—consists of less established semiprofessionals including but not limited to social workers, public school teachers, and nurses. This group of professionals has been most profoundly affected by proletarianization. The preceding analysis carefully examined the losses in skill, discretion, and decision-making authority that have colored the recent work experience of these direct practitioners. More mechanical, fast-paced, and factory-like forms of practice are increasingly structuring the work of this group of laborers. The skills needed to perform their "new tasks" can be learned in a relatively short period of time.

There are fewer opportunities for career advancement at this middle level than at the upper level of primary independent workers (Gordon et al. 1982). Like factory workers in manufacturing industries, the small band of opportunity for career mobility is reserved for those workers with the greatest seniority. The means of controlling this segment of the labor force is also consistent with the private-sector experience. These workers are increasingly directed by technical systems of control. The organization is structured to enforce certain patterns of work. Again, the particular structure that has been developed in manufacturing industries and the welfare state to manage this group of workers originated with industrial, assembly line production processes.

Although there are apparent differences between social workers or teachers at the bachelor's and master's levels, both groups are part of the primary subordinate labor market. Certain parts of the literature indicate that policies of fiscal austerity are narrowing the differences between these subgroups of workers. For instance, the differences in B.S.W. and M.S.W. job descriptions have been narrowed in states like Michigan (Austin and Pecora 1983). This merging of professional groups at different levels of training is yet another expression of the deskilling, cheapening (average salary for B.S.W.'s is $15,000 as compared with $22,000 for M.S.W.'s), and ultimately, proletarianization of this segment of the welfare state labor force (NASW 1987).

Finally, there is a third rung in the welfare state labor ladder—the secondary labor force. This includes home attendants, orderlies, and certain groups of paraprofessionals. These workers have little if any education beyond high school. Consistent with private-sector data, their jobs rarely require more than basic literacy. This "dirty work" of the welfare state offers very low pay and virtually no opportunity for career mobility. Recent efforts to unionize this part of the labor force have resulted in greater job security and proposals to upgrade salary scales for some workers. However, the overwhelming majority of these workers continue to have little job security and live at or below the poverty line (Donovan 1987). Like their counterparts in the private sector, secondary workers in the welfare state are subject to simple control measures that are shaped and enforced by supervisors. The nonunionized workers in this segment of the labor force are particularly vulnerable to the arbitrary and/or spontaneous exercise of power by management. Part of the experience of workers who function within the secondary labor market of the welfare state is described below:

Even the home attendants who can find full time work earn only $8,632 a year, which is below the poverty level for a family of three. . . .

"There is no question that the salaries need improvement," said Robert Linn, the City's Director of Labor Relations. . . . The immediate beneficiaries of salary increases would be a largely powerless constituency—workers who are only slightly less poor than the people they serve. (Roberts, March 21, 1988, p. B–1)

It has also been suggested that "contracting out," or purchase of services, has contributed to the expansion of the secondary labor market. This process spawns a group of workers whose institutional attachments and economic security are even less certain. Cousins (1987, p. 176) describes this phenomenon more fully:

The costs of contracting out are, therefore, borne by ancillary workers who suffer redundancies, reduced pay, reduced conditions of work, loss of bonus payments, loss of overtime, excessive use of part-time work . . . and reduced access to union protection. . . . Contracting out therefore restructures the labor force . . . segmenting different groups by the terms and conditions of their employment into core and casualized forms of labor.

Finally, the racial and gender divisions common to labor markets within the private sector are mirrored within the welfare state labor force. To begin with, a number of studies have indicated that minority women dominate various parts of the welfare state secondary labor market (D'Antico and Jurik 1988; Dressel 1988b). Just as importantly, John Ehrenreich (1985) and others have documented (white) male dominance at the upper levels of the social work profession, and Dressel et al. (1988b) has noted that men are twice as likely as women to be represented in welfare state administrative positions. It is important to stress that this overrepresentation of men in managerial positions is occurring in a profession that is primarily, if not overwhelmingly, comprised of women. Meanwhile, the lower end of the state labor market (the secondary labor market) is distinguished by the significant overrepresentation of minorities and women. This can be traced to discriminatory practices (both presently and historically). These tendencies are exacerbated by the heightened structural demands for the segmentation of the welfare state labor force.

Although private- and public-sector organizations share a number of parallel experiences in terms of labor force segmentation, there are also a number of striking differences. To begin with, the analyses of economists like David Gordon emphasize the broadest relationship(s) between segmentation and the private economy (Gordon et al. 1982). This macro view suggests, for instance, that secondary labor is tied to specific markets and organizations. Similar dynamics are also described for primary subordinate and primary independent sectors of the economy. These analyses of labor market segmentation in the private sector with few exceptions stress a relationship between work type, labor markets, and organizations. More concretely, particular organizations like General Motors or Genentech and markets (automobiles, biotechnology) are associated with a specific segment of the labor force.

Conversely, there is little effort to examine the extent of labor force segmentation at the micro or organizational level. It is apparent, however, that any investigation of the segmentation of the welfare state labor force must consider divisions within organizations. Welfare state organizations, such as hospitals, maintain labor forces that are segmented into primary independent, primary subordinate, and secondary workers. The range of hospital employees (social workers, technicians, physicians, orderlies, etc.) and their distinctive work processes strongly suggests pronounced labor force segmentation at the level of the organization.

An additional area of difference between private-sector and welfare state segmentation concerns the role and presence of women. It is clear that women are highly concentrated within the private sector in secondary labor market jobs (as waitresses, domestics, etc.). Although there have been some modest shifts in the representation of women (relative to men) in the primary subordinate and independent sectors, the proportion of women in these markets or job types remains relatively small. For instance, there continue to be few female construction workers, automobile workers, or engineers. On the other hand, there has been and continues to be a strong representation of women in primary subordinate welfare state jobs. The teaching, social work, and nursing professions, for example, are primarily comprised of women. It is important to keep in mind, however, that the wage structure for many of these jobs is comparable to that of semiskilled labor in the private sector (NASW 1987).

There is also greater functional overlap among the three sectors in the welfare state labor force than in the private economy. These sectors have little formal contact in the private marketplace. Their work is proscribed and distinctive. However, within the welfare state, there is far greater collaboration and contact between primary subordinate and secondary workers such as nurses and orderlies, or social workers and CETA (Comprehensive Employment Training Act) employees. These relationships are based on shared contact with clients and overlapping areas of responsibility in the delivery of service. Consequently, these segments of the welfare state labor force are far more likely than their private-sector counterparts to work collaboratively. This difference can be traced to the distinctive demands and structure of social service work. Despite these and other differences, it is clear that the segmentation and, more generally, restructuring of work within the welfare state is more similar than dissimilar to the private-sector experience.

Conclusion

As this chapter makes clear, the forces of industrialization in public-sector work have so deeply penetrated and redefined practice that there are few expressions of an ongoing struggle to preserve or develop alternative forms of service. Such resistance and struggle, however, should be evident in the daily work of voluntary agencies.

It will be the purpose of the next chapter to explore more fully how primary subordinate social service work has changed within nonprofit social service agencies. Historically, voluntary agencies have been considered a preserve for the delivery of quality social service (Kramer 1981). Equally important, it is popularly assumed that the nonprofit sector has functioned as an incubator for social service innovation (Kramer 1981). Clearly, the voluntary agency's capacity to innovate or deliver quality service is in tension with tendencies to industrialize or proletarianize service work.

The voluntary agencies' historical role, modest entitlement responsibilities, and private sources of support would seem to suggest a degree of insulation from the industrial practices redefining social services in the public sector. To some extent, the enormity and power of these industrializing forces can be measured by their impact on this relatively protected and advantaged sphere of service delivery. The next chapter will empirically examine a number of voluntary agencies' recent service experiences. The extent to which these diverge or converge with recent public-sector experiences will also be considered.

References

Austin, Michael. "Managing Cutbacks in the 1980's." *Social Work* (September–October 1984).

Austin, Michael, and Peter J. Pecora. "Declassification of Social Service Jobs." *Social Work* (November–December 1983).

Baker, Frank, and Tom Vischi. "Continuity of Care and the Control of Costs: Can Case Management Assure Both?" *Journal of Public Health Policy* 10, 2 (1989).

Bluestone, Barry, and Harrison Bennett. *The Deindustrialization of America*. New York: Basic Books, 1982.

Bowles, Sam, and Herbert Gintis. *Schooling in Capitalist America*. New York: Basic Books, 1976.

Braverman, Harry. *Labor and Monopoly Capital*. New York: Monthly Review Press, 1974.

Brodkin, Evelyn, and Michael Lipsky. "Quality Control in A.F.D.C. as an Administrative Strategy." *Social Service Review* (March 1983).

Burghardt, Steven, and Michael Fabricant. *Working under the Safety Net*. Newbury Park, CA: Sage, 1987.

Corrigan, Paul, and Peter Leonard. "Social Work Practice under Capitalism." In Roy Baily and Michael Brake, eds., *Radical Social Work*. New York: Doubleday, 1988.

Cousins, Christine. *Controlling Social Welfare*. New York: St. Martin's Press, 1987.

Cunningham, Mary. "Eligibility Procedures for A.F.D.C." *Social Work* (January 1977).

D'Antico, Marilyn, and Nancy Jurik. "Where Have All the Good Jobs Gone? The Effect of Government Service Privatization on Women Workers." *Contemporary Crises* 35, 1 (1988).

Derber, Charles. *Professionals as Workers: Mental Labor in Advanced Capitalism*. Boston: G. K. Hall, 1982.

Department of Health and Human Services. *Medicare and Medicaid Programs Peer Review Organizations, Final Rules*. Federal Register, April 17, 1985.

Donovan, Rebecca. "Home Care Work: A Legacy of Slavery in U.S. Health Care." *Affilia* (Fall 1987).

Drago, Robert. "Capitalist Shopfloor Initiatives: Restructuring and Organizing in the 1980's." *Union of Radical Political Economists* 16, 4 (Winter 1984): 52–71.

Dressel, Paula. *The Service Trap*. Springfield, IL: Charles C. Thomas, 1984.

Dressel, Paula, Mike Sweat, and Michelle Waters. "Welfare Workers as a Surplus Population: A Useful Model?" *Journal of Sociology and Social Welfare* 1 (March 1988a).

Dressel, Paula, Michelle Waters, Mike Sweat, Obie Clayton, Jr., and Amy Chundler-Clayton. "Deprofessionalism, Proletarianization and Social Work." *Sociology. Social Welfare* 2 (June 1988b).

Edwards, Richard. *Contested Terrain: The Transformation of the Workplace in the 20th Century*. New York: Basic Books, 1979.

Ehrenreich, Barbara, and John Ehrenreich. *The American Health Empire: Power, Politics and Profit*. New York: Random House, 1970.

Ehrenreich, John. *The Altruistic Imagination*. Ithaca, NY: Cornell University Press, 1985.

Fabricant, Michael. "Empowering the Homeless." *Social Policy* (December 1988).
————. *Juveniles in the Family Court.* Lexington, MA: D. C. Heath, 1983.
————. "The Industrialization of Social Work Practice." *Social Work* (September–October 1985).
Galper, Jeffrey. *The Politics of Social Services.* Englewood Cliffs, NJ: Prentice Hall, 1975.
George, Victor, and Paul Wilding. *Ideology and Social Welfare.* London: Routledge & Kegan Paul, 1985.
Gilbert, Neil. *Welfare Capitalism.* New Haven, CT: Yale University Press, 1983.
Ginzberg, Eli, and George Vojta. "The Service Sector of the U.S. Economy." *Scientific American* (March 1981).
Gordon, David, Richard Edwards, and Michael Reich. *Segmented Work, Divided Workers.* New York: Cambridge University Press, 1982.
Gruber, Murray. "Total Administration." *Social Work* (September 1974).
Hagan, Jan. "Income Maintenance Workers: Technicians or Service Providers?" *Social Service Review* (June 1987).
Hopper, Kim, and Jill Hamberg. "The Making of America's Homeless: From Skid Row to New Poor 1945–1984." New York: Community Service Society, 1984.
Hopps, Jane, and Elaine Pinderhughs. "Profession of Social Work Contemporary Issues." In *Encyclopedia of Social Work.* Washington, DC: NASW, 1987.
Hoshino, George. "Money and Morality: Income Security and Personal Social Services." *Social Work* 16, 2 (1971).
Joe, Tom. "The Effects of Workfare on the Child Welfare System." *Public Welfare* 43, 1 (Winter 1985).
Kahn, Alfred. *Social Policy and Social Services.* New York: Random House, 1979.
Kammerman, S., and A. Kahn. *Social Services for Children, Youth and Families in the U.S.A.* Greenwich, CT: Annie Casey Foundation, 1989.
Karger, Howard. "Burnout as Alienation." *Social Service Review* (June 1981).
————. "Reclassification: Is There a Future in Public Welfare for the Trained Social Worker?" *Social Work* (November–December 1983).
Kotelchuk, Rhonda. "In the Grip of PPS: How Prospective Payment Data Is Transforming Hospital Care." *Health PAC Bulletin* 16, 1 (1985).
————. "Watchdog on a Short Chain: How Good Are PPS's Quality of Care Reviewers?" *Health PAC Bulletin* (Spring 1987).
Kozol, Jonathan. *Rachel's Children.* New York: Crown, 1988.
Kramer, Ralph. *Voluntary Agencies and the Welfare State.* Berkeley, CA: University of California Press, 1981.
Lambert, Bruce. "Hospital Shortages Hurt Patient Care in New York." *New York Times,* March 22, 1988.
Larson, M. S. "Proletarianization and Educated Labor." *Theory and Society* 9 (1980).
LeGrand, J., and J. R. Robinson, eds. *Privatization and the Welfare State.* London and Boston: George Allen and Unwin, 1984.
Lewis, Harold. "The Battered Helper." *Child Welfare* 59 (April 1980).
Lieberman, Alice, Helaine Hornby, and Marilyn Russell. *Analyzing the Educational Backgrounds and Work Experiences of Child Welfare Personnel.* Washington, DC: National Child Welfare Resources Center for Management and Administration, 1989.

Lipsky, Michael. "Bureaucratic Disentitlement in Social Welfare Programs." *Social Service Review* (March 1984).

————. *Street-Level Bureaucracy: Dilemmas of the Individual in Public Service.* New York: Russell Sage, 1980.

McDonald, T. P., and Irving Piliavin. "Separation of Services and Income Maintenance: The Worker's Perspective." *Social Work* (July 1980): 264–467.

McKinlay, J. B. *Processing People: Cases in Organizational Behavior.* London: Holt, Rinehart, and Winston, 1975.

McKinlay, J.B., and J. Arches. "Toward the Proletarianization of Physicians." *International Journal of Health Services* 15, 2 (1985).

Mishra, Ramesh. *The Welfare State in Crisis: Social Thought and Social Change.* New York: St. Martin's Press, 1984.

Morgan, Pat. "From Battered Woman To Program Client." *Kapitalistate* 9 (1982).

Mullner, Ross, Odin Anderson, and Ronald Anderson. "Upheaval and Adaptation." *American Hospital* (July–August 1986).

National Association of Social Workers. *Salaries in Social Work.* Silver Spring, MD: NASW, 1987.

Navarro, Victor. *Health and Medical Care in the U.S.: A Critical Analysis.* Farmingdale, NY: Baywood Publishing, 1977.

————. "The Labor Process and Health." *International Journal of Health Services* 12, 1 (1982).

Newman, Edward and Jerry Turem. "The Crisis of Accountability." *Social Work* (January 1974).

O'Connor, James. *The Fiscal Crisis of the State.* New York: St. Martin's Press, 1973.

Palmer, David, and David Eisenstadt. "P.R.O. Program Memo." *Akin Gump, Strauss, Haver and Feld,* August 24, 1985.

Patry, Bill. "Taylorism Comes to the Social Services." In Rand Wilson, *Professionals as Workers: A Selection of Readings.* Cambridge, MA: Policy Training Center, 1980.

Pear, Robert. "Hospitals Worry over Fixed Rate Set for Medicare." *New York Times,* August 28, 1983.

Pelton, Leroy. *For Reasons of Poverty: A Critical Analysis of the Public Child Welfare System in the U.S.* New York: Praeger, 1989.

Rehr, Helen. "Problems for a Profession in a Strike Situation." *Social Work* 5, 2 (1960).

Roberts, Sam. "Leading Workers in Home Care Out of Poverty." *New York Times,* March 21, 1988, B-1.

Rosenberg, Marvin, and Ralph Brody. "The Threat or Challenge of Accountability." *Social Work* (May 1974).

Rosenthal, Stephen. "Mandatory or Voluntary Work for Welfare Recipients? Operation Management Perspectives." *Journal of Policy Analysis on Management* 8, 2 (1987).

Russell, Marilyn. *Public Child Welfare Job Requirements.* Portland: University of Southern Maine, 1987.

Schachter, Robert. "Memo Standard for Hospital Social Work Depts." New York: *NASW* (March 1988).

Schleicher, Linda. "Special Services for Children: Profiles in Failure." *Catalyst,* no. 6 (1980).

Sheafer, Bradford, and Barbara Shank. *Undergraduate Social Work Education: A Survivor in a Changing Profession.* Austin, TX: School of Social Work, University of Texas at Austin, 1986.

Sokoloff, Natalie J. "Evaluating Gains and Losses and Black and White Women and Men in the Professions." *Social Problems* 35, 1 (February 1988).

Stinchcombe, Arthur. "Bureaucratic and Craft Administration of Production: A Comparative Study." *Administrative Science Quarterly* 4, 2 (1959).

Stother, Michael. "Confessions of a Bureaucrat." Unpublished paper, Hunter College, 1982.

Teare, Robert. "Reclassification and Licensing." In Scott Briar et al., eds., *Supplement to the Encyclopedia of Social Work.* Silver Spring, MD: NASW, 1983, pp. 120–27.

Terrell, Paul. "Adapting to Austerity: Human Services after Proposition 13." *Social Work* (July 1981).

Tolchin, Martin. "Health Worker Shortage Is Worsening." *New York Times*, April 17, 1987.

Tudiver, H. "Business Ideology and Management in Social Work: The Limits of Cost Control." *Catalyst* 4, 13 (1979).

Turem, Jerry, and Catherine Born. "Doing More with Less." *Social Work* (May–June 1983).

Vladeck, Bruce. "DRG's: Their Impact." *New York Times*, January 1986.

Vondrack, Fred, Hugh Urban, and William Parsonage. "Feasibility of an Automated Procedure for Human Service Workers." *Social Service Review* 48 (1974).

Wagner, David, and Marcia Cohen. "Social Workers, Class and Professionalism." *Catalyst* 1 (1978).

Walker, John. "The Political Economy of Privatization." In J. LeGrand and J. R. Robinson, eds., *Privatization and the Welfare State.* London and Boston: George Allen and Unwin, 1984.

Weatherley, Richard, Claudia Byrum Kottwitz, Denise Lishner, Kelly Reid, Grant Rose, and Karen Wong. "Accountability of Social Service Workers at the Front Line." *Social Service Review* (December 1980).

Wedell, Kenneth. "Privatization of Social Services in the United States." *Social Policy and Administration* 20 (1986).

Wilding, Paul. *Professional Power and Social Welfare.* London: Routledge and Kegan Paul, 1982.

Wilkins, F. *The Dynamics of Labor Market Segmentation.* London and New York: Academic Press, 1981.

Winner, Karen. "State Seeks Social Work Code End." *Westsider*, March 3, 1988, p. 91.

Wyers, Norman. "Income Maintenance and Social Work: A Broken Tie." *Social Work* (July–August 1983).

4 • The Crisis and Transformation of Not-for-Profit Social Services: A Qualitative Analysis

Introduction

The welfare state of the late 1980s is a complex social organism. Its complexity can be traced in part to its myriad functions, layers of bureaucratic structure, and the types of organizations competing for its scarce resources. The latter point is particularly important to this analysis. It is apparent from the prior chapter that the most financially dominant yet least dynamic type of organization administering welfare state funds is the public-sector agency. These agencies are a direct part of the state apparatus. Their lines of authority, legal responsibilities, and funding base are tied to the executive, judicial, or legislative branches of the state.

Another type of organization that continues to play a critical role in the development and distribution of social services is the not-for-profit, or voluntary agency. Ralph Kramer (1981) has noted that since the "colonization of what was to become the United States there have been both governmental and voluntary modes of coping with the problems of economic dislocation." Historically, the voluntary agency has represented an alternative to the provision of social services through public agencies. As Lester Salamon and his associates (1984) have remarked, however, "despite its importance, precious little is known about this set of organizations."

There is substantial definitional and conceptual confusion. Voluntary agencies engage in so many different and often contradictory activities that they are difficult to locate precisely on a road map of welfare state activities or functions. For the purposes of this discussion, it is important to clarify some of the fixed and variable characteristics of the voluntary agency. Only in this way can the particular interests of this inquiry be clearly situated within the far broader confines of the not-for-profit segment of the economy.

The Internal Revenue Service has defined no fewer than twenty-five types of agencies as eligible for tax-exempt or not-for-profit status.

The activities of these agencies are disparate. They include burial and fraternal associations as well as the educational and social service organizations that are more commonly associated with voluntary agency status. All of these agencies, however, share a common structural drive that prohibits economic profit and encourages the delivery of a service. Organizations in the voluntary sector also enjoy some degree of independence from the state or public sector. They are not directly responsible to any branch of government. Instead (much like the corporation), they are self-contained structures. The critical work of the organization is divided between the staff, who carry specific daily tasks, and the board of directors, which bears the ultimate fiduciary and planning responsibilities for the organization.

Salamon's basic classification of not-for-profit agencies into four major categories is clarifying (Salamon, Musselwhite, and Abramson 1984). He divides the not-for-profit economy into (1) churches; (2) fund-raising or distributing organizations (United Way, private foundations); (3) recreational organizations that serve the needs of members (professional societies, labor unions, etc.); and (4) charitable or educational organizations (serving a community beyond the membership of the organizations). The particular interest of this inquiry is in the charitable and social service sector of the not-for-profit economy.

The scope and character of this subset of agencies, however, remains conceptually confused by either the unavailability or deficiency of data (Salamon, Musselwhite, and Abramson 1984). Although available data are highly flawed, most recent estimates indicate that approximately 60 percent of these organizations engaged in the delivery of social or legal services, 17 percent provided health care, 16 percent emphasized education or research, and approximately 7 percent focused on cultural activities. Sixty percent of the total budget of this subset of not-for-profits was devoted to health services while approximately 17 percent was dedicated to social or legal services (Dawes and Saidel 1988; Weisbrod 1988). Clearly, not-for-profit health agencies, although less numerous, are substantially larger than social service or legal agencies. More generally, there are great disparities in the size, labor force, and substantive foci of this subset of not-for-profit agencies. These differences will be more fully elaborated upon later in our discussion when the sampling strategy for this inquiry is presented.

As was noted earlier, the voluntary charitable agency can be traced back to the earliest stages of the American experience. Services for the destitute and disabled were frequently provided in the nineteenth century by voluntary agencies. These organizations, although originally conceived as a supplement, represented a dissatisfaction with public resources and to some extent attempted to replace government (Kramer 1981). These services were organized through the voluntary sector as private groups attempted to fill the gap between communal need and narrow definitions of government responsibility. As the not-for-profit agency assumed increased responsibilities that otherwise would have been unmet or fallen to government, it pressed the state to subsidize these efforts.

The subsidization of voluntary initiatives by government is critically important to the following discussion. We will argue that the contours of this fiscal relationship have been significantly affected by cost-containment policies. This emphasis on cost containment (as a mechanism in support of state accumulation functions) has intensified centralizing and bureaucratizing pressure on voluntary agencies. These forces are in turn reproducing a social service labor process that is increasingly incapable of meeting client need. The disturbing new realities associated with the recent reworking of this relationship will be more fully explored in the next section of this chapter.

A basic premise of this book is that government cutbacks (in various forms) of welfare state activities have substantially influenced the structure of services and the nature of social service work. The impact of government fiscal decision making on the functioning of not-for-profit agencies, although less immediately apparent than for public agencies, is no less profound.

The Not-for-Profits' Partnership with the State

Although a historic relationship of subsidization existed between voluntary agency and government, this relationship was both tenuous and limited prior to the 1960s. During the period 1960–1980, there was a rapid expansion of the dimensions and magnitude of this relationship at all levels of government. The two primary sources of government subsidy are direct assistance (the most popular of which is purchase of service contracts), which accounts for approximately 20 percent of government support, and reimbursement of income-eligible clients (Medicare, Medicaid, etc.), which represents more than 50 percent of the government subsidy to the voluntary sector (Salamon, Musselwhite, and Abramson 1984). The heightened dependence of not-for-profit agencies on these sources of revenue is documented by an array of data. Some have suggested that the result has been a progressive and pervasive mingling of public and private funds. This is reflected in references to the contract state, third-party government, and the mixed economy of welfare (Terrell and Kramer 1984).

This new "mixed economy" of government and not-for-profit agencies has at times blurred the boundaries between these types of organizations and heightened a relationship of fiscal dependence. Between 1971 and 1978 the percentage of social service funding under the Social Security Act involving contracting out increased from 25 percent to 50 percent (Kramer and Grossman 1987). Additionally, it has been estimated that the U.S. Department of Health and Human Services in the 1970s employed more people through contracting than through full-time employment.

An additional source of revenue for not-for-profits is direct assistance to clients, or third-party reimbursements. In the early 1980s many agencies emphasized such assistance as a means of cushioning the impact of contract cutbacks (Demone and Gibelman 1984). For instance, the number of Family Service Association agencies making this shift increased by 13 percent between 1979 and 1981 (Ostrander 1985).

The expansive flow of dollars to the voluntary sector was not without certain costs. Over time there was an increased call for accountability mechanisms to monitor elements of the client and agency experience. Of particular importance was accounting for dollars spent and numbers of clients served (Poertner and Rapp 1985). Outcome measures attempting to discern whether or not the intervention made a difference in the behavior, attitude, etc. of clients were often sacrificed (De Hoog 1984). The increased flow of dollars to voluntary agencies and reliance upon accountability measures further exaggerated trends that were increasingly shaping the character of voluntary social services.

Voluntary Agency Trade-offs

To a great extent, the increased funding directed toward voluntary agencies can be traced to a generalized dissatisfaction with government. Social Democrats such as Michael Walzer and Gunnar Myrdal suggest that government has apparently reached the limits of its capacity in numerous areas and now must incorporate greater participation in other sectors of society (Terrell and Kramer 1984). More conservative commentators like Peter Drucker (1988) agree that government has become too big and too remote for citizens to participate in it. Volunteers and voluntary agencies are perceived across the political spectrum as a viable alternative to government services. However, as the voluntary sector mushroomed, the very factors that distinguish it from government were placed at risk.

This tendency is perhaps best illustrated by the government's heightened accountability demands upon the not-for-profit agency (Kettner and Martin 1986; Barber 1986; Radin and Benton 1986; Willis 1984). The monitoring and attendant paperwork associated with both client access to voluntary social services and agency compliance with government standards have significant implications. These compliance mechanisms effectively limit a number of the historical advantages of voluntary agencies. More specifically, it has been suggested that providers are called upon to devote more and more time to paperwork requirements and therefore are less and less available to clients (Fabricant 1985). For instance, in studies of contracting-out, most complaints about state monitoring are concerned with the frequency and duplication of paperwork (Kramer and Grossman 1987). Additionally, as was noted earlier, the substantive focus of state monitoring is typically fiscal and restricted to service outputs (effort) rather than outcomes (effectiveness).

This reflexive drive on the part of the public bureaucracy (due to its scale, broad public responsibility, and struggle to provide services during a period of contracting resources) to define its measures of compliance in the most simple, uniform, and quantitative terms has affected the structure and character of voluntary social services. Again, what these trends have most fundamentally reinforced (during the past twenty-five years) is the convergence of government and voluntary social services. The motor force during this merger has been the increasingly valuable and dependent fiscal relationship between voluntary agencies and the state.

Quite clearly, one of the primary trends for voluntary agencies (as a result of the confluence of these forces) is a loss of autonomy. As Ostrander (1985) has noted, these tendencies "raise the issue of the tension between voluntary agencies' demands for autonomy and the state's demands for accountability." The extent and nature of these losses are not entirely clear. However, a basic premise of this analysis is that losses in autonomy and shifts in the structure of services have accelerated as the competition among voluntary agencies for increasingly scarce public dollars has intensified.

Additionally, as Kramer and Grossman (1987) have indicated, underfunding is a recurrent condition confronted by agencies receiving grants or contracts for services. It should also be noted that restrictions on reimbursement formulas (DRGs, etc.) have exacerbated these tendencies (Coulton 1988; Walsh 1987; NASW 1988). One major study discovered an average dollar loss of 15 to 20 percent to voluntary agencies on most government contracts and grants (Kramer and Grossman 1987). The underfunding of not-for-profit grants (and restriction of reimbursables) has affected salary scales. In general, not-for-profit workers are expected to engage in the same type of service work and produce the same results as their public-sector counterparts for less money. The only countervailing force for salary parity between voluntary and government agencies is the capacity of the not-for-profit to raise funds privately. Ultimately, the underfunding of agency work represents a deemphasis of governmental responsibility for the provision of various services. The costs associated with this partnership have been at least partially enumerated. It is equally important, however, to explore the benefits and incentives that continue to propel voluntary and government agencies to deepen their relationship.

Despite the various challenges associated with purchase-of-service contracts and third-party reimbursement, these new and expanded sources of revenue have helped both to solidify the funding base and to expand the services of not-for-profit agencies. As has been noted, government funding increasingly represents a major portion of the resources available to nonprofit agencies. Without such support, many agencies would have been left with the equally unsatisfactory choices of shutting down their operations or dramatically restricting the types of services they make available to the community. Even more specifically, services related to children (adoptions, residential treatment), disability (cerebral palsy, muscular dystrophy), and socialization/assimilation (settlement houses, recreation centers)—historically identified with not-for-profit activity—would have been curtailed at the very least.

Just as significantly, new areas of services recently associated with not-for-profits, such as senior citizen centers, feeding programs, housing projects, homeless shelters, or employment training programs, might never have existed. To the extent that government subsidies are more available to provide particular kinds of services (the most recent examples of which are homelessness and feeding programs) not-for-profit agencies revised their substantive (or service) focus to incorporate these new opportunities. Conversely, if less funding is made available, agencies may have to withdraw from specific fields of service or alter the kinds of service they deliver.

How the Partnership Benefits the Public Sector

The benefits for government of an expansive, subsidy-driven partnership are numerous and complex. Any discussion of these benefits must begin with cost reduction. It has been consistently suggested that not-for-profit agencies can provide the same services as the public sector at a lower cost. For instance, between 1970 and 1981, five empirical studies were undertaken to determine why human service agencies were rapidly increasing their use of purchase-of-service contracts (Booz-Allen and Hamilton 1971; Wedel 1974; Benton, Field, and Millar 1978; Pacific Consultants 1979; American Public Welfare Association 1981). A principal consideration cited in each of these reports was fiscal. These government agencies were specifically expected to lower the cost of services and increase control over fiscal accountability (Kettner and Martin 1985).

While voluntary agencies are able to reduce the labor costs associated with service provision through the use of unpaid and low-paid staff, various formal and informal labor agreements severely restrict public-sector agencies from drawing as extensively upon the same range of cheaper labor options. Public-sector managers have identified a number of economies associated with contracting out for services. As Kramer and Grossman (1987) have indicated, these strategies include the use of low-paid paraprofessionals, preprofessional interns, unlicensed professionals, lower paid part-time staff, consultant staff ineligible for benefits, and subcontractors or consultant staff who accept lower fees in exchange for guaranteed work. Additionally, public-sector managers have indicated that cost savings are available through donated funds, which essentially represent resources that are raised privately by voluntary agencies and then are used to supplement government grants. These dollars may be used to reduce administrative costs, supplement a benefits package, or contribute to the basic salary of staff. Their specific use is less important than the general conse-quence: these donated funds absorb costs that otherwise would have been assumed by government (De Hoog 1984).

It is important to note that a substantial literature is emerging which questions whether voluntary agencies are cheaper or more cost effi-cient than the government. As Lipsky and Smith (1989, p. 16) note, however, the findings of these studies are mixed.

> There is some reason to believe that savings may be available through private sector contracting because of the lower wages private providers are able to pay and lower administrative costs.

Other factors that the literature suggests contribute to the strength of the voluntary sector (relative to government) are its innovation, flexibility, and responsiveness to changing community needs. The pre-vailing view is that not-for-profit agencies are less burdened by many of the operational constraints associated with government bureaucracy. In effect, voluntary agencies are smaller, relatively independent, and located in the community. These characteristics are perceived as en-abling nonprofits to respond more effectively to the changing needs of the community. Equally important, these agencies are less insulated from community turbulence. Consequently, they are better positioned to develop innovative or experimental responses to changing condi-tions. In effect, voluntary agencies are forced to struggle with practice approaches or problem foci that may be increasingly out of touch with the changing character, culture, or needs of their target populations. For instance, many voluntary agencies working with the homeless or unemployed white working-class youth were the first to report an in-creased use of crack. Their working assumptions regarding viable in-terventions were therefore modified earlier than those in other service organizations. In sum, it has been suggested that the process of identi-fying such changes and integrating the lessons of these experiences into the daily work of the agency can occur far more rapidly and experimen-tally for voluntary agencies than for the government.

Most recently, however, the very nature of the partnership between the public sector and voluntary agencies is being restructured by the intensified cost-containment policies of the state. These new fiscal policies are increasingly affecting the daily operation of voluntary agencies. Before considering the specific impact of these budget cuts

and/or fiscal constraints upon the work of voluntary agencies, it is important to focus attention on the magnitude and nature of these intensified
cost-containment policies. These policies threaten the viability of voluntary agencies and, relatedly, the historic trade-offs of state subsidies.

Cost Containment and the Redefinition of the Partnership

The recent cost-containment policies of the state can be traced to an
international economic crisis (as was noted in chapter 2). A range of
commentators also acknowledge that the welfare state is in crisis. The
inability of the welfare state to solve fundamental employment, crime,
health, and housing issues, to name but a few, is defined by the Left
and Right as a fundamental failure of its institutions and structure.

As Salamon has noted, this crisis is double-edged. On the one hand, it
is associated with the inability of Western democracies to continue to
support the expansion and maintenance of traditional levels of service. On
the other hand, there is widespread dissatisfaction with the structure and
organization of the welfare state, which is characterized by red tape,
distance from the community, elitism, and fragmentation. As a consequence of fiscal pressures and ideology, intensified forms of cost containment were developed and implemented during the Reagan administration.
A number of these policies specifically affected the functioning of voluntary agencies (Salamon, Musselwhite, and Abramson 1984).

Agencies providing day-care, counseling, child and family services,
assistance to the elderly, legal services, and employment training suffered the most substantial losses of federal support between 1982 and
1986. Abramson and Salamon have noted that these agencies lost $12
billion in federal funding during this period. The income received by
these not-for-profits in fiscal year 1986 was projected to be approximately 40 percent below what it had been in fiscal year 1980 (Abramson and Salamon 1986).

Additionally, not-for-profit health agencies are increasingly vulnerable to cuts and cost-containment strategies. Recent data indicate that
federal support for outpatient clinics has declined. By fiscal year 1985
the level of support had fallen 33 percent below the 1980 allocation
(Abramson and Salamon 1986). Not-for-profit hospitals and nursing
homes are also affected by cost-containment policies. The prospective
payment system is increasingly regulating Medicaid spending. More
specifically, this regulatory tool is being used to control the costs of

third-party reimbursable spending under Medicaid (Coulton 1988; Walsh 1987; NASW 1988).

The impact of these cost-containment policies has been experienced in various ways by local communities. The Urban Institute's Nonprofit Sector Project is very instructive in identifying the variable impacts of these policies on the service areas and particular populations of communities. For instance, Salamon and associates note reductions in government support between fiscal year 1981 and 1983 for nonprofits in cities such as Chicago (6.3 percent), Atlanta (15.4 percent), Phoenix (4 percent), and Pittsburgh (13.8 percent) (Salamon, Altschuler, and De Vita 1986). Alternatively, nonprofits in other areas experienced an expansion in government support during the same time period: Rhode Island (2 percent), San Francisco (6 percent), Flint, Michigan (6 percent), Minneapolis/St. Paul (5.2 percent), and New York City (6 percent) (Salamon et al. 1986).

The most recent data available from this project indicate that there was a loss of 4.5 percent in government support for not-for-profit agencies between the years 1981 and 1983 (Salamon et al. 1986–87). The differences in government support can be traced to the variable commitment of states and city governments to support the work of nonprofit agencies and thus replace the loss in federal revenue.

It is also important to note that the loss of government support was not shared equally by every type of not-for-profit agency. One theme that emerges from the Urban Institute Project is that not-for-profit agencies providing a range of social services were particularly hard hit by these budget cuts. Multiservice agencies in Chicago (34 percent), Atlanta (11 percent), Phoenix (22 percent), and Providence, Rhode Island (11 percent) experienced far greater losses in government revenue than the broader sample of nonprofits that were surveyed. Similarly, social service organizations (Providence 25 percent, Chicago 11 percent, Atlanta 9 percent) and employment, housing, and legal services (Rhode Island 11 percent, Twin Cities 3 percent, Phoenix 38 percent, Chicago 34 percent, and Atlanta 7 percent) suffered a disproportionate share of government funding losses during this period.

The not-for-profit social service organizations that experienced the greatest expansion of government revenue were providers of health, mental health, and residential services (Salamon et al. 1986–87). This additional support can be traced in part to the greater availability of third-party reimbursables in these areas of service work. As Ostrander (1985) has noted, one of the ways of coping with cuts in government support has been to emphasize services covered by third-party payments such as Blue Cross and Medicare/Medicaid. Such an approach is particularly pertinent for health/mental health agencies. However, this strategy has become increasingly untenable as regulatory mechanisms have been developed to contain the costs of these third-party programs.

Losses in government revenue for voluntary agencies have also had a differential impact on clients. In general, not-for-profits serving poorer communities experienced substantial decline in such revenue (Chicago 19 percent, Rhode Island 28 percent, Atlanta 23 percent, Flint, Michigan 21 percent, Twin Cities 3 percent, Phoenix 3 percent, Pittsburgh 18 percent). Even more dramatic reductions were reported for voluntary agencies that were primarily serving black and Hispanic clients (Rhode Island 42 percent, Atlanta 20 percent, Twin Cities 6 percent, and Phoenix 44 percent) (Salamon et al. 1986–87).

The demands for nonprofit services mounted at precisely the moment when various sources of public funding contracted. The most dramatic examples of intensified need that emerged during the 1980s are homelessness, hunger, and drug abuse. Mounting crime, teen pregnancy, and domestic violence also contributed to the increased volume of clients seeking services from local not-for-profit agencies. Equally important, these problems represented a shift in the locus of agency work. The community agency was increasingly working with clients who were in crisis. With ever greater frequency, people seeking services presented problems that had festered for years but had been untended. The work of the not-for-profit agency thus has been altered not only by the increased demands for services from the community but also by the more complicated crises of clients. The voluntary agency in turn is under siege from two directions. It is expected to meet the growing, ever more complex problems of communities in crisis with less and less public resources. Clearly, the circumstance of the voluntary agency is becoming more and more untenable. It is unable unilaterally to fill the gap between changing community needs and the government's fiscal disengagement from various social problems. There is also nowhere for voluntary agencies to run and hide.* They are contractually, historically, and organizationally committed to

---

*The increased emphasis throughout the 1980s on informal community support networks supports this point. These networks emerged because voluntary agencies were less and less able to meet certain basic needs.

the continued provision of social services to particular communities. However, these cross-cutting pressures have taken a significant toll on the work of the voluntary agency.

The intersection between cost-containment policies, rising demand for services, and the quality of work life within voluntary agencies is of particular interest to this inquiry. There have been a number of studies that document the macro issues associated with the cost-containment policies of the government. Recent investigations have been particularly concerned with calculating the impact of these policies upon particular types of services. In effect, the data and findings of these studies are structured to consider policy questions that are pertinent to specific service areas within the welfare state, such as disability, health, and mental health services. Rarely, if ever, are the more discrete consequences of these policies upon the voluntary agency or worker seriously considered. It will be the purpose of the next section of this chapter to briefly identify the threads in the literature that detect general shifts in the nature of social service work.

Changes at the Level of the Agency and Worker

As has been suggested, a number of instruments have been developed by the federal government to contain costs: Quality Control for AFDC, RUGS (Resource Utilization Group System) for nursing homes; and PPS (Prospective Payment System) for hospitals. Perhaps the most notable method is the Prospective Payment System, which is structured to limit expenditures associated with Medicare. Under PPS and its reimbursement system, known as Diagnostic Related Groups (DRGs), hospitals are reimbursed for a patient's stay at a predetermined fixed amount for various diagnostic categories of disease. Hospitals tend to gain financially when the length of stay for patients is less than that specified by DRGs and they lose income if patients' stays exceed those standards (Coulton 1988; Wolock et al. 1987).

The containment of federal spending during the 1980s provoked a number of disturbing yet fiscally necessary responses by voluntary agencies. With a relatively fixed resource base, yet increased demands for services, not-for-profit agencies were faced with the choice of controlling their costs by enlarging the caseloads of workers or expanding the waiting list of clients (and extending the waiting period between the request and receipt of services). Often agencies mixed their responses and consequently asked both staff and clients to shoulder the burden of these policies. Ultimately, extended waiting periods and ballooning caseloads further exaggerated the difficulties already associated with access to agencies and the declining quality of social services (Lipsky 1984).

Perhaps the most striking outcomes associated with the containment of costs are the new managerial practices and structures being implemented by voluntary agencies. More and more, the new systems of managerial control intended to husband scarce resources are ill suited to voluntary agencies. The rapidly changing and uncertain environment of agencies increasingly exposes workers to obscure and contradictory pressures. As Burton Gummer (1984, p. 10) notes,

> Managerial control systems can be expected to increase in importance both as a device for protecting increasingly scarce resources and as a reflection of the mounting influence of the professional manager. . . . The rise in the importance of management control systems in social agencies is paralleled, however, by evidence that these organizations are less suited to these kinds of controls than ever before. The social agency's environment is increasingly characterized as rapidly changing, full of obscure and contradictory pressures and highly uncertain.

The fundamental contradiction between the gathering force of centralization and heightened managerial control to produce cost savings, on the one hand, and the divergent needs of workers and agencies for discretion and loose internal structures in order to invent effective responses in a rapidly changing environment, on the other, will be more fully explained in the empirical sector of this chapter.

Although the literature is sketchy regarding the impact of cost-containment policies upon staff and clients, certain themes have emerged. The Urban Institute Project suggests that specific staffing and management changes were implemented by voluntary agencies because of federal revenue losses (Salamon et al. 1986–87). The agency staffing patterns were increasingly marked by larger case loads, unfilled positions, and the reduction of administrative support staff. Management changes that were consistently cited in this survey involved the reorganization of administrative staff and the initiation of new management efficiency programs. The data also indicate that agencies characteristically made certain programmatic changes in response to fiscal pressures. Many agencies chose to eliminate programs, reduce levels of service, and tighten eligibility standards.

This general information, however, offers the reader only a very limited understanding of the relationship between cost-containment policies and the changing texture of social service work within voluntary agencies. Other strains in the literature speak of shifts in the behavior and attitudes of social service workers and the structure of social work departments (Cohen 1986; Dinerman et al. 1986; Dressel 1982; NASW 1988). However, these changes are either partial and thus not sufficiently developed in relationship to other agency/environmental shifts, or represent secondary analytic themes that are barely developed. For instance, there is a burgeoning literature on burnout in the field (Fahs-Beck 1987; Jayaratne et al. 1986; Lewis 1980). However, each of these studies reflects the increasingly specialized tendencies of the field. With few exceptions, they simply miss the more general implications of the spreading cancer of worker burnout. The authors' insights are generally restricted to describing the phenomenon of burnout and identifying specific variables in the agency or service field that may trigger this psychic drain (Fahs-Beck 1984; Jayaratne et al. 1986).

Flowing from the structure of these analyses are a range of technical proposals intended to improve the mental health of workers. These include the use of yoga, diet, breathing exercises, and various forms of counseling. Although each of these analyses and proposals have some merit, they collectively fail to consider burnout within the broader context of economic/political change, cost-containment policies, and shifts in organizational structure and demand. By framing the problem of worker burnout in such a limited manner, the prescriptions for altering this condition have limited utility because they fail either to comprehend or to consider sufficiently the origins of the "disease."

Taking the disease model one step further, an analogous situation might exist in the health field if, for instance, the medical researcher or practitioner only focused on the cells of the patient as the source of cancer. To the extent that pollution, hazardous waste, and other rapidly changing environmental factors contribute to the increased risk and incidence of cancer, such emphasis is shortsighted at best. For staff burnout and cancer alike, highly focused definitions of the problem and responses will do little to affect either the recurrence (within the individual) or reproduction (with at-risk populations) of the disease. An increasingly toxic environment is affecting the quality of work life for line staff and services for clients (Donovan 1987; Lewis 1980).

Burnout is only one of the final outcomes of a dynamic process that is transforming the nature of social services and social service work within voluntary agencies.

Another visible outcome associated with the interplay between cost-containment policies and the restructuring of services is increased difficulty in retaining staff. Across the country, professional groups, government commissions, and interagency associations are troubled by the difficulties associated with retaining professional social service workers (COFCA 1989; Massachusetts Department of Human Services 1987; Gallagher et al. 1988). A New York City survey of voluntary human service administrators reported that 82.6 percent of the respondents felt that staff recruitment and retention was one of their top three problems (Gallagher et al. 1988). Approximately 75 percent of those interviewed indicated that recruitment and retention were more difficult today than either two or five years ago. A survey in Massachusetts also reported that staff recruitment and retention are the most significant problems not-for-profit human service managers expect to face in the next three to five years (Massachusetts Department of Human Services 1987). These reports and others clearly associate retention and recruitment difficulties with the deteriorating working conditions in human service agencies. Low salaries, high work loads, and loss of worker autonomy are some of the causes cited.

Although this essentially descriptive literature is reasonably attentive to the crisis confronting social service work and the interplay between specific variables that explain this circumstance, it is insufficiently concerned with fully and richly presenting the changing nature of work within voluntary agencies. Only by developing such a portrait can we begin to identify and explain the complex array of micro forces affecting burnout or retention. Equally important, the reports pay scant attention to broader macro currents (cost-containment policies, etc.) that trigger and reinforce the new micro trends and structure of service work.

Analyses of the impact of these practices and policies on the client is similarly limited. Length of stay, access, quality of service, and satisfaction are emphasized (Coulton 1988; Wolock et al. 1987; Demone and Gibelman 1984). However, these trends and attitudes are not tightly fastened to a recent agency history. Consequently, the meaning of these new behaviors and attitudes, if not entirely lost, is only very partially understood.

It will be the purpose of the rest of this chapter to offer a fuller explanation of the impact of cost-containment policies upon voluntary agency service work. As has been noted repeatedly, it is critical that the deepening crisis of the welfare state, which in great part can be explained by declining resources, be traced from its macro origins to the consequent restructuring of micro practices. The broader political and economic forces affecting profound agency changes were presented in chapters 1 and 2. The specific public agency practice changes and bureaucratic pressures provoked by this turbulent fiscal environment were conceptually and partially considered in chapter 3. However, the emergent experience and structure of social service work within voluntary agencies has yet to be portrayed empirically through the use of primary data.

This is an important omission because it has been assumed that the greatest opportunities for human service workers to develop a professional practice (autonomous, flexible, and skill-based) exist in nonprofit agencies. Equally important, voluntary agencies are frequently described as the field's incubator for practice and programmatic innovation (Kramer 1981). The extent to which voluntary agencies are presently able to perform these functions, however, is unclear. Additionally, the various issues identified as characteristic of the changes affecting voluntary agencies (turnover, burnout, centralization, etc.) must be verified, organized into a coherent whole, and more richly understood. Finally, the dilemmas, contradictions, and implications of this new service structure need to be examined in relation to the specific experiences of workers. For these reasons, an exploratory study of line workers in an array of not-for-profit agencies was undertaken in the fall of 1988. The findings of this investigation will be presented in the subsequent section of the chapter.

The following analysis presents anecdotal data on the interplay between intensifying cost-containment processes of bureaucratization and worker experience. This information was drawn from a sample of fifty-three line workers employed by three voluntary agencies. The names of the agencies have been altered to assure the anonymity of respondents. The programs targeted by this inquiry specifically include TEP (Training and Employment Program), CAFCA (Children and Family Counseling Agency), and Evergreen Hospital. The TEP programs that were of particular interest included Mothers in Transition (MIT), a training program for AFDC recipients, and Youth on the Move, an employment/training program for high school students. Each agency is located in the New York City metropolitan area. A range of methods was employed to collect and develop the anecdotal material presented. A description of these methods (Appendix 4–A) and a listing of respondents by pseudonym, agency, and key characteristics (Appendix 4–B) are provided in the appendices.

The Feel of a Workday

The daily routine associated with social service work is increasingly tense. Every client encounter and meeting is tightly structured because of the volume of daily tasks that have to be met. There is little slack time in the worker's schedule. Instead, the day feels like a headlong rush from one set of tasks to the next. More and more, these demands are overwhelming the worker. The daily pressure cooker associated with social service work is illustrated in the following passages:

> They keep you very busy around here, there is really no time wasted, pretty much every minute of the day is mapped out. . . . It's like a religious camp, you never get a chance to catch your breath. . . . A typical day around here is busy and frustrating. I'm frantically consulting my calendar and everyone else's to find common time for things. . . . Even such free time as I've got is hectic because it's spent catching up, hovering outside people's doors to catch them for a few minutes when the client leaves or whatever, it's fast paced. (C–17 Family and Children's Counseling)

> One of the great complaints of staff is that the only purpose of work is to get through it. It often seems that the only purpose of the training interview is to schedule it and get through so the client can move on to the next stage and we move on to the next interview. We're just freed for the next wave of interviews. Too often the work seems overwhelming and the staff feels helpless. The constant feeling is let's just move the clients through this process. We are just thinking about moving them from step A to step B because there is so much pressure. (B–15 Employment Training)

> There's so much frustrations with hospital social work at this point. There's just a constant feeling you can't catch up. They expect quality

services and excellent documentation, but the time is not built into the job. During the course of a day, you're just pulled from one part of the job to the other. There's just a chronic feeling that you're under water and can't get to the surface. (A–20 Hospital)

The workday of line staff is influenced by the urgency of client problems. With increasing frequency, agency workers are required to intervene with poor individuals and families who have multiple problems. Often, these clients' presenting problems are part of a mosaic of economic, social, and personal histories that require broad-based and time-consuming responses. Specific crises rupture the daily functioning of clients and color the staff person's encounter with people seeking services: the dire need for child care in order to remain in an employment training program, housing upon discharge from the hospital so as to avoid becoming homeless, or intense therapy to alleviate violent behavior are the types of problems workers are being asked to manage.

Of course, as the intensity of the client's problems burns ever hotter, the worker is asked to mobilize personal and other resources more rapidly. The worker is expected to tailor an immediate response to the narrowed choices, volatility, and/or relative deprivation of the client. As the number of clients with such needs swells, the social service worker is increasingly required to redirect her attention from routine daily tasks to crises. The apparent tension for the worker, however, is that each crisis absorbs substantial amounts of scarce time. More specifically, the paperwork, service encounters, and meetings associated with the rest of the caseload do not disappear when the worker is meeting the needs of a particularly troubled client. Instead, the amount of work multiplies. Essentially, the worker is expected to meet the distinctive needs of an entire caseload. As the number of crisis cases rises, the social service worker is flooded by the breadth and depth of the demands upon her time. The crosscutting pressures upon staff associated with this expansive pool of emergencies is presented below:

We're dealing with one crisis layered on top of another and still expected to address all of our daily noncrisis work in a timely manner. It creates so much stress. It just seems as though there's always a crisis. Of course, often the hospital stay is so short it's difficult to get at any of the issues underlying the crisis. (A–6 Hospital)

We're under greater and greater pressure to move people in and out of the hospital. But we're getting more and more patients in here with no identification. They're confused and disoriented. I'm still under pressure to get them out of here between three and five days. In order to do that though, I have to start with something but I have no information. I'm like a detective trying to identify and place this person so we don't release him to the streets. More and more often I'm being asked to be a miracle worker. (A–11 Hospital)

If too many clients call me and they are in crisis, I'm in trouble. No matter what, I still have to see my three new people every morning, an hour and one-half apiece, so the pipeline into training is filled. It's getting harder and harder to meet the needs of both sets of clients. (B–10 Employment Training)

More and more we seem to be moving from one student to the next. We're doing a lot more crisis management. As a result, outside of these crises often we just seem to be babysitting students. If I hear that an issue sounds urgent, I respond. This kind of problem is just occupying more and more of my time. (B–2 Employment Training)

The number of chaotic families we're seeing is increasing. I don't know where to start with these families and that certainly contributes to the pressure around here. They need therapy more than once a week, but it's not available. (C–4 Family and Children's Counseling)

As has already been suggested, the pressures and demands upon workers have necessitated a highly structured workday. For many line staff, each hour of every day is scheduled with prescribed tasks or meetings. There is little, if any, time to reflect upon particular cases. Instead, each workday has a constant and intensifying rhythm.

The drain of energy and compassion associated with the workday has a particular impact upon workers who provide counseling services. The strain of attempting to participate in a dynamic therapeutic process, often with little recovery or reflective time between clients, has exacted a specific cost upon mental health workers. By the end of a workday they are frequently less able to focus their energy or attention. They are less able to identify key emotional issues and develop an appropriate service plan. The strain of providing mental health services in an environment that is highly pressured also has a cumulative and corrosive effect. The fading concentration of mental health workers who are daily confronted with the mounting pressures of increased caseloads and crises is illustrated in the following passages.

> What do we have to look forward to? At the end of each workday, I'm exhausted and drained. I often wonder why am I doing this? Am I masochistic? (C–11 Family and Children's Counseling)

> At the end of the workday I'm just not as alert, I'm exhausted. I'm just not there for the client. There is also a cumulative effect, this exhaustion spills into the next day. Again, I'm just not there for them in a way that I need to be or should be. (C–10 Family and Children's Counseling)

> By the end of the day if I'm with a client that is low functioning, I'm glad because I don't have to think as much. When clients come late, I'm glad because at the end of a day it means I have to invest less energy. My schedule is such that I'm really feeling fatigued. Consequently, you just really don't have the energy to focus or address client resistance in ways that you might if you were less tired. Ultimately, I just tend to space out in many more of these sessions or I don't take it where it should go therapeutically. (C–3 Family and Children's Counseling)

Heightened Demands and the Intensification of the Workday

New Client Profile

The pressures, crises, and often chaos that are increasingly characteristic of social service work can be traced to a mixture of highly interactive elemental parts of the service experience. Certain key elements of the service experience are undergoing rapid change. These distinct changes have had the similar affect of multiplying the work load of line staff. The agency, and in turn its workers, has been buffeted by the cross currents of a changing clientele, reduction of community support, an intensified drive for productivity, and increased paperwork. Each of these variables has independently influenced the quality and nature of social service work. The combination of these forces has contributed to a dramatic restructuring of the social service labor process.

As was briefly noted earlier, more clients are in multiple crises during their initial and subsequent encounters with an agency. At least one of the factors that continues to fuel the rapid reproduction and expansion of these more vulnerable populations is the greater deprivation that seems to mark the experience of clients presently seeking services. The clients of a cross section of agencies are more likely to be burdened by deficits that cripple their immediate capacity to function within a community or family and on the job. The combination of economic, social, and emotional deprivations reduces the clients' functional capacity (by creating significant breaks in emotional balance) and also limits the choices available to workers. Clearly, there are few effective interventions for clients that are so highly and historically marginalized. Furthermore, a predicate of any effective intervention is continuity and frequency of contact. The resources necessary for sustained and intense client contact, however, are increasingly unavailable to workers. The worker's circumstances (intensifying resource scarcity) then mirror the client's. The following passages more fully describe the harsher conditions and deprivations that define the experience of clients prior to seeking services from social agencies.

> Yes, the diagnoses are getting worse. I don't know if I'm regressing or they're getting more screwed up. I've seen a 100 percent rise in multi-problems, abuse, and dual diagnosis; you name it. People don't seem to be getting better. In the midst of these more demanding clients, the agency is asking us to cut down our length of treatment. I just don't know what we're going to do. (C–14 Family and Children's Counseling)

> All I know for sure is that CAFCA reports with its own statistics, things are getting worse. People require more drastic interventions, hospitalization, for instance, and people who have been admitted once are likely to be back with the same problem. They say this means problems are worse. (C–17 Family and Children's Counseling)

> The dilemma is we're getting more and more people needing hospitalization and psychiatric help. We don't have the resources to work with them as therapists. (C–2 Family and Children's Counseling)

> It's hard to get employment opportunities for students when they have so many survival problems. . . . The students are asking for services they desperately need, but which we can't really respond to. (B–8 Employment Training)

> The clients are becoming more and more problematic. They need so many more support services than our agency provides. All we focus on is the employment not their emotional needs which will affect their success in the program, but of course, when you mention this to the

director, all she can say is this an employment not a counseling program. (B–9 Employment Training)

Oh, there are so many people coming in here with worse and worse problems. You wonder how have they hung on for so long with so little. There are so many families hanging on by a thread. They have no family or nurturing or housing. (A–7 Hospital)

Clients are coming in here with so many more problems and deficits. There is no question we now have a more difficult population. Equally important, we must understand our limits. (A–17 Hospital)

To some extent, the cost-containment policies of the past decade have also contributed to an intensification of community and family problems. Increased homelessness, for instance, can be traced directly to reductions by the federal government in low- and moderate-income housing creation (Fabricant 1987; Hopper and Hamberg 1984). The loss of Food Stamps' purchasing power during this period has further diminished the capacity of poor families and individuals to avoid extended periods of hunger (Burghardt and Fabricant 1987). As crack addiction and AIDS have coursed through many communities and affected the lives of innumerable families and individuals, the government has been slow to respond. This lapse is at least in part attributable to policies of fiscal restraint that make it increasingly difficult to maintain the status quo, much less develop the new initiatives necessary to respond to emergent crises.

In a sense, the quality of life and social supports recently available to an array of communities are endangered. The losses experienced by these communities have combined to increase their problems and vulnerability. Where do the individuals and families of these communities turn when food is less available, housing lost, or the crack epidemic touches their lives? In the absence of new social services, these citizens will either independently locate or be channeled to existing resources. The consequence of these funding and migratory patterns is that voluntary agencies are being expected with greater frequency to respond independently to the more complex problems of an expanding pool of clients. A number of the communal tensions that increasingly define the worker's encounter with clients are presented below:

We're seeing an increase in homelessness among poor pregnant young teens. We have more and more kids coming in here who are likely to be malnourished, perhaps substance abusers and often without housing.

They have nowhere to go when they leave the hospital. The maternal grandmother is often the primary caregiver. What are we to do with these kids? I don't know. (A–12 Hospital)

I just have tremendous client pressures. More than half of my caseload is experiencing domestic violence. Housing for these mothers is a big problem. The housing is often overcrowded, inadequate, or drug infested. More and more often I find five or six kids living in one room, or in a welfare motel or shelter. I'm also seeing more drug abusers. I feel so locked in and overwhelmed by these problems. (B–10 Employment Training)

So many of these students just have so many survival issues to talk about. They want to know how I can help them find a place to live, help their parents who are substance abusers, or clean up their blocks of crack abuse. These kids are also seeing shootings on a weekly basis on their blocks. Our services, such as Narleen, in the face of drugs, shootings, housing problems, and no food, just seems inadequate. It's frustrating and getting worse. (B–8 Employment Training)

We're seeing more and more of a poverty population. Of course, it's so much harder to work with them on emotional issues. I've been at this sixteen years. There are just so many more chaotic families. The parents are so needy and clearly not in control. . . . Often I don't know where to start with the issues of housing, food, violence, or drugs. . . . All of this just adds to the pressure I'm feeling. (C–4 Family and Children's Counseling)

Reductions in Community Supports

As social service agencies independently struggle to address the mounting needs of their clientele, they find themselves less able to meet the challenge. Consequently, voluntary agencies have attempted to adapt to this situation by drawing on the resources of other agencies. At the earliest stages of the service encounter, line workers are expected to assess whether the client's problem(s) can be addressed by the mix of services available through their agency. These screening devices are applied with increasing frequency, for instance, by the mental health or counseling agency. However, these organizations' subsequent capacity to refer clients to other more appropriate "service outlets" is quite limited. The needed services are often either unavailable or nonexistent.

The dearth of service options reduces the worker's chances of sharing responsibility on particular parts of a case with other agencies. Each agency is struggling in greater and greater isolation to manage its own expansive caseload. In effect, the distress, disorganization, and survival issues that mark recent client experience are overwhelming agencies. Each agency, however, has been required independently to absorb these new pressures. The degenerative cycle of greater resource scarcity, multiplying client problems, and an intensified focus on survival have had as profound an impact on agencies as clients. One of the consequences of this narrowing focus on survival has been to isolate affected individuals, communities, and agencies. It is within this context that agencies are less and less prepared or able to establish collaborative relationships with each other. The process and outcomes associated with this withdrawal of interagency (community) support is illustrated in the following statements.

> It feels like other agencies are just reluctant to help us address serious problems of the client. . . . For me it means trying to touch base with other agencies, it's time-consuming. You call them up . . . they tell us to call other agencies . . . call back. Because of their caseload and problems, they're passing the buck. But it gets frustrating when you have student after student with sexual abuse problems and nowhere to send them. (B–6 Employment Training)

> Resources in the community are also overwhelmed and drying up. So when you send them out, there's not much hope they'll receive services. If they're homeless or substance abusers, there are so few services. It's increasingly frustrating identifying needs the system cannot or will not meet. (B–15 Employment Training)

> We're finding more and more people dumped in the emergency room. They have so many different kinds of problems—housing, drugs, mental illness—I could go on. . . . Ten years ago there were more community agencies to pick up. There are simply fewer available services today. (A–12 Hospital)

> I spend a lot of my time fighting with social service agencies to get them to see the crisis and expedite the process . . . but when I call the agency, all I get is a fight. They don't want, for instance, homeless cases that aren't reimbursable. . . . They see us as money hungry and dumping problems on them. (A–14 Hospital)

> The resources in the community are drying up. Housing, child care—it goes on and on. Because we can't get these services, often the kids have to

stay home. They don't go to school or can't take advantage of our employment services. They wind up taking menial, dead-end jobs. (A–19 Hospital)

The tensions (budget cuts, expanding client need, etc.) now characteristic of social service work have placed more and more agencies in the difficult position of having to default on their historic obligations to respond rapidly to survival needs. The inability of children's agencies to protect their clients' physical safety and of hospitals to provide timely services to patients backlogged in emergency rooms are but two examples of such breakdown. Consequently, line workers are less and less able to have the basic needs of even their most desperate clients met by appropriate and/or responsible service structures.

It's increasingly difficult to get other agencies to pick up on our most difficult cases. They have these waiting lists. I had a suicidal child . . . I couldn't get a bed for, agencies are telling us to wait three months. The kid's going to jump out of a window though, and can't wait. (C–6 Family and Children's Counseling)

They really don't even want to take kids away from mothers who are substance abusers. We report it [from the hospital] to the state agency but you get the feeling that it's not a high priority. . . . They're so overloaded, they're only dealing with twenty-four- to seventy-two-hour response rates for physical abuse. Their caseloads are so high, it's hard for them to deal with anything else. (A–8 Hospital)

I have women who have real financial need. I call an agency and I'm on the phone for fifty minutes with a service person. Then I'm told she's the wrong person and I'm transferred. This happens again and again. It's another fruitless experience. What's the point? (A–4 Hospital)

Cost Containment and the Productive, Efficient Budget: Leaner and Meaner

The budgets of social service agencies are more and more likely to be tied to reimbursement formulas. For instance, hospitals must comply with the various recording, definitional, and clinical requirements associated with DRGs. Equally important, the particular problems of patients must be made to conform to DRG definitions of an illness, and length of stay cannot exceed the limits established by the guidelines if the hospital expects continued reimbursement. The Training Employment Program has a number of enumerated steps in its service process. The agency's contract stipulates that a fixed amount of dollars be reimbursed for a client's progression from one step in the process to the next. The most substantial rewards are tied to the client's graduation from the program. Similarly, CAFCA must comply with daily caseload quotas established in its contractual relationship with the city.

The agency budget, then, also reflects a more uncertain and volatile fiscal environment. Voluntary agency contracts have always emphasized standards of performance in exchange for grant dollars. However, the new contracts being forged by government and voluntary agencies are generally more demanding and less flexible. They describe with greater specificity the particular service requirements that must be met. They thus limit the not-for-profit agency's discretion in identifying or meeting the "extracontractual" needs of a client. These reimbursement procedures are structured to heighten bureaucratic impulses toward specialization and uniformity. The intensified, fiscally driven expectations of the state are at least partially illustrated below:

> The City of New York specifies units in terms of a "patient visit" which is a minimum of 30 minutes. The visit is multiplied times the number of people in the session. The City has set as its level of expectation that a worker will have four patient visits a day. The City figures . . . 800 visits per year. . . . The aggregate productivity of all professional staff, some of whom such as psychiatrists, supervisors, and administrators, may not be doing as much direct service as line workers, must meet this standard. (Union Minutes, CAFCA)

> Throughout the hospital DRGs have shifted thinking to dollars. It's a business. We're expected to maximize dollars. We do this through DRGs by emphasizing length of stay. (A–11 Hospital)

> The issue here with DRGs is how long patients remain. We're paid for discharges, people leaving. . . . But we have to keep filling the beds. What it comes down to is keeping numbers up. We must keep our census up to survive. (A–1 Hospital)

> Everything is written down with the students to make sure as an agency,

> we get credit. Every phone call, every student or teacher contact is documented. (B–3 Employment and Training)

> All of the reimbursement is tied into the structure of moving people from one step in the training process to the next. We have little discretion in how we can work with these women. Our job is to get them through each reimbursement step. These steps include initial workshops, vocational exploration, training, and employment. (B–11 Employment Training)

The new reimbursement procedures place greater emphasis upon moving substantial numbers of clients through the service process. Each client effectively represents raw material that has time-limited value. It is the line worker's responsibility to shepherd these resources through the service marketplace. The service worker is expected to focus on matters of productivity. The work, or "efficiency," of staff is measured by their capacity to process substantial numbers of clients through the service experience in relatively brief periods of time.

The push for greater productivity is particularly acute in the discharge planning unit of the hospital and in the employment agency. These fields of service employ a relatively high proportion of less formally educated workers. For instance, discharge planning is conducted by a cohort of workers who have bachelor's degrees. The TEP employs a mix of bachelor's level paraprofessionals and master's level workers. Alternatively, the mental health counseling agencies and other units of the hospital exclusively employ master's level workers. It is important to note that the increased drive for productivity differentially affects line workers with less formal education. The middle and lower rungs of service workers are expected to manage particularly large caseloads and stressful time demands.

Every agency, however, has been significantly affected by the heightened demands for productivity. No service or line worker was left untouched by the new evolving fiscal relationship between the state and voluntary agencies. This point is generally illustrated below:

> I think at the clinic we get mixed messages. The director seems to be empathetic . . . we understand about your struggle to keep up . . . he says, "I don't know how you do it." They know I'm carrying thirty cases. On the other hand, they'll ask me to pick up another case on an emergency basis. The pressure just grows. (C–11 Family and Children's Counseling)

My main contention here with administration is that we're working with patients, not numbers of people. As a social worker, I'm supposed to look at personal needs, but it is less and less the case. (C–15 Hospital)

I'll tell you all this hubbub for numbers makes me angry. I feel as though I'm not a social worker because everything is so quick and impersonal. I'm part of a social work unit but all they're interested in is numbers. (B–10 Employment Training)

The expanded number of clients moving through the service pipeline has affected both the caseloads and the quotas associated with service work. Each worker is potentially a budget-maximizing mechanism. The dimensions of time and volume define service productivity and in turn have a pronounced impact upon service work.

The counseling agencies, for instance, have developed a point system that weighs the relative value (fiscally driven) of specific tasks performed by the worker. At the end of each week, the worker is expected to achieve an acceptable point or productivity total. Similar pressures on worker output exist in the employment and health services. The line worker's struggle to manage these expanding responsibilities within a fixed period of time is perhaps the dominant new feature of the service experience.

My caseload is comprised of people with AIDS. My caseload just keeps going up. It started one year ago and my caseload has gone from twenty to sixty. I got three new people today. . . . I have all these meetings. Each month I'm also supposed to go to eight different extended meetings. (A–10 Hospital)

My caseload is between 150 and 200. To some extent the size depends on the time I have to close cases. . . . Our schedules are booked. I have between 9:00 and 1:00 to see clients in the morning. In the afternoon all I do is go to meetings. . . . The whole sense of the place of getting people in and moving them out doesn't work. (B–10 Employment and Training)

There's a push here to overbook. For instance, I'm responsible for 22.5 case contact hours per week; usually I'm doing more . . . I book thirty-seven cases once a week. . . . I usually get about ten cancellations. But I never know how many will cancel. If its less, of course, I'm way overbooked. . . . It's like an airline—we're always overbooking. (C–8 Family and Children's Counseling)

Ethical Dilemmas

Workers in each of the agencies have indicated that the rush to produce greater numbers and revenue in shorter periods of time generates certain ethical dilemmas. The hospital line worker must be increasingly concerned with the implications of releasing patients "quicker and sicker" into the community. Often these patients are not prepared to manage their lives independently after hospitalization. Yet, as has already been suggested, the critical support services that ease this transition are often nonexistent. Consequently, the worker may be in the position of having to release patients or terminate treatment despite continued and perhaps acute needs. In the employment agency (TEP) particularly high caseloads affect the worker's ongoing capacity to identify the training strengths and weaknesses of the client. This breakdown often undermines the client's chances of completing the program. Finally, because of expansive caseloads and quota formulas, mental health agencies (CAFCA) find it increasingly difficult to engage clients in an ongoing therapeutic process.

A richer depiction of the contradictory outcomes associated with service productivity will be presented later in this analysis. It is presently apparent that service workers are increasingly experiencing a tension between the quantitative fiscal obligations of the organization and the qualitative service needs of the client. The worker is essentially the locus of the push–pull between the state and the community. The state's primary focus on accumulation functions (leading to fiscal constraints) and the community's swelling need combine to place service workers in the untenable position of having to address this deepening dilemma independently.

> I feel the hospital is doing things that are unethical and immoral and I don't want anything to do with it. We're releasing people who are sick, placing them in unsafe situations, and sometimes sending them right out onto the streets. I've tried to do things about some of these problems and been shot down by the hospital. (A–13 Hospital)

> As a result of the large numbers of people we deal with, mistakes are made in terms of decisions regarding training or employment. We had a client . . . good potential for business training. Good reading, speaking, typing skills. . . . She was mistakenly sent to a work internship. . . . She

finished the work internships three months later and is no further along than when she came to us. She'll be a file clerk. (B–13 Employment and Training)

The volume here is self-defeating in terms of creating success. I don't know how this small program can provide the myriad of necessary services to such a large number of people and still be effective. (B–15 Employment and Training)

Whatever therapeutic impact we may be making is at the surface of a person's life. . . . We just don't have the time. That's just built into the structure of this place. (C–3 Family and Children's Counseling)

Documenting Productivity through Paperwork

The weight of responsibility shouldered by line staff has also been affected by paperwork. Perhaps the most onerous feature of the changing social service work environment is the proliferating welter of paper that must be filled out by each worker. These forms document more and more details of the service encounter, from contact through departure or graduation. To the extent that an agency has multiple funding or reporting requirements, this process may often seem redundant. In effect, workers are more frequently duplicating information on different forms.

The rapid expansion of paperwork is a logical consequence of the production priorities of state-financed service agencies. If agencies are to raise output, then there must be a visible expression of this upward spiral. Similar demands are successfully enforced in the private sector when more units of a product are produced with a fixed investment of labor, thus increasing profit margins. The voluntary agencies' outputs, however, are far more subtle and therefore less easily measured than those of the private sector. In effect, it is far easier to track quantitative leaps in automobiles, washing machines, and profits than dimensions of service process or outcome. Ironically, it is precisely the subtlety of the service experience that triggered new demands for documentation.

In an environment that increasingly values concrete measures of performance, voluntary social service agencies had to locate their indices of "success." Equally important, a concrete ongoing expression of such output had to be developed. Paperwork is the device that ultimately addressed the need to specify measures of output while providing an ongoing record of relative accomplishment. In classic "goal displacement" terms, the paper became an end in itself. There developed an operable presumption that a direct relationship existed between the volume of paperwork and the productivity of an agency. This was a natural outgrowth of the nonprofit sector's search for a product analog comparable to the private sector's. The concrete and/or material properties of such output found their most literal translation in paperwork.

Paperwork reinforced the new fiscal relationship between the state and voluntary agencies through its emphasis on "outputs." Forms emphasized those elements of the service experience that were reimbursable. The paperwork, then, was also a concrete expression and reminder of the shifting contractual relationship between the state and voluntary agencies. Even more specifically, these records provided the documentary evidence necessary for reimbursement.

The dynamic interplay among cost-containment policies, the shifting fiscal underpinnings of voluntary agencies, and the mushrooming work load of line staff has been most directly captured in the restructuring and expansion of paperwork. These increased record-keeping requirements are of primary concern to line staff.

> The paperwork is just ridiculous. . . . Let me give you a rundown of my responsibilities. I have to document medical charts one time a week, social work charts for liability, closing summaries, statistics once a month, and billing information. . . . I have to be part of a witnessing process for doctors so they're not sued. Nine out of my twenty-one hours a week are spent on paper. (A–14 Hospital)

> The amount of time I'm spending on paper is definitely increasing. About 30 percent of my time is spent on paper. For instance, last week I had a sixty-two-year-old man who had been in the hospital a year. He nas had one medical disaster after another. . . . After three days, I got him back in Marlboro State. But I spent days filling out paper and making calls. I could go on with one illustration after another. More and more of my job is spent filling out paper. (A–12 Hospital)

> Look, I have more paperwork than I can handle. I have about fifteen different kinds of forms that have to be filled out on the kids. About 70 percent of my time is spent filling out these forms. (B–2 Employment and Training)

There's just so much paperwork, I can't keep up. Somewhere between 33 percent and 50 percent of my time is spent on paper. I do prescribing interviews that must be documented. Every phone contact must be recorded. Each individual case requires quarterly, biannual, and annual comprehensives. These are very comprehensive psychological profiles. They also lay out a thorough treatment plan. You should know that groups are treated as individuals. I have seven people in a group and must do separate papers on each of them. By the end of the day you just don't want to pick up a pen again. (C–7 Family and Children's Counseling)

The increased volume and tighter time deadlines associated with agency paperwork are yet another source of pressure for service workers. Paperwork must be in on time. The absence or delay of service documentation will disrupt the flow of expected public-sector support. Paperwork is the mechanism that regularly cements the contractual relationship between the state and the service agency. Documentation establishes that the level of service specified in the contract has been delivered and charges the state for these efforts or outputs. Reimbursement is tied to the timely delivery of paper. If particular workers fail to meet time deadlines, they are affecting the cash flow of the agency. Chronic tardiness by many workers can seriously impair the agency's capacity to continue functioning. Agency managers are particularly mindful of the consequences associated with such delay. These administrators are ultimately responsible for the prudent fiscal management of the organization. They therefore consistently remind staff in a variety of ways that the prompt completion of paperwork is not a secondary but rather a primary task.

The techniques employed by administrators to refocus staff attention can be as benign as a simple statement of concern at a meeting, or as threatening as directly punishing staff members who are consistently tardy. These conditions are particularly troubling for staff. Even with the best of intentions, they simply may be less and less able to meet all of their obligations. With substantial quantitative jumps in paperwork and caseload, as well as qualitative shifts in client makeup and community support, the workers' standards of performance must decline if they are even cursorily to tend to all of their responsibilities. However, paperwork can claim a disproportionate share of the staff's time if they are responsive to managerial messages. The environmental and personal pressures that the workers associate with mounting paperwork are presented as follows:

It seems as though it's only the paperwork that counts. Just accountability and statistical things. They [administrators] scream if you don't get it right or get behind. It makes me angry. (C–17 Family and Children's Counseling)

All this paperwork, it's so much, too much. Every time we reach an audit, our attention has to be almost entirely focused on the paper. We just have so much to do it feels like there isn't a minute to spare. I just don't feel in control. I feel like I should come in on Sundays. (C–3 Family and Children's Counseling)

The overall guidelines have forced the hospital to become a business. Its attention is on making money. The paperwork could really be done by a non–social worker. There's so little time to search for appropriate nursing home placements or alternatives, for instance. Now from day one you must push on the paper and get patients thinking about a specific nursing home. It's all about the machinery of referral. (A–12 Hospital)

Today you'll be stepped on if you mess up files. We're under lots of stress. You walk out of here in a daze. You just can't have loose pieces on a case. Everything must be signed off and supervisors must check your work. There's a threat if there are loose pieces of paper, we will lose days of pay. (A–5 Hospital)

The paperwork is just so difficult. Some days I just spend the whole day trying to catch up. After 2:30 I try to do paperwork without interruption, but that's impossible. There's just all kinds of pressure to take the paperwork home with you. (B–6 Employment Training)

Workers in mental health or counseling agencies are particularly aware of the contradictions between the demands of paperwork and the needs of clients. In part, this can be traced both to the greater discretion available to these workers in their encounters with clients and the structure of the therapeutic or counseling service. For instance, mental health workers (as opposed to the discharge planning personnel of the hospital or the staff of the employment agency) expect paperwork to have a positive influence on the service experience. Their training suggests that case notes, treatment plans, and other elements of the recording process are critical tools in assessing and reflecting on the condition of the client. Yet the quantitative recreation of these devices to meet fiscal priorities is perceived as having seriously compromised the therapeutic process.

Equally important, record keeping is more likely to be defined by these workers as an exercise in magic and manipulation. To a far greater extent than their counterparts in hospital or employment social services, these workers indicate that they shade and shave their paperwork to increase the amount of time they have available to clients. They repeatedly indicate that their commitment is to the client and not the paper. Furthermore, they note that the agency's claims regarding levels or types of services delivered does not reflect the service experience, but rather contractual obligations to the state. Respondents suggest that the agency manipulates client numbers and categories of service to maximize the potential for reimbursement. These findings indicate that relative to hospital and employment training staff, mental health workers effect a more independent posture regarding paperwork and more fully understand (perhaps because of the content of their work) the costs and fantasy associated with paperwork demands.

> The paperwork is an annoyance because it has no relevance to my work with patients. Sometimes it seems as though the paperwork that matters, session notes and such, don't mean anything. . . . (C–17 Family and Children's Counseling)

> We're in the mental health field, yet the fictions we create around this paperwork are unbelievable. For instance, our comprehensives are supposed to be completed after three months. In fact, they are supposed to be used to develop a timely treatment plan for the clients. . . . But I'm completing comprehensive assessments for the audit now that should have been completed a year ago. The psychiatrists cooperate in this fantasy, so do the utilization review people. They are of no value in the treatment process. . . . What's the point? We're all part of this fiction. (C–9 Family and Children's Counseling)

> The paperwork is intense . . . and yet it's all so bogus. We're told to exaggerate client problems and stuff, you know, to make things look worse so we get our funding and it looks like we are really serving a needy population. If the truth be told, most really seriously troubled clients . . . don't have the types of problems that are reported. No way. (C–12 Family and Children's Counseling)

Look, most people are able to manipulate the state forms. I've come up with key phrases or words. I won't allow state forms to alter my work, their concreteness, time limits, uniformity . . . I'll put something on the line to pacify them. What you put on the forms is your business. (A–7 Hospital)

Narrowing the Service Encounter

Briefer Encounters with Clients

One consequence of the multiplying and more complex demands being made upon social service workers is that in various ways they are less and less accessible to clients. The new service gospel of speed and volume narrows the amount of time available to meet with any single client. In the past, workers had greater discretion in defining both the length and the nature of their encounters with citizens seeking services. This kind of discretion, however, has been eroded by the waves of demand and pressure crashing about the line worker.

The preciousness of time in the new service environment has had a leveling impact. In agencies such as Evergreen Hospital and TEP, where new incentives exist to process larger numbers of clients more rapidly, each encounter is defined by its brevity. The line workers simply do not have the time to engage in extended dialogues or sessions with specific clients. Instead, they must identify and address issues of concern in very short time bits. Quite frequently, these brief and often "one time only" encounters last no longer than thirty minutes.

Alternatively, the fiscal underpinnings of mental health services are structured to encourage practitioners to meet with a prescribed number of clients for a fixed period of time once a week. Reimbursement is keyed to the number of face-to-face encounters with different clients. Although volume is emphasized, it is also constrained by the forty-five-minute block of time that must be devoted to each counseling session. Clearly, the client contact work of mental health practitioners is less rushed than their hospital and employment training counterparts. In the past, however, sessions were more frequently allowed to run past forty-five minutes. The practitioner also had greater latitude to schedule second appointments during the course of a week for particularly complex or difficult cases. These options of more extended or frequent contact with the client are now less available.

Eleven years ago you could sit and talk with people about their dying. There was lots of time. . . . Now we simply touch hands or heads with our patients and move on. The fifteen or twenty minutes we had in the past just doesn't exist anymore. (A–11 Hospital)

Look, my caseload is just so high. It's difficult to do quality case management. Every client can't talk about their problem in 15 minutes. (A–19 Hospital)

I spend between fifteen minutes and half an hour working with clients. I feel guilty when I spend more time, it slows down the flow into the clinic. I have a waiting backlog then of eight clients. It just short-circuits the process. (B–6 Employment and Training)

I look to get more involved with each of these kids. They are so desperate for employment training. But if I stay too long, I have two or three others who are waiting and can't see me. Each of them may have serious problems. (B–1 Employment and Training)

Look, if we're going to do decent workups so these mothers can get employment, we need more time. We're asked to do effective assessments. They want us to get them to share critical information and trust us all in one hour and usually one time only. The numbers coming through this program are so large we can't do it. And God forbid they have to come back with a problem. The numbers on initial assessment are so large, it's hard to squeeze anyone in for a second visit. (B–15 Employment and Training)

There's no flexibility if you need to see a client more than once or more than forty-five minutes; you better have a good reason . . . and even then. . . . (C–14 Family and Children's Counseling)

Skimming the Surface

These briefer, less frequent, and often time-limited encounters between client and worker affect the quality of service provided by the practitioner. In general, workers are required to partialize and simplify their contacts. They are increasingly unable to address the more subtle, complex, or persistent issues influencing clients' lives. In fact, such matters are consciously avoided because the constriction of time and focus forecloses opportunities to develop more in-depth, open-ended service processes with the client. This more superficial service agenda and relationship is generally illustrated in the following passages:

> I don't work with clients in the same way. I keep it narrowly focused and superficial so I don't get into things that require more time. (A–20 Hospital)

> Sure, I skim the surface with these kids. I don't have time to get into their emotional issues or even complicated concrete needs. I just want to get them enrolled and onto the employment program. Even though it's a lot of time, this is what's needed if there is to be a successful program. . . . But I don't touch these issues because of the size of my caseload and the paperwork. Time is what prevents me from getting into these issues with the kids. (B–6 Employment Training)

> People are coming with substantial needs. This has implications for longevity and frequency of treatment. . . . I feel we do a patchwork job. . . . But we can't keep them forever, we have a waiting list of a year. . . . Also, I think we're starting in the wrong place, we're so focused on the emotional, yet their concrete needs are getting worse and worse . . . but there's no time to deal with these needs and it's not valued. (C–11 Family and Children's Counseling)

Reduced Interventive Choices

In an environment that emphasizes quick and superficial encounters, the choices available to workers are less satisfactory. The line staff are simply unable to utilize an array of available methods and resources. There is not enough time to thoughtfully develop and apply relatively complex service plans. Such an approach would challenge the more programmed format of services offered by agencies. Increasingly, agencies and line workers are restricted to the delivery of concrete or counseling services.

In the hospital, discharge planning service workers can pay little attention to the emotional needs of clients or families. Instead, these workers must perform the shepherding function of relocating patients out of the hospital. This movement must occur in a timely manner. Any breakdowns may jeopardize the continued funding of a particular hospital bed. Consequently, the staff person is focused upon consistently updating and utilizing appropriate residential or nonresidential support services in the community. These workers' jobs have become both more specialized and more demanding as the length of stay for various categories of patient has been restricted by new federal regulations. Clearly, the discharge planner's work is principally, if not exclusively, focused on certain concrete needs of the patient.

A heightened emphasis on concrete need has also influenced the practice of social service personnel in Evergreen Hospital and TEP. A number of departments within the hospital, such as neonatology, women's health, and pediatrics, employ personnel to deliver specific social services to in-and-out patients. In general, this staff's concerns are far broader than those of the discharge planner. For instance, pediatric social workers are expected to identify and describe the history, mood, and present options of an abusing mother. Similar tasks are carried out by the women's health unit, which is in frequent contact with pregnant mothers who are malnourished, homeless, or substance abusers. Although the function of these workers is less circumscribed than that of discharge planners, the services they dispense are no less concrete. The pressure of time and urgent need has compelled these workers to ignore certain emotional dynamics. Additionally, only the most critical and attainable concrete needs of patients are inventoried or emphasized. This decision-making framework, then, is shaped by immediate opportunity and personal as well as structural constraints.

What unifies the non–mental health social service personnel in the hospital is their singular focus on concrete need. However, these workers are also distinguished by the nature and scope of their responsibilities. A clear hierarchy of responsibility exists. The discharge planner's work is most restricted. Her tasks relate to the single function of moving patients out of the hospital. Social service personnel located in other departments of the hospital are expected to have a broader field of vision in both identifying and addressing patient problems. The discharge planning function is carried out by bachelor's level workers while employees with master's degrees deliver the other departmentally based services to patients. Thus, the hospital has subclasses of social service workers that are primarily distinguished by the scope of their decision-making responsibilities.

Similar to the hospital, the interventive choices available to TEP workers are quite restricted. Little, if any, of the workers' time can be spent tending to the emotional needs of clients. Their caseloads, which number in the hundreds, and task responsibilities generally prohibit workers from establishing counseling relationships. Instead, they are expected to engage in highly specific and concrete tasks with each client.

Again, there are distinctions within this narrow concrete format of social services. The master's level worker has the smallest caseload, the greatest range of responsibilities, authority over paraprofessionals, and more service choices, including very modest opportunities to address the client's emotional needs. The B.A. social worker has a large case load, relatively broad overarching case management responsibilities, and tacit authority over certain paraprofessional staff. Finally, the largest caseloads and most concrete tasks are assigned to paraprofessionals. These subclasses of workers share the common ground of restricted interventive opportunity.

Interestingly, the services provided by mental health workers in the hospital and by the family and children's counseling agency represent the other side of a convex mirror of services. The line personnel of these programs have master's degrees and are specifically focused on the emotional rather than the concrete needs of the client. Again, however, *the needs of the client have been partialized and recreated to fit the specific fiscal and productivity requirements of the agency.* It is on this basis that mental health service workers simply do not have the time to consider or address the mounting concrete needs of their clients. Instead, they maintain a relatively myopic focus on psychological dynamics and ignore the intensifying material needs of their caseloads. Despite the shared tendency to neglect an entire dimension of client need, mental health workers enjoy a privileged professional position as compared to their colleagues in the hospital or employment programs. Their smaller caseloads and more extended encounters with clients (weekly sessions for relatively long periods of time) offer different service opportunities to this cadre of workers. The countervailing and intensifying drive for productivity, however, continues to reduce the choices and interventive opportunities of mental health workers.

Summarizing the above, subclasses of workers (representing various tiers of primary subordinate work—see chapter 3) are emerging within and between agencies, reflecting increasingly narrow definitions of service. These workers' choices are generally restricted to the provision of either concrete or mental health services. Consequently, they are more frequently forced to ignore significant aspects of the client's experience. The worker's interventive choices will depend on her class position and agency location. In general, the lowest subclass of workers, such as paraprofessionals in the employment training programs, function on the narrowest isthmus. They are structurally consigned to a few concrete tasks. There is a middle range of workers who, although focused on concrete services, have to juggle more varied and complex tasks. Finally, mental health workers essentially ignore concrete need. Their smaller caseloads and opportunities for continuity mark them as perhaps the most privileged service workers.

The worker's singular preoccupation with either concrete or mental health services is a unifying trend that has been intensified by the new environment of social services. There is simply less time available to address both dimensions of need. Even more to the point, the worker is increasingly required to focus on subdimensions of the client's circumstance. Productivity demands and narrowed pockets of choice available to workers have had the paradoxical impact of heightening differences between workers (subclasses of workers performing different tasks), while requiring clusters of workers to homogenize their practice. The context and contradictions of the most recent separation of concrete and mental health services is more richly illustrated below:

> When I came out of undergraduate school, I had the notion that I would provide counseling and concrete services. Good social work was not one or the other, but both. . . . But our exclusive focus is on the concrete and not counseling . . . maybe it has to do with the separation and discharge planners not having time to do counseling. (A–11 Hospital)

> The department head says make sure you're covering the concrete and paper needs of all the patients, then you can provide therapeutic services. . . . That leaves me no time . . . maybe in the hospital now all you can provide with the size of the caseload and amount of the paper is concrete service. . . . Maybe there just isn't an opportunity to do counseling anymore. (A–14 Hospital)

> It's just such a contradiction. I mean we need more time, not less, to work with people on their counseling needs. If these women are going to finish this employment program, they are going to need to be able to address certain emotional issues. To stay employed, these women must

tap into their history, their behaviors. I could go on. We just don't have the time to address these questions here. At best, all we can offer are some concrete services. (B–6 Employment Training)

Look, I tell my supervisor we're starting in the wrong place. Yes, of course, there are psychotherapeutic issues that need to be addressed, but that's all we have time to look at. . . . Increasingly, what's needed is an ability to address concrete needs, but that's not valued. How can they engage in a psychotherapeutic relationship when there are more and more concrete problems—housing or other needs—pressing in on them? It's an either/or situation for the worker, only address the psychological needs. But the client doesn't live that way. What we are ignoring is affecting their ability to even utilize our service. (C–11 Family and Children's Counseling)

The clients really have to take responsibility for themselves here and that's good. For instance, the delivery of concrete services doesn't require a master's degree. The agency really discourages us from delivering such services. But therapeutic services are much more gratifying professionally. I would feel as though I was wasting my talent if I were offering concrete services. Let's face it, even if I could get a mother food stamps or AFDC, big deal. . . . It's not enough to live on or eat well on. . . . Instead I can focus on the more pervasive issues of fear and poor self-esteem. (C–16 Family and Children's Counseling)

Follow-up

Often, the workers in each of these agencies are unable to follow up on the specific needs of a client. The critical capacity of social service workers to (a) engage in community outreach in order to systematically update their knowledge of available resources, (b) monitor specific referrals to assure the delivery of expected services, and (c) visit the homes of clients to sharpen assessments has been minimized. The flexibility and time necessary to engage in each of these follow-up activities are less available to the worker. The same variables that have restricted the duration of a single encounter, continuity of service, and interventive choices are also affecting the worker's capacity to engage in any type of follow-up. The agency and workers' unloading of these activities like so much excess baggage has functioned to further narrow and redefine the service encounter. In effect, the historical role of the service worker to extend beyond the agency and into the community is being lost. Any active connection between the worker and the community is being dismembered by the service experience. The stripping away of this service element, and the consequently more barren encounter between worker and client, is presented below:

> Our caseload is overwhelming. We need more time to tighten our follow-up and tracking of [employment] services. A lot of what they need is follow-up work, but they're just not getting it. You want to move them onto other services they need, but because of time, you can't do it. . . . (B–10 Employment Training)

> I'd like to do more outreach in the community, but there's no time. (A–4 Hospital)

> We have so many kids who are seriously ill or where abuse is a problem. They need visiting nurses, homemakers, or an aide. . . . But there's no manpower to go out and locate these services. (A–6 Hospital)

> I just don't have time to do follow-up for concrete services. . . . More and more I'm trying to get the parent to do that work. . . . But it's very difficult for them to locate and gain access to services. (C–5 Family and Children's Counseling)

> It's a dilemma, we're getting more and more people needing hospitalization and appropriate services. We need the time to get them booked with appropriate services. But this is time-consuming and I don't have the resources to do the follow-up and make the appropriate connection. In order to do it, I have to steal time from other needy cases. (C–2 Family and Children's Counseling)

Alienation from Client and Service

The social service labor process is increasingly alienating for workers. This trend is especially important because social services have frequently demanded that line workers be alert and fully engaged in their daily encounters with clients. These qualities are expected to affect the critical rapport between worker and client. Such trust and bonding is essentially the foundation upon which the structure of quality services might be built. For instance, citizens who experience consistent disappointments in their efforts to locate stable employment often require an array of support services to strengthen their job and education skills. The need for such services may reflect deficits in the client's education, emotional development, or job history. The various disappointments or frustrations embedded in this experience often affect the client's initial and ongoing capacity to utilize needed services. One of the functions of the service worker is to enable the client to identify her needs and accept particular services. Perhaps even more fundamentally, line staff must frequently breathe into distrusting clients a faith that the service experience can make a difference in their lives. This hope is particularly vital for the increasingly troubled clients requesting services.

This connection is equally critical to the delivery of other social services. The worker must effectively apply engagement and relational skills to pierce the alienation of the client and more tightly fasten her to a service experience of positive possibility. However, heightened productivity demands have distanced line staff from the service encounter by narrowing the scope and possibility of their work. They are increasingly separated and alienated from the client by these demands. The increased alienation of workers, however, cannot be isolated from the service process in the same way that communities may be insulated from communicable diseases. To the contrary, it is the worker's role, at least in part, to offer an antidote to the client's alienation. The festering and spreading alienation of workers, therefore, has the dual effect of reducing the staff's connection to their own labor and in turn diminishing their capacity to convey or support the sense of possibility associated with social services. The loss of relationship between worker and client in the service process casts a deeper shade of meaning onto an alienated labor force.

> Look, all these demands prevent me from doing what I know needs to be done with patients. . . . All of this is just put on a back burner . . . sometimes I think the hospital is not suitable for anything other than a clerk. (A–14 Hospital)

> Forget about trying to establish relationships with clients. For instance, these women call me and are in crisis and I'm in trouble. Basically we're an intake service before they get to the training. Between that and my meetings with the school's supervisors, team, and other staff, there's no time left. This is something I should do, but I can't squeeze them in. (B–10 Employment and Training)

Sure, I feel as though I have insufficient discretion in working with these families and kids. . . . When working with a child, for instance, you need to see their teacher and significant others outside the family. This is not even a goal now. What I do is send out a form to the school rather than run an interview, but the information is so limited and usually not helpful. These limits really force me to face service problems of integrity in my practice. I'm just not able in many ways to do the job for the kids. The question is, how much integrity am I willing to sacrifice to stay here? (C–9 Family and Children's Counseling)

The restriction of decision-making opportunities available to service workers also drains their encounters of creativity and spontaneity. The time and productivity demands that restrict their ability to identify a need or establish a service relationship (with clients) also deny opportunities for creative work. This is yet another facet of the hardening and alienating labor process associated with the delivery of social services. One of the primary expectations of social service workers, and more generally professional or semiprofessional groups, is that they will be able to apply their skills creatively in a problem-solving process. The opportunity to engage client problems imaginatively is a fundamental premise of effective service work. The fainter creative pulse has had a particularly arresting effect on the content of hospital and employment social services.

I find myself losing the impulse to be creative. There's little time to be creative. There's too much going on. So you have A, B, or C solutions to a problem and pick which one is best. You try to use one of them to get them through the night. (A–19 Hospital)

Look, the process is packaged and preprogrammed. This, of course, affects my ability to creatively meet the individual and specific training needs of the client. (B–13 Employment and Training)

Creativity just goes in this environment. You try to be creative, innovative, and use different methods, but because of paperwork, the caseload, and types of kids, you barely keep your head above water. . . . We're barely doing maintenance case management. (B–8 Employment and Training)

Yes, in the delivery of our counseling services we are being pushed toward a kind of routinization of service. . . . But it hasn't happened here because we push back against it. . . . But sometimes it just feels impossible. (C–4 Family and Children's Counseling)

The Devaluation of Essential Work

The worker receives various cues from the agency indicating that the delivery of essential services is undervalued. Agency policy regarding emphasis or credited work is often in tension with the daily experiences of staff. The gap between what are essentially prescribed areas of reimbursement (or agency priority) and needed services as perceived by line staff is yet another source of worker alienation. This contradictory circumstance places another wedge between workers and their labor.

The tensions between agency priorities and worker experience have specific implications. For the staff of TEP, support services essential to the accomplishment of particular training milestones are not incorporated into the productivity equation. The staff's need to track the progress of trainees and/or students is also undervalued. The mental health practitioners employed by CAFCA receive little incentive to work with children, families, or groups. As has already been noted, they are also not encouraged to provide concrete services. Finally, hospital service workers experience few, if any, rewards when they attempt to provide counseling services.

> Look, the only priority in counseling is when there is a possibility of liability. For instance, where parents are potentially abusive or neglectful. Outside of that the hospital doesn't see or want to see many patients' critical need for counseling. (A–13 Hospital)

> Whoever created this employment program has no sense of the needs of this population. If you're going to serve a population that for many generations hasn't worked, been in foster care, and lost stabilizing parts of their lives, you need support services separate and apart from training. But that's not done and is self-defeating. (B–15 Employment and Training)

> Support services are not part of the process of these women achieving their milestones. We are rewarded X amount of dollars for moving each woman step by step to employment. But there's no reimbursement for support services and so we're discouraged from providing them. (B–11 Employment and Training)

> It's a misnomer to say we're dealing with families or groups. Although

we provide some of these services, the structure really discourages us. We only get 2.5 credits for groups and 1.5 for families, yet we may have to fill out separate paperwork for a six-person family or group. That absorbs so much time. . . . It creates a disincentive, for instance, to work with families, and clouds your clinical judgment. (C–1 Family and Children's Counseling)

If you see the child, you must see the parent. From my point of view, that's a disincentive . . . because files must be opened on both. So you see less children. (C–11 Family and Children's Counseling)

The Contradictions of Paperwork

The "credited existence" of certain service efforts clearly influences the direction and content of the service worker's labor. If substantial investments of worker time in the delivery of a particular service cannot be captured by the agency's recording forms, then that effort does not formally exist. Equally important, if certain services require greater amounts of paperwork, then there is a clear disincentive to provide them. Finally, the proliferation of paperwork also independently limits the worker's opportunities to meet with clients. The new and more alienated relationship of worker to services is greatly defined, then, by paperwork. Of course, the existence of accountability mechanisms is not alienating by definition. To the contrary, such documentation can enhance the delivery of effective services. The form and content of paperwork will affect its value. In general, to the extent that recording requirements encourage workers to evaluate or reflect upon their efforts and are carefully delimited to minimize time demands, the greater their benefit to line staff. The recording requirements of Evergreen Hospital, TEP, and CAFCA, however, fail to comply with either of these criteria. Even more to the point, the proliferating and substantial paperwork in each of these agencies adds to the numbing alienation of workers by redirecting an increasing proportion of their time to (mechanical) tasks that do not contribute to the delivery of effective services.

Paperwork is growing and we have less time to see patients. It's slapped together and has no value. I remember when we did paper progress notes once a month and it was supposed to be meaningful. (A–9 Hospital)

Look, I need more time to see the children and families . . . can't make the time to see the child with behavioral problems because of all of the hospital's paperwork. (A–6 Hospital)

This is very similar to a profit-making business. For Macy's everything is documented through profit forms, it's paper. How can we slim down the paper when the state demands more and more? We want to work with these kids around their employment needs but we're victims of paperwork and we can't work with many kids because of it. (B–3 Employment and Training)

So much of our time is spent filling out paper, it's frustrating. There are a number of forms that could be collapsed into one. So many forms are redundant. I spend more time filling out forms than helping people and that's frustrating. (B–10 Employment and Training)

I've been here seven months and everything is beginning to feel rote-like. . . . There is so much documentation and you feel like a robot filling it out. Consequently, you can't spend time, thoughtful time with the clients. (B–1 Employment and Training)

The paperwork feels like a lot of work. . . . Right now all of my comprehensives are overdue. It's so difficult to keep up . . . I have to stop the flow of treatment to get information for the forms. (C–10 Family and Children's Counseling)

The recording requirements for the treatment process are counterproductive. They don't add to our understanding of the client. . . . To begin with, everything is based on three-month intervals and our clients don't change that quickly. . . . Secondly, so much of what is recorded is intrapsychic and it becomes difficult to translate the change into behavioral terms. If the paperwork were year to year, it might be more possible. We're being asked on paper to show subtle progress, yet given the time intervals, categories, and volume of cases, the record requirements just aren't helpful to the treatment. (C–11 Family and Children's Counseling)

Machine Work

The partialized tasks, briefer encounters, and work quotas that are increasingly critical to the production of social services have further contributed to the alienation of the worker. Through this emergent structure, the line staff are further distanced from the client, from their own critical abilities, and, most importantly, from any sense of control over the work process. The worker's narrowing functional responsibilities are tightly enforced by new service production processes. This environment's emergent structure and demands are producing increasingly alienating forms of work that line staff define as machine-like.

> When I first came to this hospital I thought it would be a way to serve sick inner-city kids. . . . But all I feel like is a processing machine. They take a bed and immediately we're responsible for getting them back out in the community. It's all so overwhelming, impersonal, and almost factory-like. (A–16 Hospital)

> This job just feels so much more mechanical. It's not what I was trained to do. When I first came here, the job was so much more satisfying. (A–20 Hospital)

> Sometimes it feels like a factory. Social workers are trained to be supportive and caring and to use skill. I feel so much of the time we are cold, distant . . . just moving people through as we fill our their forms. . . . This makes me angry. I feel like I'm not really a social worker because everything moves through here so quickly and impersonally. (B–10 Employment and Training)

> The clients also feel it's like an assembly line. They feel like a pushpin. Just take them out and stick them into a process. It's one thing to feel that at welfare, but to come here and be treated the same way . . . that's especially difficult. (B–13 Employment and Training)

> My job feels limiting and mechanical. The kids come in and I'm the first step in the process and then they move on to the next step. It feels like I'm just an echo with no real voice. (B–6 Employment and Training)

> This place can and does feel factory-like. We have one client right after another. As the shadow of one is leaving and another person comes in, there is a moment of anticipation. . . . The feeling is that I'm seeing one after another. . . . Sometimes I just feel like saying "next, next." (C–9 Family and Children's Counseling)

The physical environments of certain social service agencies also increasingly have the feel and look of a factory. The line staff at the hospital and employment agency have indicated that the waiting areas, and deteriorating, overcrowded physical plant affect the mood and content of their work.

> This place is no different than people walking into welfare for Food Stamps. People are treated like cattle in the waiting area. . . . (A–5 Hospital)

> There are physical site issues. The building is overcrowded; there aren't enough offices to go around. . . . I don't know how they do it; I couldn't work without an office. (A–9 Hospital)

> The way people line up here and people are given offices feels like a factory. We have no privacy . . . offices are divided by partitions . . . conversations can be overheard. The lack of privacy and noise levels limits what can be shared. . . . Also, the traffic back and forth in and around our offices affects our ability to focus. (B–6 Employment Training)

Unable to Meet Basic Needs

As has already been noted, the clients seeking assistance from service workers have less and less social, economic, and emotional margin. Their problems are both more urgent and more complex than before. This new client profile would at least appear to require more skilled, flexible, and creative interventions. Such interventions, however, have become less available. Perhaps the fundamental social service contradiction of the 1970s and 1980s is that at precisely the time when service needs became more complex, agencies were restructured to narrow their substantive contact with clients. In short, the social services analog to the media's sound bite has been created. What is of special importance to this segment of the analysis, however, is that these smaller service bites have a lethal impact upon the quality of social services. Clients more likely to have significant personality disorders, housing problems, or diseases (AIDS) cannot be partially and rapidly strained through the service experience if there is any expectation of making a difference in their lives. Such an experience will likely contribute to the persistence of the problem and to recidivism.

The new service structure offers the appearance of productivity and efficiency. This image, however, is little more than illusion. The combination of briefer and briefer service bites and the greater difficulties experienced and expressed by clients leave workers in a kind of no man's land. On the one hand, they often represent the best line of hope to beleaguered and desperate clients. On the other, they are objectively less and less able to deliver services that make a meaningful difference in the lives of clients.

Clearly, social service workers have always been constrained by limited knowledge, skills, and resources. These variables have historically defined the modalities and possibilities of social services. However, it was precisely these modest possibilities that distinguished the boundaries and legitimated the enterprise of social services. Equally important, there was always the hope that this perimeter could be expanded over time (by more resources, new skills, etc.). What is rapidly being lost is this sense of modest possibility and hope associated with the domain of social services. Instead, service workers are increasingly confronted with various signs of their failed labor. The pride that professionals take in the product of their labor is less and less available to service workers. The increased realization of the inadequacy of their service interventions has further alienated line workers from their own labor.

> This population is just so difficult. We are an increasingly small part of their life. I have less and less time to work with these pregnant teens. It's so frustrating, they come back five or six times. A few years later they're pregnant again. Maybe I've invested twenty hours. . . . Let's face it, all we can see them is max one hour a week over a number of weeks. It's just not enough given what they're up against. (A–8 Hospital)

> We're pushing these patients out so quickly, there's no time to work with them. . . . For many, you know what the consequence is. They're back a week and a half later because the family can't handle the problem. . . . This is happening again and again. (A–15 Hospital)

> This program is so short-term, there's no time and so much pressure. We can't have the time to address the crises of these clients. So the clients wind up dropping out and not completing the training program. We just don't have the time to work with them around so many problems that they have and of course it comes back to haunt us. (B–8 Employment and Training)

I feel the time constraints are just impinging on me all of the time. I'm not serving kids like I want to. I'm just not giving them enough of anything. I just don't feel effective. I'm bogged down in minutiae. (B–4 Employment Training)

It happens in so many situations where you know the clinically effective approach, but don't have the time . . . can't get together the appointment calls or reflective time. You just can't do it adequately. . . . You feel ineffective. (C–4 Family and Children's Counseling)

I just can't get what I need. Theoretically I have Black and Hispanic clients. Culturally, there's a missing piece in my treatment. I just don't have the time to learn about or apply the critical pieces of class, culture, or race to my clients. It hurts the therapy, because these clients have different experiences and orientations that need to be tapped and understood. But who has the time for this extra but necessary work? It's a great loss and part of the reason we're not very effective in working with minority clients. (C–9 Family and Children's Counseling)

Devaluation of the Social Service Worker

Skill Loss

One of the defining characteristics of craft or professional work is the development and application of skill. Traditionally, skills incubated and evolved to a very great extent through the daily practice experiences of the service worker. The discretion and autonomy traditionally associated witn such work provided opportunities for the application, refinement, and extension of skill. Within such an environment, medical doctors were likely to have the opportunity to sharpen diagnostic or surgical skills, social workers could build on their counseling or advocacy crafts, and workers with lesser degrees often were able to apprentice and develop an array of techniques for on-the-job effectiveness.

The conditions necessary to refine or develop certain skills through agency-based practice are rapidly changing. In effect, the underpinnings of a skills-based practice—autonomy, discretion, etc.—are gradually being eroded by more constricted frameworks of social service that emphasize productivity and accountability. It is within this context that workers are being deskilled.

We have to be more concise and quick in our assessments. We do more crisis work. I think in those areas of work, that is, rapid assessment and diagnosis, I've sharpened my skills. . . . But there clearly isn't as much time to do clinical work. We don't have the time to enter into the kinds of counseling relationships when stays were longer. Much of the personal gratification has been lost . . . I just don't use the skills I did in the past to see a case all the way through. (A–3 Hospital)

When I first started here, I was able to be creative and experimental. It really helped me develop my practice. . . . Now the focus is to do more in less time. How to get by with the least that you can do for someone. . . . I feel like my skills are atrophying. I feel like there's a skill drain. . . . Everything now has to be fit into shorter and shorter periods of treatment. (A–20 Hospital)

There has been definite loss of skill. I was taught to do individual counseling, group work, and assessment. . . . But I feel that I may be losing basic skills because of the demands and nature of this environment. I was taught to listen to clients, not to rush them, work through a process where they can draw their own conclusions, but who has the time? Consequently, you're more directive, push harder because you have to see hundreds of kids a month. . . . (B–8 Employment Training)

Skills dry up here. I have a social worker who has real strengths in conducting interviews and assessing clients. . . . The most difficult clients engage in a counseling process with her. She was applying and further developing her skills . . . but as the volume increased and the number of clients multiplied, her skill diminished. She pulled back because she just didn't have the time for such work. She verbalized her frustrations to me about having to limit her use of skills. . . . The client of course also leaves with a sense of not being heard or valued. (B–15 Employment Training)

I feel as if I'm able to do the work I need to do with my patients and develop needed skills . . . although I can foresee a time when that may be difficult if the agency goes over to short-term family work. I can see it coming. There are just too many clients seeking treatment. (C–14 Family and Children's Counseling)

Salary and Mobility

The salaries associated with social service work have always been relatively low. Recent studies indicated that master's level social service workers, for instance, are among the lowest paid civil service employees (NASW 1987). Line workers repeatedly indicated that their salaries were a source of disappointment and resentment. Many indicated that they were finding it increasingly difficult to live on their incomes. Others suggested that entry-level, relatively unskilled work in the private sector (such as secretarial functions) often paid more than professional social service work. Social service workers uniformly experienced low salaries as perhaps the most fundamental expression of the value attached to their daily labor. The incongruity of low salaries and increasing demands is a particularly critical and characteristic tension of social service work.

This tension has traditionally been moderated by opportunities for upward mobility within service agencies. Workers were rewarded with supervisory, mid-management, or, over time perhaps, executive responsibilities and salaries. This safety valve, which enabled agencies to retain and reward able workers, is less available today than in the past. To begin with, in the 1960s and 1970s as the welfare state expanded, increased numbers of line and administrative positions were created. However, since the middle or late 1970s, most service agencies have experienced far more modest rates of growth. Consequently, the pool of administrative positions has remained relatively fixed. Line workers have indicated that these more scarce administrative positions are experiencing less turnover.

The more business-like role of the service manager is also less attractive to line workers. Managerial positions tend to emphasize features of service work that are least appealing to line workers; monitoring paperwork, meeting statistical quotas, and learning reimbursement procedures are but a few of these functions. Consequently, managerial positions are less and less able to satisfy specific career aspirations of line workers. Although the salaries are higher, the substantive content of the work is considered more oppressive and alienating. For all of these reasons, the line worker's traditional pathways to upward mobility are rapidly disappearing. This is yet another expression of the devaluation of the labor and contribution of line workers.

> We just posted a managerial position. No senior clinician or supervisor applied. . . . Does this say something about the perception of the job? (A–2 Hospital)

> Here there are few supervisory slots. There's no place to go. You can

work twenty years as a social worker in this hospital and go no place. (A–6 Hospital)

As long as I've been here, which is two years, I've seen no one make an upwardly mobile move. (B–7 Employment Training)

I see little opportunity for mobility in this employment training program. . . . I don't see them recognizing or affirming education or experience as much as they should. They just don't hire professionals trained in the field. They're hiring B.A.'s and B.S.'s to do master's level work to save money. . . . (B–6 Employment Training)

There are no administrative positions I would be interested in. I'm not interested in administrative bookkeeping, I want to develop as a clinician. . . . That's my goal. (C–2 Family and Children's Counseling)

There is very little sense of mobility here. . . . You move in very tiny increments. (C–8 Family and Children's Counseling)

The only group of line workers that perceived viable pathways to upward mobility were prebachelor's and bachelor's level workers in MIT (Mothers in Transition). These workers indicated that mobility into senior line positions, not administration, was available. Their opportunities for career advancement can be traced to the agencies' unwillingness to hire master's level workers for more senior roles. Ironically, the relatively low salaries of these jobs may explain their availability to prebachelor's and bachelor's level staff. Workers with a master's degree simply cannot be consistently recruited for these positions. The agency's accommodation to these conditions perhaps most fundamentally represents a devaluation of certain standards of certification. The mobility opportunity available to this segment of line workers is more fully illustrated below.

There are many opportunities for career mobility. . . . When I got my B.A. I was promoted to assistant supervisor of a residence. Since then they wanted to promote me to supervisor and I turned it down. From there they offered me a day treatment job. It was a master's level position that I got with a B.A. I've never been held back by my lack of degrees. Now I'm a senior social worker in this training program and of course I still don't have my master's. (B–11 Employment Training)

Staff Turnover

The multifaceted devaluation of direct social service work has had many repercussions. To begin with, low salaries and limited opportunities for skill development or upward mobility have loosened the bond between worker and agency. Consequently, the turnover rate in voluntary social service work has accelerated. Workers simply do not expect to remain in a single agency for more than two to three years. TEP, for instance, experienced nearly 100 percent turnover of its personnel within a year and a half. The hospital social service staff neatly clustered at the ends of a seniority continuum. One group of workers accumulated fifteen to twenty years of seniority while the other, much larger cohort of line staff regularly turned over every two to three years. Finally, CAFCA's staff remained on the job for approximately two years and frequently defined their practice as an apprenticeship. Upon completion of their apprenticeship many of these practitioners hoped either to open a private practice or to locate employment with organizations (institutes or agencies) that paid higher salaries and allowed for the development of more sophisticated forms of practice. In general, line staff indicated that they were preparing to leave the field entirely (accept a private-sector position) or were seeking a hard-to-find social service position that offered greater autonomy and salary. The most powerful consequence of the devaluation of the social service labor force is the increasingly nomadic career patterns of line workers.

The extent of this turnover and its impact upon the quality (skill level) and continuity of social services is presented below:

There is such a high turnover rate here. I feel like a dinosaur. . . . As people leave, it discourages you from staying. People leave because of money, mobility, and not enough input into decision making. (A–18 Hospital)

I'm thinking of leaving to do in-vitro counseling. . . . Here I feel as though social work is just above housekeeping. (A–20 Hospital)

The average life of a worker is one and one-half to two years. This of course creates problems in continuity of care for these kids. People just come and go, yet stability is such an important part of what we need to offer these kids. They come from such unstable backgrounds. We just seem to mirror their experience and of course it is harder and harder to connect with them. . . . Unfortunately, we're just reinforcing what they've come to expect. (B–3 Employment Training)

Staff gets their experiences and some training and then leave. . . . Because of this turnover clients aren't getting what they need. . . . New inexperienced workers keep rolling in here making the same mistakes in judgment and having to learn all the procedures while delivering the service. . . . It's just not fair to clients. (B–13 Employment Training)

We're losing people here every two to three years. We're getting inexperienced workers as the seasoned ones leave. . . . It's outrageous turnover. If the client is here five years they could have four or five therapists. Clearly, the breaks in continuity of service and lesser skill level of new workers affect the quality of the therapy. And the client of course pays the price. (C–2 Family and Children's Counseling)

The Struggle to Preserve Craft and Service

In the recent past (approximately thirty years ago) workers had more opportunity to shape various parts of their daily practice. The lower case load and slower pace of social service delivery in many not-for-profit agencies provided workers with the autonomy necessary to engage clients more fully—through frequency and long-term service—and reflectively—using an array of skills. As we noted earlier, the welfare state's uninterrupted period of expansion between the end of World War II and 1973 also offered a greater proportion of service workers a chance for upward mobility. It is important, however, that these "halcyon" days of social services not be romanticized. The productivity and effectiveness of services during this period has been questioned. Voluntary agencies only addressed a very small fraction of the community's needs. To some extent, these agencies' relatively focused efforts (given the breadth and depth of community need) were influenced by their greater commitment to long-term interventions. Whatever deficits, limits, or tensions that marked voluntary social services during this period, it is clear that workers had a greater opportunity to define their encounters with clients and to develop skill or craft.

As the work environment of not-for-profit social service agencies has changed, the workers' commitment and sense of what is possible has also been altered. Various workers continue to struggle to develop their craft and bring some meaning to their encounters with clients. However, the workers' aspirations have been substantially reduced and the parameters of their struggle more modestly framed. The present demands of agency work have essentially forced line personnel to lower their expectations. As the agency and wider community have dramatically restructured the nature of line practice, the workers' initial response has been both reactive and restricted.

Workers have increasingly come to view their work as transitory. They maintain less commitment to a single agency or substantive area of interest. To some extent, this shifting sensibility enables workers to distance themselves from the daily work routine and locate specific areas of opportunity. The single most powerful weapon workers possess to fend off the attacks of heightened demands and restricted choices is the freedom to leave the agency or field. The workers' "disengagement from agency" has contributed to new ways of defining work life and the reinforcement of old commitments. For new workers, the agency has become a training ground. It is a place where for an abbreviated period of time they may be able to develop specific skills and build upon their experience. In the tradition of apprenticeship, workers are prepared to accept low wages and poor working conditions in exchange for the opportunity to develop their craft. This highly specific and short-term commitment to an agency was most evident in Evergreen Hospital and CAFCA.

> I haven't been on the job long enough to see it as a routine. I'm trying to be as clinically creative as possible to learn as much as I can while I'm here. . . . I don't plan on being here more than a total of two to three years. I'll learn as much as I can and then move on. (A–15 Hospital)

> I guess I enjoy the clinical work. . . . This place is difficult. . . . None of the other places in the city have the reputation of CAFCA in terms of what it expects of people and training. . . . I was pleased to get hired but I doubt I'll stay. I see myself moving on in a few years, but this is a good place to hone my skills. (C–13 Family and Children's Counseling)

The less stable labor force of voluntary agencies is comprised more and more of younger workers who are recent graduates of master's or bachelor's programs. These workers often maintain a particular commitment to service delivery. Perhaps their interest in skill development, relative enthusiasm, and dedication to clients combine to make them an especially productive work force. Whatever the explanation, these novice personnel are more likely than other staff to exceed certain work norms

> Look, I've become a workaholic. I'll work fifteen hours a day five days

a week if necessary to make certain that the catastrophic illness of the child doesn't exacerbate the problems of the families. (A–13 Hospital)

I feel overwhelmed by the number of youngsters coming through. I often have to test the students and do paperwork the next day and often have to take the paperwork home and I'm not compensated for it. (B–5 Employment Training)

The day is just so intense and every hour is accounted for. I'm paid for four days but I'm really working four and a half to five days with the extra hours and need to get everything done. (C–3 Family and Children's Counseling)

Sometimes I just try to be too productive. Often I'll have twenty-four contact hours of direct service when I only need twenty. That in turn generates all kinds of extra paperwork. Of course, I don't get any type of extra credit or comp time for this extra work. (C–6 Family and Children's Counseling)

Service Encounter and Autonomy

The worker's struggle to preserve or develop craft is multifaceted. As we have already noted to some extent, a predicate for this struggle is the worker's reduced career or substantive commitment to a single agency and willingness to extend the workday. Yet the very redefinition of this relationship also represents an area of struggle. Novice workers are essentially resisting the agency's need for labor force continuity and bypassing its definition of a service encounter (in terms of length, frequency, or nature).

These struggles are in part propelled and renewed by line personnel at CAFCA, Evergreen Hospital, and TEP who maintain a firm commitment to meeting the needs of the client. Despite restricted opportunities and mounting demand, they continue to struggle to respond flexibly and appropriately. Ultimately, client contact and change is a principal source of gratification for these service workers.

This is what it's about. . . . I feel I can still make a difference and help them tie up the loose ends as they're dying with AIDS. With all the problems, it's making this kind of difference that enables me to go on. (A–10 Hospital)

> The kids that you can make a difference with, that makes you feel good. Two kids who graduated from our program cut a record. . . . I've been a part of many kids' development. That's still possible and its a shot in the arm. (B–4 Employment Training)

> The clients here of course make the work palatable. There are very few clients here I can't like. (C–6 Family and Children's Counseling)

The worker's capacity to effect a constructive process or outcome with clients is greatly dependent upon her autonomy. As we have noted repeatedly, worker autonomy was substantially diminished by the new demands and structure of service work. Yet service personnel continue to struggle both to preserve and to extend their discretionary authority. These efforts, however, generally do not congeal about collective interest but are limited to the turf battles of individual workers.

> I see myself as a patient advocate. . . . I'll do whatever needs to get done to assist the patient. . . . I've pushed back against M.D.'s to do right. You push for more time in the hospital, that the process of dying cause minimal pain for the family and so on. It's a constant fight. (A–16 Hospital)

> There are so many personal problems clients are trying to handle. If a client says "I'm really sorry I can't stay until 3:00, I couldn't get someone to pick up my child," I tend to say OK, whereas my supervisor wouldn't do this. She'd make them take the workshop and reschedule, which means another two to three weeks wait. You can't imagine the impact, they just drop out. It's so rigid. It's a lack of recognition of their issues. So in my own way, behind closed doors, I make different choices. (B–13 Employment Training)

> The type of intervention or therapy style you develop here is generally your own business. This is one area where we do have discretion and it's been maintained. It allows me to work in ways that I think are most effective with clients and it can continue as long as I don't shout it down the hall. In a sense I'm being allowed to develop my own clinical style. (C–15 Family and Children's Counseling)

The Struggle to Develop Skill

Professional groups highly value skill and technical judgment. As we have noted, social service workers' opportunities to develop skill are being increasingly minimized. To begin with, there is very little chance to develop a broad, generic base of skill. Instead, worker skill development has been pressed to conform to narrowed interventive choices available within the agency.

Even within these more restricted *boundaries* for craft development, the workers' needs to increase their skill are in tension with the heightened productivity demands of the agency. The practitioner's relatively modest opportunities to develop skill and be creative are richly illustrated below:

> I have to be creative in locating community resources. We just can't do the job at the hospital. Increasingly, the community churches and agencies also can't handle our clients' problems so I have to be able to maintain a rolling inventory of available services, identify contact people, and make the appropriate referral. There is some creativity or skill required to do this work well. This is about the only area of my work where I can create something new. (A–8 Hospital)

> I have sharpened my ability to make quick assessments. These skills are more fully developed. You must size up the patients' needs quickly and know your community services. You have to be very flexible as needs arise. In effect, you need greater skill in these areas to cope with shorter time frames. (A–5 Hospital)

> We've lost the opportunity to see a process or situation unfold organically. Everything moves too quickly around here for that kind of service. What we push to develop and we've gotten very good at around here is assessment. You must work on developing your assessment skills in this environment or else risk drowning. (B–8 Employment Training)

> There aren't very many opportunities in social work like those at CAFCA. By that I mean it is very clinically oriented. I've learned a great deal about assessment, diagnosis, and treatment . . . of course, other types of intervention and skill development are discouraged— concrete work, advocacy. . . . (C–14 Family and Children's Counseling)

The ongoing need for worker training and skill development is recognized by many agencies. To some extent, they have attempted to respond to this need by offering training programs and structured supervision. These pockets of support, however, have received a mixed response on the part of workers. Frequently, training sessions are experienced as either insufficiently rigorous or rudimentary. Many programs fail to address the most pressing or immediate concerns of workers and clients. Similarly, learning opportunities available through supervision are greatly influenced by both the skill level of the supervisor and the extent to which accountability or productivity issues define the session. These factors clearly affect the quality of supervision for many workers. Despite these difficulties, the staff in our study almost without exception consider supervision and training as the single most important agency contribution to their professional or craft development. In the midst of intensifying routines and heightened demands, these supports represent a veritable lifeline. These structured periods of potential pause and reflection offer workers the opportunity to extract insight and develop skill from their daily work experience. This process also strengthens the worker's belief that her "daily" efforts have value.

> I do see a real opportunity for in-house and out-of-house training development. I can go to local conferences and have found it very useful. The psychiatrists' presentations on issues like domestic violence or substance abuse have also helped strengthen my work with clients. . . . I also feel supported by my supervisor. I've learned a great deal from him. Frankly, these sessions are very important in helping me to sort out my work with clients. (A–18 Hospital)

> Supervision is so important here, it makes a big difference given the craziness of the agency. . . . It has helped me to develop certain skills and ventilate some of my frustration. Supervision helps me make sense out of this crazy situation. I'm supposed to get supervision once a week; because of her intense schedule, I'm lucky if I see her once a week. Now training used to be a critical learning tool, but they're taking it away. You can't go to conferences anymore. This was such an important resource in learning about AIDS, drugs, and other problems. The conferences offered up-to-date information and direction. None of this slack has been taken up by in-house training. The in-house training is very infrequent. (B–10 Employment Training)

> Supervision has been very good. I've gotten a lot out of it. I could have gotten a lot more if it wasn't so pressured and infrequent. But given the circumstances, I've learned a great deal. It's part of what keeps people here. . . . The training here has been very useful to my work. This agency values learning. They are going to pay for some of my advanced training. These are the things that have kept me here for four years. (C–11 Family and Children's Counseling)

A Deepening Crisis

Despite the workers' struggle to preserve autonomy and develop skill or craft, the heightened demands of agency work life continue to narrow their sphere of influence. The intensification of the work process and proletarianization of workers has been quite costly. In addition to its relatively hidden structural inefficiencies (client recidivism and dropouts), this service strategy also "burns out" workers. The emphasis on speed, productivity, paperwork, and narrowed encounters with clients are but a few sources of tension and frustration spawned by an industrial service structure. The new service environment tends to drain workers physically and emotionally. Over time it is effectively using up more and more workers. This process might be likened to increased dependence upon and exhaustion of certain natural resources in advanced industrial societies.

The rapid depletion of these scarce worker resources contributes to breakdowns in behavior and ultimately affects turnover. This point is more fully illustrated below:

Sometimes I have no energy because I feel totally drained. Sometimes I feel there is nothing I can do to solve the problems, that I never accomplish anything. I start a lot of things but see no accomplishments. These feelings cause me to be a bit more numb and irresponsible when I meet with clients. (A–6 Hospital)

In this field of work there is just so much burnout. I'm trying to avoid it, but more and more my mind and body are saying "you need a break." It's just overwhelming doing this work on a continuing basis. (B–7 Employment Training)

I'm just feeling so burnt out. The symptoms are subtle. For instance, when the client comes late I'm just glad that I'm spending less time with them. I have less clarity in sessions and space out, or when I'm working with a client who is low functioning I say good because I don't have to think as much. (C–3 Family and Children's Counseling)

But this kind of agency work is putting all of us at risk of burning out. I'm here single-handedly with no supports. (A–14 Hospital)

There is a huge turnover in staff here. I've been offered a corporate job for more money and I'm about to give notice. People leave though because they are demoralized and burnt out. (B–13 Employment Training)

All the frustrations of this job are driving people to private practice. Of course, private practice is isolating. This is work best done in a team and you lose that when you leave an agency or clinical setting. (C–8 Family and Children's Counseling)

An Endangered Labor Force

The not-for-profit social service agency is experiencing a deepening labor crisis. For instance, only 23 percent of this study's participants had been employed by their present agencies for more than three years. The ruptures in continuity of care, skill development, and leadership produced by such turnover have already been noted. The rapid loss of this fundamental human resource is as profound an occurrence within service agencies as has been the out-migration of basic industries in many midwestern communities. Clearly, these communities were as dependent for their survival on basic industries such as steel, rubber, and automobiles as the not-for-profit agency is on the development of a skilled and committed labor force. Will these forces deplete a cross section of not-for-profit agencies of purpose and capacity to the extent of, for instance, Flint, Michigan, or Youngstown, Ohio?

Of course, this is an imperfect analogy. In the case of Flint or Youngstown, it was the corporation that migrated and the worker or community that was economically dislocated. In social services, the worker is dislocated but the organization remains fixed. Clearly, however, both agency and worker are forced to accommodate to this wrenching change.

Such subtle differences should not shroud the similar centers of gravity in these situations. Both disruptions can be traced to economic crisis and the push toward cost containment. Equally important, despite the differences in organizational mobility between the corporate and not-for-profit sectors, each situation has functioned to dislocate substantial numbers of workers.

It is important to note that in social services the most visibly dramatic change is being triggered by relatively isolated and powerless workers. Their individual responses to an increasingly alienating work environment have cumulatively resulted in substantial labor flight. The crisis has deepened for service agencies as they find it more difficult to fill available positions with workers whose skill, training, and/or experience approximates that of their predecessors. The diminished quality of this labor pool partially explains the greater number of jobs in not-for-profit agencies that remain unfilled for extended periods of time. These patterns are particularly evident in Evergreen Hospital and TEP. The clinical orientation and training opportunities in CAFCA, while not arresting the turnover rate, do contribute to a steadier stream of qualified applicants for unfilled positions. The extent and consequences of these staff shortages is illustrated below:

> It can take a year to get someone of any caliber to work here. In the past two years it has been especially difficult to get qualified social workers to work here. (A–5 Hospital)

> Across the board, we may be filling in for workers who have left and have not been replaced. It creates a lot of double work. Sometimes you feel like you're doing two jobs. (A–9 Hospital)

> We wait to hire for awhile but then we're in a sense forced to hire underqualified candidates. We just have fewer and fewer people with the necessary skills and degree and of course it affects our work with clients. (B–13 Employment Training)

> The turnover of staff affects the availability of skilled people for clients. Our case loads also go up because positions go unfilled. My caseload just went up about 25 percent and now another person left; how much more will it go up in the next few weeks? The cases wait until the person is replaced and the cases are shuffled to others who at best can only offer crisis services. The new people who are hired almost always represent an erosion of skill. There is little opportunity to build on anything. People are always leaving and we always seem to be starting at ground zero. (B–15 Employment Training)

Conclusion

To the extent that not-for-profit social service agencies are unable to provide services that make any appreciable difference in the lives of communities or clients, their legitimacy is at stake. As the data indicate, however, the greater scarcity of resources (due to cost containment) in combination with increased demands for service has brought about a profound restructuring of agency process and outcome. This transformation of services can be traced to heightened tension between the accumulation and legitimation functions of the welfare state. The state's emphasis is shifting toward a primary focus on its need to foster accumulation. The elevation of these functions is in great part a consequence of the crises affecting the larger economy. As chapters 1 and 2 make clear, dislocations of industry, mounting debt, and increased bankruptcies are but some of the present symptoms of the economic crisis that demand state attention.

The outcome has been fiscal retrenchment, resulting in the contradictory mix of tax cuts, deficit reduction, and diminished growth rates for social services sponsored by the federal government. The states and municipalities are increasingly unable to make up the differences in federal spending. At the same time, the emphasis on accumulation functions has intensified poverty and increased demands on the state and its social service agencies who are charged with the responsibility to meet citizens' needs. Unable to resolve the push of accumulation demands against heightened social needs, the state has opted for new organizational measures that increasingly favor quantitative, output definitions of service (fiscal accumulation) over qualitative, outcome-focused services (legitimation). The state's emphasis is driven by economics. Services organized to produce more quantitatively are seen in the short run as less costly. The trade-offs and long-term costs of this more productive model of services have not been considered.

As the data suggest, the new emphases of government have contributed to the intensifying bureaucratization of services and professional work within not-for-profit agencies. The bottom line for the not-for-profit agency, like the private-sector corporation, is its level of productivity. The number of people processed through the agency and the volume of documentation are increasingly emphasized as measures of success. In order to process more and more people in shorter periods of time, the *structure of services and professional work had to be altered.* Shorter, more focused, and frequently superficial encounters and higher caseloads are characteristics of the new service work. Line staff are more often engaged in short-term crisis work. The skills they can develop or draw upon are more modestly framed. Finally, some of the skills service workers bring to the job evaporate.

As the discretion of the worker has diminished and the work load has grown, *not-for-profit bureaucratic structures that reflect the new service priorities have also begun to emerge.* Proliferating paperwork and early stages of assembly line practice are but two structural expressions of the increased emphasis on productivity. This new industrial service structure is in different stages of development in the three agencies that were investigated. CAFCA maintains high quotas and substantial paperwork requirements. Caseloads, however, are relatively small, and the opportunities for skill development and autonomy are significant. TEP, on the other hand, enforces the most industrial definition of services. It places high productivity demands upon workers (caseload, quotas, etc.) and offers the fewest opportunities for both discrete, continuous work with clients and skill development. As compared to CAFCA and TEP, a middle range of productivity demands and practice losses (autonomy, skill) are experienced by service workers in Evergreen Hospital. The trend in each of these agencies, however, is toward a more industrialized and productivity-driven model of services.

The consequences of this transformed and proletarianized labor process have been profound for the professional service workers. They are increasingly alienated from their own work and from the agency. Yet workers continue to struggle against these tendencies during their contact hours with clients. The line service workers in these not-for-profit agencies have maintained a commitment to clients despite the growing volume and complexity of need. These professionals' persistent dedication to client and service is reflected in their effort to preserve autonomy and skill. The data suggest, however, that over time workers are being worn down by the demands, frustrations, and tensions of industrial service environments. Consequently, staff turnover has reached crisis proportions for each of these service agencies. Clearly, the present conditions in not-for-profit agencies are producing contradictory consequences and certain dilemmas.

First, professional workers are losing discretion, autonomy, and skill at precisely the moment when the growing complexity of client or community needs demands flexibility and craft. Second, both paperwork and the structure of services increasingly ignore critical facets of the clients' circumstances. Finally, paperwork requirements intended to record the productivity of workers significantly reduce the practitioner's contact hours with clients. Fundamental inefficiencies such as recidivism and high client dropout rates are a by-product of the intensifying bureaucratization and industrialization of services, yet are rarely recorded or considered.

It is also troubling that as not-for-profit agencies are implementing more industrial and bureaucratized service structures, they are rapidly losing legitimacy with clients and the community. Although certain short-term goals may be met through a service ideal of productivity (contact and processing, or the appearance of serving a larger number of clients), the consequent neglect of fundamentally complex issues affecting individuals and communities will have costly long-term consequences. This litany of contradiction and dilemma could be continued, but it is unnecessary. This listing was only intended to underscore the very substantial visible and not-so-visible costs of this new structure—costs that ultimately threaten to undermine the legitimacy of the not-for-profit social service agency. Only some recognition of this threat can provide the catalytic spark necessary to strike a new service balance between the fiscal concerns of the state and the pressing multiple needs of social service workers and the communities they serve.

APPENDIX 4–A

Methodology

The purpose of this inquiry was to reconstruct the work experiences of various line social service staff. The study was exploratory. It was not intended to test particular hypotheses or measure specific outcomes. Rather, the investigation employed participant observation techniques to develop a preliminary understanding of the social service labor process. This approach was particularly appropriate given the paucity of literature or data on the labor process of social service work. For this reason, various welfare state scholars have called for exploratory or qualitative investigations on the changing nature of this work (Cousins 1987; Gough 1979).

The principal methodological tools utilized by the investigators were observation and open-ended interviewing. This included qualitative interviews with line staff and a small number of middle managers. In addition, upon entering the agencies sampled for this study, the investigators spent brief periods of time observing line staff engaging in their daily tasks.

It is not the purpose of this discussion to describe the weaknesses or strengths of this method. A full account of this debate can be located in various social science texts and journals. In general, this methodology has been criticized for being less structured, rigorous, valid, generalizable, and reliable than more quantitative or experimental methodologies. However, there also seems to be an emerging consensus that qualitative and participant observation techniques are particularly appropriate and useful in developing an understanding of social processes and situations that are particularly complex or fluid and about which little is known. The greater flexibility of this method allows researchers to redirect their inquiries on the basis of data coming in from the field (Dean 1969). Such flexibility is absolutely essential in social situations that are relatively unexplored.

The first stage of the research process is devoted to developing an analytic description of the phenomena under investigation. This analytic description must systematically classify and report on facts as well as generate new empirical generalizations. A notable tradition of qualitative research exists in both cultural anthropology and sociology. These methods have been employed to understand more fully social groups and/or cultures (delinquents, criminals, the homeless, South Pacific Islanders, etc.) about which little is known. It is on this basis that the less structured and standardized but more dynamic and flexible techniques of participant observation have been employed.

The recent complex and relatively unexplained changes associated with social service work mark this labor process as particularly fertile for qualitative or exploratory research. A more specific description of the sampling, data collection, and data analysis procedures of this investigation is presented next.

Sampling

Health care, child welfare, and employment/training are central activities of the welfare state. Yet these service areas do not represent either an exhaustive or critical short list of welfare state activities. Given the time and resource constraints of the investigation, however, only three service areas could be selected. After much discussion, it was decided that the relative size of health care and the historic role of children's services as well as employment training required that they be included. The next step in the sampling process was to locate appropriate agencies.

Two additional criteria that influenced the selection of agencies were location and size. The agencies included in this study were located in the metropolitan area of New York City and were restricted to the largest not-for-profits.

These choices have both visible and hidden consequences and therefore should be explained. To some extent, the study was limited to

New York City and New Jersey by budgetary constraints. However, New York City has historically been at the cutting edge of certain kinds of change. In the last fifteen years, for instance, New York was among the first cities to experience intense fiscal crises, significant cutbacks in service, inefficiencies of scale, and the rapid expansion of homelessness, AIDS, and crack. New York City's social service work force is also in rapid and advanced stages of change. The combination of scale, centralization, magnitude of community problems, and resource scarcity is dramatically affecting the structure of social service work in the New York metropolitan area. Similar changes are also at work (albeit perhaps in earlier stages of development) in mid-sized and small urban areas throughout the country. At the present time, the clearest snapshots of the emergent social service labor process exist in New York City and a few other very large metropolitan areas (Los Angeles, Chicago). However, these changes are both incubating and in earlier stages of development in other metropolitan areas. Various aspects of the new service experience most clearly manifested in New York City and a few other metropolitan areas are rapidly becoming a defining feature of the service experience elsewhere, as tendencies toward centralization, increased scale (of service agencies), resource scarcity, and intensified community problems rage unopposed.

Equally important, not-for-profit agencies with multimillion-dollar budgets were selected into the sample. Conversely, smaller and mid-sized agencies were eliminated from the sample. Clearly, the agency experience presented in the empirical section of chapter 4 is not representative of all not-for-profits, but rather of the largest examples of this species of organization. This decision was made for the following reasons: (1) most social service workers in the voluntary sector are employed by the largest not-for-profits; (2) tendencies in the field toward centralization and increased scale suggest that in the future, service work may increasingly be conducted in agencies of this size; and (3) there is a direct relationship between agency size, or centralization, and the changing nature of service work. A purposive sample was selected, then, of agencies that employ a majority and growing proportion of service workers and are the increasingly dominant organizational instrument for restructuring the service experience.

The specific agencies selected into the sample include: TEP (Training and Employment Program), CAFCA (Children and Family Counseling Agency), and Evergreen Hospital. These agencies were selected because of their accessibility and history of delivering the types of services of interest to this investigation. Equally important, these agencies are highly regarded by a broad cross section of the service community.

The TEP programs that were of particular interest to this study included Mothers in Transition (MIT), a training program for AFDC mothers, and Youth On the Move (YOM), an employment program for high school students. The social work, partial care, and mental health units of Evergreen Hospital were also investigated. Finally, three community counseling agencies of CAFCA were studied. In order to assure confidentiality, pseudonyms were created for every program and respondent selected into the study sample. Two of the programs being investigated maintained more than one site location. Consequently, three of eighteen local family and children's counseling clinics and two of the four high school employment programs were randomly selected into the sample. Finally, with but one exception, 50 percent or more of the employees for each of the program units being investigated were randomly selected into the sample. Randomization procedures could not be employed for the MIT program. Various attempts to gain entry into this program failed. Access was finally established through a line staff person who took a personal interest in the investigation and who provided access to seven employees of the program. These employees worked in three specific areas that were of interest to the investigation (child care, training, and mid-management). However, they were selected because of their relationship to the key respondent.

Fifty-two workers were included in the sample. More specifically, the sample distributed itself in the following manner: hospital, 20 respondents; CAFCA, 17 respondents; and TEP, 15 respondents. The educational achievements of study participants varied substantially by agency. The hospital's work force was almost evenly split between workers whose last degree received was a master' and those holding a bachelor's. TEP line employees were less likely than the hospital staff to have a master's degree (33 percent) and more likely to have an associate's degree (20 percent). Finally, 93 percent of the line service staff of CAFCA had at least a master's degree. On an average, these staff had been employed two years at TEP, two and a half years at CAFCA, and four and a half years at Evergreen Hospital. Approximately 25 percent of the hospital staff, 66 percent of the TEP participants, and 20 percent of CAFCA respondents were people of color. Finally, less than 20 percent of the total study sample were men.

Data Collection

Face-to-face interviews were conducted with each of the fifty-two respondents. An interview guide was created to identify key areas of the inquiry. Follow-up questions were developed for each of these general areas of inquiry. These follow-up questions evolved out of the particular or collective experiences shared by respondents. Substantive themes or issues raised by participants affected the direction of the interview. For instance, respondents influenced the proportion of an interview spent on a particular question. Additionally, emergent data provided the interviewer with signposts for specific follow-up questions. The follow-up questions helped to clarify the particular and more generally shared experiences of respondents. They also provided illustrative and more concrete data. The essential point is that by using techniques of semistructured interviewing, emergent data and themes were able to influence the direction of future data collection. This dynamic process enriched the study's data base and sharpened analytic insights regarding the interrelationship of certain themes. Of course, these benefits are not surprising. As was noted earlier, these strengths are characteristic of semistructured interviewing and qualitative research.

The length of an interview ranged between one and two hours. The longer interviews were conducted with respondents who either had more flexible work schedules and/or offered the investigation a relative abundance of data. Each interview was recorded through both handwritten notes and tapes. These data were analyzed weekly. The regular analysis of data affected both the direction of data collection and represented the earliest stages of categorizing and interpreting data. The data collection process was initiated in September 1988 and concluded in June 1989.

Data Analysis

After the data were collected, the process of analysis intensified. The raw data had to be converted or translated into categories and subcategories of analysis that explained the labor process of social service workers. As the data were reviewed, general and particular themes of shared worker experience began to emerge. The relative strength of a particular theme and consequently the choice of whether or not to weave it into the analysis was based upon the number of respondents who shared specific experiences. The clustering of responses then provided the central clues to locating and creating the primary themes of the analysis.

In order both to locate these clusters and to organize the analysis, the data had to be coded. In the most preliminary stages of data analysis, very general categories were established and associated with discrete coded data. Each anecdote was coded with an alphabetical and numeric symbol that enabled the investigator to identify its location in the field notes. Over time, more discrete subcategories emerged and their relationship to broader categories of analysis became apparent. In part, this movement toward greater clarity was underpinned by hours of manipulating the various pieces of the analytic puzzle until they fit into a coherent, empirically supported whole. It should be noted that often this process required that categories be created only to be eliminated or recreated at a later point. In effect, the birth, death, and rebirth of analytic categories were linked in a creative cycle that ultimately gave life to a more accurate representation of the social service labor process.

Two final points need to be made. By definition, qualitative research is intended to capture complex, changing, and unexplored social processes. These realities do not generally lend themselves to numeric representation. Any effort to convey the richness of shifting, complicated experiences demands a less precise type of data. Numeric data forms would be particularly artificial and inappropriate for this research task. Consequently, the anecdotal data collected and displayed for this type of research, although less uniform and objective, meet the demands of research that is struggling to explain various phenomena in historically unlighted places.

Finally, the research was intended to explain both differences and similarities in the labor processes experienced by various types of voluntary agencies. The differences are particularly important. It is critical that differences in experience be located and explained. Only in this way can such information help to determine where these labor processes are in their most and least advanced stages of development. Why such variation exists also needs to be explored. Alternatively, the similarities of experience between agencies and workers provides insight regarding the generalizable, characteristic features of this emergent labor process.

APPENDIX 4–B

Key Characteristics of Study Respondents

Evergreen Hospital

Name	Title	I.D. no.	Education
John Rubin	Director of Social Work	A–1	M.S.W.
Janice Doyle	Outpatient Coordinator	A–2	M.S.W.
Eileen Sands	Coordinator Pediatric Social Work	A–3	M.S.W.
Sarah Swain	Adult Outpatient Therapist/Social Worker	A–4	Master's Education Counseling
John Myers	Adult Outpatient Therapist/Social Worker	A–5	M.S.W.
Linda Parl	Pediatric Social Worker	A–6	60 credits toward M.S.W.
Joan Smith	Adult Outpatient Therapist/Social Worker	A–7	M.S.W.
Rona Chambers	Women's Health Social Worker	A–8	M.S.W.
Jonas Strauss	Psychiatrist	A–9	M.D.
Elaine Dunne	AIDS Social Worker	A–10	B.A.
Jennifer Blake	Discharge Planner	A–11	B.A. candidate for Social Work degree

Jane Pettis	Discharge Planner	A–12	B.A.
Randi Green	Clinical Pediatric Social Worker	A–13	M.S.W.
Sandi Press	Neonatal Social Worker	A–14	M.S.W.
Marlene Magnusson	Discharge Planner	A–15	6 months from her M.S.W.
Bessie David	Discharge Planner	A-16	B.A.
Ronald Cantor	Asst. Administrator Partial Care	A–17	Master's in Counseling
Bobbi Sherman	Intake Coordinator Partial Care	A–18	B.A.
Judy Merton	Community Liaison Partial Care	A–19	Master's in Counseling
Mary Dean	Women's Health Social Work Supervisor	A–20	M.S.W.

TEP

Name	Title	I.D. no.	Education
Jim Kent	Community Liaison	B–1	Associate's Degree
Joan Jefferson	Senior Case Manager	B–2	Master's in Counseling
Deanne Brown	Unit Director	B–3	Ph.D.
Jim Johnson	Outreach Counselor	B–4	Associate's Degree
Bernice Davis	Diagnostic and Education Evaluator	B–5	B.A.

Maria Lopez	Case Manager	B–6	Master's in Education Counseling
Greg Hudson	Outreach Worker	B–7	Associate's Degree
Janice Mays	Unit Administrator/ Case Manager	B–8	Master's in Education Counseling
Angela Rose	Social Worker	B–9	M.S.W.
Pauline Rivera	Social Worker	B–10	B.A.
Eileen Conroy	Senior Social Worker	B-ll	B.A.
Donna Pinero	Community Resource Specialist	B–12	Associate's Degree
Rachel Shapiro	Prevocational Trainer	B–13	B.A.
Carol Viola	Community Resource Specialist	B–14	B.A.
Lannie Blair	Supervisor	B–15	M.S.W.

CAFCA

Name	Title	I.D. no.	Education
Carl Benn	Social Worker/Therapist	C-l	M.S.W.
Davita Paulino	Social Worker/Therapist	C–2	M.S.W.
Nicole Cohen	Social Worker/Therapist	C–3	M.S.W.
Rona Albert	Senior Social Worker Supervisor	C–4	M.S.W.
Betty Siu	Senior Social Worker	C–5	M.S.W.

Edie Sender	Social Worker/Therapist	C–6	M.S.W.
Clara Romero	Case Aide	C–7	B.A.
Sarina Mott	Social Worker/Therapist	C–8	M.S.W.
Rebecca Silver	Social Worker/Therapist	C–9	M.S.W.
Kate Driscoll	Clinical Psychologist	C–10	Ph.D.
Barbara Ward	Caseworker Therapist	C–11	M.S.W.
Elana Buhl	Social Worker/Therapist	C–12	M.S.W.
Bill Daitz	Social Worker/Therapist	C–13	M.S.W.
Louisa Shmerz	Social Worker/Therapist	C–14	M.S.W.
Mary Ford	Social Worker/Therapist	C–15	M.S.W.
Christine Beal	Social Worker/Therapist	C-16	M.S.W.
Pam Meadowcroft	Social Worker/Therapist	C-17	M.S.W.

References

Abramson, Alan, and Lester Salamon. *The Nonprofit Sector and the New Federal Budget*. Washington, DC: Urban Institute, 1986.

Altschuler, David, Lester Salamon, and Carol De Vita. *New York Nonprofit Organizations: The Challenge of Retrenchment*. Washington, DC: Urban Institute, 1987.

American Public Welfare Association. *Study of Purchase of Social Services in Selected States*. Washington, DC: American Public Welfare Association, 1981.

Barber, Daniel, "The New Revenue Crisis in Human Services: California's Proposition 62." *New England Journal of Human Services* 6, 4 (1986).

Benton, B. T., T. Field, and R. Millar. *Social Services: Federal Legislation vs. State Implementation*. Washington, DC: Urban Institute, 1978.

Booz-Allen and Hamilton. *Purchase of Service: A Study of the Experiences of Three States in Purchase of Service under the Provision of the 1967 Amend-

ments to the Social Security Act. Washington, DC: Social and Rehabilitation Services, U.S. Dept. of Health, Education, and Welfare, 1971.

Burghardt, Steven, and Michael Fabricant. *Working with the New American Poor.* Newbury Park, CA: Sage, 1987.

Council of Foster Care and Childrens' Agencies (COFCCA), Task Force on Turnover and Recruitment. *The Work Force Crisis: The Weakening Ability of Voluntary Child Care Agencies to Provide Foster and Preventive Services to Children and Youth.* New York: COFCA, 1989.

Cohen, Neil, "The Quality of Care for Youths in Group Homes." *Child Welfare* (September–October 1986).

Coulton, Claudia. "Perspective Payment Requires Increased Attention to Quality of Post Hospital Care." *Social Work in Health Care* 13, 4 (1988).

Cousins, Christine. *Controlling Social Welfare.* New York: St. Martin's Press, 1987.

Dawes, Sharon, and Judith Saidel. *The State and the Voluntary Sector: A Report of New York State Project 2000.* Albany, NY: Nelson A. Rockefeller Institute of Government, 1988.

Dean, John. "Limitations and Advantages of Unstructured Methods." In George McCall and J. L. Simmons, eds., *Issues in Participant Observation.* London: Addison Wesley, 1969.

De Hoog, Ruth Hoogland. *Contracting Out for Human Services: Economic, Political and Organizational Perspectives.* Albany, NY: State University of New York Press, 1984.

Demone, Harold, and Margaret Gibelman. "Reagonomics: Its Impact on the Voluntary Not-For-Profit Sector." *Social Work* 129 (September–October 1984).

De Vita, Carol, and David Altschuler. *Flint Nonprofit Organizations: The Challenge of Retrenchment.* Washington, DC: Urban Institute, 1987.

Dinerman, Miriam, Richard Seaton, and Efriede Schlessinger. "Surviving DRG's: New Jersey's Social Work Experience with Perspective Payments." *Social Work in Health Care* (Fall 1986).

Donovan, Rebecca. "Stress In The Workplace: A Framework for Research and Practice." *Social Casework,* no. 5 (1987).

Dressel, Paula. "Policy Sources of Worker Dissatisfactions: The Case of Human Services in Agency." *Social Service Review* (September 1982).

Drucker, Peter. "The Non-Profits' Quiet Revolution." *Wall Street Journal,* September 8, 1988.

Fabricant, Michael. "The Industrialization of Social Work Practice." *Social Work,* (September 1985).

———. "The Political Economy of Homelessness." *Catalyst,* no. 21 (1987).

Fahs-Beck, Dorothy. "Counselor Burnout in Family Service Agencies." *Social Casework,* no. 1 (1987).

Gallagher, David, Debra Markowitz, and Ying Zhou. *Short Staffed:The Personnel Crisis at New York City's Voluntary Human Service Agencies.* New York: The Greater New York Fund, 1988.

Gough, Ian. *The Political Economy of the Welfare State.* Cambridge: Cambridge University Press, 1979.

Gummer, Burton. "The Changing Context of Social Administration: Tight Money, Loose Organizations and Uppity Workers." *Administration in Social Work* (Fall 1984).

Hopper, Kim, and Jill Hamberg. *The Making of America's Homeless: From Skid Row to New Poor—1945–1984*. New York: Community Service Society, 1984.

Jayaratne, Srinika, Wayne Chess, and Dale Kunkel. "Burnout: Its Impact on Child Welfare Workers and Their Spouses." *Social Work*, no. 1 (1986).

Kettner, Peter, and Lawrence Martin. "Making Decisions about Purchase of Service Contracting." *Public Welfare* (Fall 1986).

———. "Purchase of Service Contracting and the Declining Influence of Social Work." *Urban and Social Change Review* 18, 2 (Summer 1985).

Kramer, Ralph. *Voluntary Agencies and the Welfare State*. Berkeley, CA: University of California Press, 1981.

Kramer, Ralph, and Bart Grossman. "Contracting For Social Services: Process Management and Resource Dependencies." *Social Service Review* (March 1987).

Levitt, Theodore. *The Marketing Imagination*. New York: Free Press, 1983.

Lewis, Harold. "The Battered Helper." *Child Welfare*, no. 4 (1980).

Lipsky, Michael. "Bureaucratic Disentitlement." *Social Service Review* (March 1984).

Lipsky, Michael, and Steven Rathgeb Smith. "When Social Problems Are Treated as Emergencies." *Social Service Review* (March 1989).

McQuaide, Sharon. "Human Service Cutbacks and the Mental Health of the Poor." *Social Casework* (October 1983).

Massachusetts Department of Human Services. *Personnel Needs and Opportunities in Health Care Services (Executive Summary)*. Boston, MA: Massachusetts Department of Human Services, 1987.

Mullner, Ross, Odin Anderson, and Ronald Anderson. "Upheaval and Adaptation." *American Hospital* (July–August 1986).

National Association of Social Workers. *Salaries in Social Work*. Silver Spring, MD: NASW, 1987.

———. Health, Mental Health Commission. "The Impact of Prospective Payment Systems on Health Care: A National Survey of State Chapters." Silver Spring, MD: NASW, 1988.

Ostrander, Susan. "Voluntary Social Service Agencies in the United States." *Social Service Review* (September 1985).

Pacific Consultants. *Title XX, Purchase of Service: A Description of State Service Delivery and Management Practices*. Washington, DC: Health, Education, and Welfare, 1979.

Poertner, John, and Charles Rapp. "Purchase of Service and Accountability: Will They Ever Meet?" *Administration in Social Work* (Spring 1985).

Radin, Beryl, and Bill Benton. "The New Human Services Manager." *New England Journal of Human Services* 6, 1 (1986).

Salamon, Lester, David Altschuler, and Carol De Vita. *Chicago Nonprofit Organizations: The Challenge of Retrenchment*. Washington, DC: Urban Institute, 1987a.

Salamon, Lester, David Altschuler, and Carol De Vita. *Pittsburgh Nonprofit Organizations: The Challenge of Retrenchment*. Washington, DC: Urban Institute, 1987b.

Salamon, Lester, David Altschuler, and Carol De Vita. *San Francisco Bay Area*

Nonprofit Organizations: The Challenge of Retrenchment. Washington, DC: Urban Institute, 1987c.

Salamon, Lester, David Altschuler, and Carol De Vita. *Twin Cities Nonprofit Organizations: The Challenge of Retrenchment.* Washington, DC: Urban Institute, 1987d.

Salamon, Lester, David Altschuler, and Carol De Vita. *Atlanta Nonprofit Organizations: The Challenge of Retrenchment.* Washington, DC: Urban Institute, 1986.

Salamon, Lester, Carol De Vita, and David Altschuler. *Phoenix Nonprofit Organizations: The Challenge of Retrenchment.* Washington, DC: Urban Institute, Washington, D.C., 1987.

Salamon, Lester, James Musselwhite, and Alan Abramson. "Voluntary Organizations and the Crisis of the Welfare State." *New England Journal of Human Services* (Winter 1984).

Salamon, Lester, Lisa Tunick, and Carol De Vita. *Rhode Island Nonprofit Organizations: The Challenge of Retrenchment.* Washington, DC: Urban Institute, 1987.

Terrell, Paul, and Ralph Kramer. "Contracting With Nonprofits." *Public Welfare* (Winter 1984).

Walsh, Anne. "Impact of D.R.G. Reimbursement: Implications for Intervention." *Social Work in Health Care* 13, 2 (1987).

Wedel, Ken. "Contracting for Public Assistance and Social Services." *Public Welfare* (Winter 1974).

Weisbrod, Burton. *The Nonprofit Economy.* Cambridge, MA: Harvard University Press, 1988.

Willis, David. "Purchase of Services: Another Look." *Social Work* 29, 6 (1984).

Wolock, Isabel, Elfriede Schlessinger, Miriam Dinerman, and Richard Seaton. "The Post Hospital Needs and Care of Patients: Implications for Discharge Planning." *Social Work in Health Care* (Summer 1987).

5 • Charting A New Direction: Generative Social Services

Even in the best of times, social service practitioners have been required to balance daily tensions that are built into the structure of their work. The demand for social services always has outstripped what can be supplied by agencies. Waiting lists, the shutting down of intake, and a scarcity of referral sources in the community did not suddenly appear in the last two decades. Equally important, the agencies' tendencies toward specialization of skill, centralization of authority, and routinization of service have deep historical roots that frequently limited opportunities to develop an autonomous, flexible, and skill-based practice. There are many accounts of workers struggling throughout the twentieth century against these constraints (Lubove 1973; Fisher 1980).

The workers' resistance to these forces has been propelled by a desire to develop a more professional practice both to improve the quality of work life and to meet the needs of clients. These interests are not always complementary. Too often, agendas advanced by professional associations have further insulated and isolated workers from community needs. However, autonomy, skill, and craft reflect both the dominant social imagery and core aspirations of a range of professions. These qualities also represent the critical underpinnings of any intervention that is intended to improve the quality of life for individuals and/or communities. Although the intensity may vary according to historical period or professional group, the struggle to carve out a more autonomous, skill-based practice has remained constant. The push–pull between the worker's desire for greater independence and the organization's need to control its labor force is part of a long-standing tradition within and outside of the welfare state.

During the past two decades, however, the intensity and balance of

195

this struggle has clearly shifted. Public and not-for-profit agencies have been squeezed by the instability and contraction of their budgets while faced with rapidly expanding community need. These intensified realities have ruptured old ways of doing business within social service agencies.

The Findings and Their Implications for the Future

Today's agency budget is more volatile because of a social environment that constantly threatens and acts to cut service allocations. Equally important, new reimbursement and accountability procedures have increased the uncertainty of the total dollars that will be available, for instance, to hospitals (DRGs) in a given year. The fields of control of various agencies have been further limited by increased need. Agencies throughout the country report alarming increases in the number of pregnant teens, homeless families, substance abusers, and unskilled youth. The resource drain of these expanding populations on service agencies is exacerbated by clients whose problems are more complex and urgent. Practitioners have repeatedly noted that as you scratch the surface of presenting problems, you discover other compelling emotional and/or concrete needs that require immediate attention. Families and individuals with multiple problems have been a persistent source of challenge and stress to social service workers. However, recent examples of such cases are both more plentiful and complicated than before. For instance, the social worker in the 1950s or 1960s was not as likely to encounter deeply troubled young mothers on the verge of homelessness with a history of substance abuse. Other examples of the more demanding cases that have largely redefined the nature of social service work can also be found in the areas of child welfare (crack-addicted babies), manpower (highly unskilled trainees with an array of emotional problems), and health care (substance abusers with AIDS).

The agency's loss of control can be explained in part by the tension between policy decisions made in the broader political environment that reduced the allocation of service dollars, and a cross section of poor/working-class communities that are finding it increasingly difficult to house, feed, educate, and emotionally stabilize their residents. The social service agency is expected to provide the concrete and discrete services necessary to ameliorate many of the communal problems within the budget allocated by government. (As was noted in the previous chapter, the not-for-profit agency budget is more varied in as much as it includes funds from individuals and foundations. However, government funds constitute the largest part and an increasing proportion of the not-for-profit budget.) The agency's efforts are expected to balance the contradictory functions of the state to: (1) *legitimate the social order* (feed the hungry, house the homeless); (2) *reproduce the labor force* (socialize pregnant teens or welfare mothers to the low end of the labor market); and (3) constrain spending or maximize other more productive uses of capital (lower taxes, more dollars available to the private sector), all of which *preserve the ongoing accumulation of capital.* Such contradictions have led to a tenuous balance at best. Even this balance has been weakened by intensifying demand. In such an equation, the quality and even nature of services cannot remain constant. As Michael Lipsky (1980, p. 173) has noted:

> the problem of managing the fiscal crisis consists of reducing expenditures while minimizing the apparent impact of cuts . . . rationing typically means increasing the costs to clients of seeking services while maintaining the service shell or reducing services to decrease potential benefits.

The consequences of this new balance of interests have been explained in chapter 4. The increased needs of the community are effectively subordinated to the agency's more pressing concern to ration resources. However, the agency must still struggle to preserve some measure of legitimacy for its work. Consequently, it must in some way respond to the various claims that are being made upon scarce resources. These essentially conflicting demands have contributed to the industrialization of the structure. measurement, and delivery of social services (Fabricant 1985).

The agency's paramount interest is in processing as many clients through its stream of services as rapidly as possible. Such processing may result in a single truncated episode for a patient in a hospital who is then referred back to the community, or in abbreviated weekly encounters between social workers and clients in a family service agency. This rapid processing of clients is further reinforced by reimbursement procedures and productivity measures that emphasize volume and output. Agency measures of productivity are less and less concerned with outcomes such as physical health or skill development, which to some extent encourage a struggle to provide quality services. Instead, only the quantitative component of the service is measured. The volume of clients seen face to face, the number of telephone or collateral contacts in a day, or the amount of time a patient occupies a bed effectively define the productivity of the agency. The historical tension in social service agencies between quality (legitimation) and quantity (accumulation) may some day be an artifact of a bygone era, for more and more, there is no tension, simply a singular preoccupation with quantifying and maximizing the productivity of every facet of service work.

These tendencies are especially apparent in the work of mid-sized to large public and not-for-profit agencies. While there has been some agreement that such tendencies were intensifying in public agencies, not-for-profit social service organizations have been viewed as a kind of oasis that preserves quality in social services and encourages innovation. The data in chapter 4 indicate that the new balance in service work, which emphasizes quantity and increasingly ignores questions of quality and outcome, is also substantially redefining the work of not-for-profit agencies.

The pressures to increase productivity have affected every facet of service work. The employment training agency (TEP) developed an almost assembly line structure to process clients rapidly through the service experience. The existence of segmented functions for the employment workers, which only allow them to assist clients in a single area of need, such as child care, counseling, community resources, or training, might be likened to automobile factories where "line workers" repeat the same specialized tasks over and over again. Any sense of the whole human being is lost in such a production process. Equally important, the client is reduced to a commodity in such a service process. The difficulties and costs associated with the commodification of clients will be more fully discussed later in this section.

In the hospital (Evergreen) and family service agency (CAFCA), the structure was not as explicitly organized around principles of industrial or Taylorist production. Instead, management simply assigned substantial work loads to line workers and implemented structures of accountability that assured quotas were being met and particular services delivered. Although the client did not flow through a service process that can be likened to an assembly line, certain industrial features did define the provision of these services. The substantial quotas limited workers' time with any single client. Productivity measures were determined not by the quality of service provided but rather the number of clients seen. The increased centralization of authority and heightened accountability of workers within these agencies was partially illustrated through the proliferation of paperwork requirements. These forms assigned value to particular kinds of work and outputs. Equally important, they devalued relatively subtle outcomes and processes.

Swelling caseloads and paperwork have significantly contributed to the redefinition of social services during the past decade. The demands of the paperwork and caseload leave the worker with little time to engage client need. There is little if any time for skillful discovery. Frequently, even the presenting problem is lost in the rush to keep things moving. What the worker does address during an encounter is proscribed by paperwork or managerial demands. The rushed quality of these encounters has an industrial rhythm and intolerance for worker discretion. Lost in this process are the particular and multiple problems of clients that fall outside the limits of this time-limited and rigidly framed encounter, and the discretion, autonomy, and skill necessary to respond to such complex needs.

As the nature of service work is increasingly focused on movement and output, the need for a skilled work force diminishes. The kinds of skills, necessary to develop relationships with clients, fulfill fundamental client needs, create innovative responses, or press for resource expansion outside the agency are lost. The more mechanical approach to social services requires a less skilled work force. This represents yet another short-term saving for the state.

It is important to reiterate that the focus on cost and quantity has contributed to the subtle loss of process and outcome in social service work. The discretion, flexibility, and skill necessary to innovate and meet the qualitative needs of clients are being lost. More specifically, the agency's capacity to positively affect the lives of individuals and communities is reduced within such a climate. Over time, the agency's and worker's capacity to carry out basic social reproduction functions (labor market training, socialization, counseling, health care, education, etc.) or to maintain even a semblance of legitimacy with the community will disappear. We know that social service agencies have always been constrained in their capacity to contribute to the social reproduction of the labor force and to maintain legitimacy with the surrounding community. These boundaries have always been defined by cost or resource constraints as well as imprecise knowledge. However, the struggle (both in and outside of welfare state agencies) to develop effective interventions or encourage the provision of quality services has been muted during the past twenty years.

The abandonment of this struggle for a more industrial model of social services has been fraught with problems. To begin with, the manufacturing structure is a poor fit for social service organizations. As has already been noted, there is a critical yet very subtle interrelationship between process and outcome in social services. Friere, Schön, and others have remarked that frequently in social services, the process defines the outcome (Friere 1970; Schön 1983). Embedded in the process is the structure and content of the service. If we alter the process in health care or manpower, the fundamental nature of social services will be changed. As Morgan (1986) notes, the delivery of a service is more like the process of thinking than of manufacturing a commodity. Private managers have changed manufacturing production processes, and still produced the same basic product, be it an automobile or a computer. However, if the thought process attached to services is altered, perceptual and/or analytic outcomes are likely to be significantly changed. Karasek and Theorell (1990, p. 291) have noted, "services are being turned into commodities to be packaged and transferred to the customer like barrels of oil . . . many nonmaterial aspects of service disappear altogether, humor, empathy, exchange of personal information, social network building, potential for human growth. . . ." These and other process variables greatly define both the nature and the outcome of services.

Too often, output measures capture only the most concrete and evident aspects of social service work. The more subtle and often decisive dimensions of service work are either too difficult to measure or do not appear to contribute to the new quantitative industrial agenda of the agency. As Lipsky (1980, p. 169) has noted,

> It is not sufficient that people are assigned a social worker. . . . We also expect that they will be processed with a degree of care with attention to their circumstance or potential. Thus there may be an . . . inverse relationship between quantitative indicators of service and quality.

Social service organizations are faced daily with confusing and difficult situations. Many of these situations demand innovative responses on the part of workers if they are to be effective. Yet the new industrial social service structure denies the worker the necessary discretion and autonomy to respond creatively to the confusion and uncertainty that is an inherent part of social service work. This is especially troubling because the needs of individual clients and communities are increasingly complex. As Karasek and Theorell have indicated, rigid hierarchical management strategies that limit worker responses in times of high job demand not only take a toll in terms of individual stress, but also limit learning.

An industrial model of services is also more likely to neglect primary and secondary problems of clients. As has already been noted, primary attention is paid to the most concrete expressions of productivity. Consequently, workers' encounters with clients are highly regimented. In the rush to meet quotas, the opportunity to address the persistent needs of clients is often lost. This displacement of goals (from affecting client functioning to processing people) has significant implications (Lipsky 1980). Over time, the client may simply become discouraged and drop out of the service process. Perhaps a higher mortality rate is simply built into a service structure that responds more and more mechanically to complex human need. In the short term, this deflection of clients back to the community represents a savings for both the state and social order. Clients who do not return for additional services are less taxing on the agency's scarce resources. If such responses can be structurally encouraged, this represents at least one answer to the fundamental dilemma of swelling community need and increasingly scarce resources. Any ledger, however, that assesses the costs and benefits of a service structure must also review the longer-term trade-offs.

The industrial service structure does produce a number of toxic externalities. As the primary and secondary problems of clients are neglected, their difficulties are likely to multiply and become more intractable. There may be substantial long-term social costs associated with teens who drop out of training programs or children who do not receive appropriate counseling or supports from nonresidential family agencies. We know that youngsters in poor and working-class communities more frequently engage in behaviors that are costly to the social order. Substance abuse, children having children, violent behavior, and illiteracy are now more likely to define the experience of these youngsters. Service agencies that systematically ignore the complexity of this situation have little hope of preventing or stemming the tide of individual and collective problems.

Ultimately, the costs to the private sector of a labor force that cannot read or abide by certain norms will be substantial. Similarly, the longer-term social costs and expenses of hospitals that return patients "quicker and sicker" to the community, shelters that warehouse families and provide few support services, or community agencies that effectively ignore the mounting problems of teenagers will be steep.

The capacity of any social service structure to respond effectively to these problems is at best questionable. Resource scarcity, limited knowledge, and the complexity of the problems are but a few of the variables that will fundamentally limit the power of any particular intervention or combination of interventions. It is clear, however, that the present structure is organized essentially to implement a policy of nonintervention, or benign neglect. This emergent structure is neither interested in nor capable of the knowledge building, innovation, or community creation necessary even to modestly affect the problems that are destabilizing individuals and communities. In effect, industrial service structures further limit the opportunity to incorporate such activity into the daily practice of line workers. Yet, as will be discussed in far greater detail later in this chapter, the development of such practice opportunity is particularly critical at this historic moment, precisely because of the increased complexity and scope of human need in working-class and poor communities. In effect, practitioners and agencies now more than ever need the autonomy to develop innovative responses to human need. The contraction of such space can only contribute to the exacerbation of communal problems and, ultimately, to a mounting list of social expenses.

As was suggested in chapter 4, the imposition of an industrial structure on social service work has also produced a more disaffected and alienated labor force. The line worker's diminished control over the content, structure, pace, and outcome of work have combined to cause a profound disengagement from the labor process. The worker is less likely over time to retain a commitment to dimensions of practice that are fundamental to the service process. For instance, the relational dimensions of the service experience are likely to be consciously minimized. In addition, the practitioner's interest in critically reflecting upon practice choices will recede in a service process where automatic or more mechanistic responses are emphasized. Finally, the worker's commitment to client growth and change will be diminished in an environment that restricts such opportunities. These and other aspects of the new service experience function to alienate the worker from her own labor and history, and help to clarify the attraction of private clinical practice. Fundamentally, even with market constraints, private practice offers the worker greater autonomy and discretion in the use of skill.

These outcomes are especially significant in social service work. If the worker is alienated from the labor process, both the *quality* and *nature* of the services she provides will be altered. Alienation from the labor process, however, also alienates service workers from their personal history. To some extent, service agencies have historically depended upon the values, commitments, and energy of new workers. These and other qualities of the new service worker have provided at least part of the spark necessary to struggle against limitations. As Lipsky (1980) has noted, part of the job of agencies is to keep new workers new. Such a process is revitalizing for both the agency and worker. A new labor force continues to nourish an expectation to provide quality services.

The industrial service structure more rapidly divorces workers from their own history and expectations. It makes new workers old more rapidly. The service worker's alienation from her own history or expectations affects the sense of opportunity or possibility associated with the delivery of social services. This more alienated labor force in turn produces certain costs for the agency. The absenteeism, burnout, and turnover being reported throughout social services can be attributed in part to a service process that severely restricts the worker's capacity to control her own labor and concomitantly to actualize her historical commitments.

Finally, as was suggested earlier, the new service structure places at risk the fundamental legitimacy of social service agencies. Hospitals, schools, child welfare agencies, and employment training programs that are increasingly incapable of performing even their most basic functions will ultimately alienate and lose legitimacy with the surrounding community. This degenerative process is likely to contribute to further budget cuts, avoidance of public and many not-for-profit agencies, and possibly the accelerated privatization of social services. This downward spiral will profoundly affect poor and working-class individuals that do not have the resources either to seek or afford other options. Those individuals and communities, often in the greatest need, are likely to have access only to the most inferior and ineffective forms of social service. This is historically consistent. However, there have been few (if any) periods since the emergence of the welfare state that have witnessed as dramatic a mismatch between available services and need.

It is increasingly apparent that the deficits of the industrial service structure may outweigh its benefits. The structure's systematic neglect of problems is becoming intolerable. The rising tide of social problems and ineffectiveness of this structure have provided part of the stimulant necessary to rethink the purposes, structural predicates, and provision of effective social services. Specific experiments have functioned as a counterpoint to industrial forms of service inasmuch as they are concerned with outcome over output, staff–client relationship over staff productivity, and practice innovation over practice standardization. Equally important, these new approaches may contribute to the development of a service structure that is able to respond more effectively to community and worker need. Such experimentation and the broader implementation of effective interventions represent the best hope of the welfare state (and its agencies) to seriously address mounting personal and communal crises.

The rest of this chapter is principally intended to look at alternative social service structures. Our discussion will initially focus on intensified forms of social services. These limited but important experiments are perhaps best exemplified through the experience of the Homebuilders' Project. A more sweeping discussion of structural and practice reform will be developed in the subsequent section. The dilemmas associated with this broader experiment will be identified and briefly discussed. Finally, the stakes associated with such experimentation and its potentially transformative effect on social services will conclude the chapter.

An Alternate Direction: Limited Pragmatism and the Development of Intensified Forms of Social Services

In their work *Within Our Reach* (1989), Lisbeth and Daniel Schorr remark that people are becoming increasingly tired of throwing money at problems that are only growing worse. As noted in the prior section, this reaction accounts to some extent for the ceilings imposed on public spending in states like California. This sentiment also explains at least in part the reluctance of federal legislators to raise taxes and/or fund new services. The public desire to limit government spending, however, is mitigated to some extent by public interest in addressing the housing, health, and educational breakdowns that directly or indirectly affect a larger proportion of the population.

A number of intensified forms of service innovation have emerged in response to highly focused definitions of agency failure. In general, these new approaches share a common commitment to "offer comprehensive and intensive services, . . . respond flexibly to a variety of needs, . . . and [develop] programs not with bureaucratic or professional blinders but open eyes to the needs in a family and community context" (Schorr and Schorr 1989, p. 2).

Perhaps the most visible and effective example of this new service form is Homebuilders. This program provides services to families who are at risk of having their children placed in foster care. The central objective of the program is to provide the support and services necessary to maintain the present structure of the family and thus avoid placement in foster care. It has developed a comprehensive package of services and implemented a relatively unique service structure in order to achieve its primary objective.

This type of intensified service delivery is not unique to family and children agencies. For instance, the GAIN (Greater Avenues for Independence Program) program in California is comparing the impact of traditional and intensified forms of service provision on AFDC recipients who are required to participate in work programs (Riccio et al. 1989, p. 2). Social researchers and the state are specifically interested in the differential impact of these approaches on the recipients' training and post-program work experience. The program experimentation of GAIN, like Homebuilders, was attached to a highly specific goal. It was intended to "enable recipients to move off the welfare rolls and into unsubsidized employment, ultimately reducing the cost of welfare" (Riccio et al. 1989, p. 2). This intensified service experiment also structurally maximized the worker's capacity to respond flexibly and immediately to client need. Other experiments of this kind exist in the areas of health care, homelessness, and child welfare. What is striking about each of these programs is the substantial overlap in their practice commitment. For the purposes of this discussion, however, the Homebuilders experience will be used to explain and illustrate the intensified model of service delivery.

In Homebuilders, each worker is assigned a small, limited caseload of families at risk. In general, cases are assigned for four weeks and the worker's caseload does not exceed two families. Equally important, workers are often in the neighborhoods attempting to intensify their relationship with clients. The worker, or "therapist," is expected to be available to the families twenty-four hours a day, seven days a week. The reasons for Homebuilders' commitment to smaller caseloads are described below:

> We believe that the disadvantages of having therapists see more than two families at a time outweigh the advantages. The size of the caseload has a direct impact on the therapist's accessibility, flexibility and responsiveness, as well as the program costs and the length of the intervention. Caseload size also has serious implications for client safety and worker burnout. (Kinney 1988, p. 7)

In general, services delivered by the Homebuilders line staff range from the therapeutic to the very concrete. A single worker is expected to respond to the multiple needs of the client. The organization's rationale for this less specialized approach to service delivery is varied. To begin with, the agency expects that by using one worker to provide hard and soft services, the compartmentalization of family difficulties will be reduced and a better service plan created. Likewise, the division between concrete and therapeutic services is perceived as difficult to coordinate and confusing for the family. The emotional and material needs of the client are viewed by Homebuilders as being interrelated. They suggested that

> clients are often the most open and willing to share information when they are involved in doing concrete tasks with their therapists. Somehow when people have part of their minds on other things, it becomes easier for them to share their deeper, more complicated, more vulnerable feelings and beliefs. (Kinney et al. 1990, p. 46)

The program encourages home visits and practice experimentation. It also retains a basic commitment to the notion that a flexible and diverse practice (granting the worker a degree of autonomy and discretion) is more likely to respond effectively to complex client needs. The form of practice being developed by Homebuilders is more generic, more attuned to learning from clients in different environments, and more cognizant of the intimate connection between concrete and emotional needs than its industrial counterpart.

The worker is expected to develop empathic working relationships with families. It is understood that the rapport and trust developed between the worker and client in process will significantly influence outcomes. The training and supervision provided by Homebuilders is structured to facilitate this process.

Equally important, this approach cannot be disassembled and implemented piecemeal. Instead, the practice and structure must be viewed as an organic whole. It has been suggested that

> All aspects of the model are important . . . rapid response to referrals, accessibility of workers at home during evenings and weekends, the time available for families, the location of the services, the staffing patterns, low caseloads and the brief duration of services . . . combine to produce a much more powerful intervention than one that utilizes only 1 or 2. (Kinney et al. 1990, p. 53)

The primary rationale for the program's continued existence and expansion is its cost effectiveness. Recent data (outside New York City) indicate that 80 to 95 percent of the families served by Homebuilders remain intact one year after the intervention. It has been estimated that the cost of placement is between $3,600 and $19,000 a year. Alternatively, the cost of intensive family services is between $2,600 and $4,000 annually. Recent analyses strongly suggest that the development and expansion of high-intensity family preservation services can largely be achieved through self-financing over the short term. At least one of the tensions for the program is that continued efforts must be made to balance a high enough service intensity to achieve adequate family functioning within a sufficiently compressed time span, in order to assure strategically defensible per case costs (Kinney et al. 1990).

Intensive forms of social service are increasingly used in areas of practice that are generally considered to be both socially and economically wasteful. For instance, workfare, nonresidential support services for families and home care for the elderly are being substituted for welfare, the residential placement of children, and extended hospitalization of the aged. The costs of the latter programs are viewed by many as substantial and the social utility questionable at best. A fundamental premise of these experiments is that *ongoing* institutional relationships between the target population and the welfare state are socially counterproductive and economically inefficient. Consequently, more time-limited, focused, and intensive forms of service have been developed to move the client toward independence. Even if the costs are equal, the experiment is philosophically preferable. Each of these experiments emphasizes highly focused objectives (maintenance of an intact family, work, and stabilized health in a home environment). The comparison of per case costs between the experimental and traditional programs represents the single most important (and, in most instances, the only) measure of effectiveness.

The strengths of the intensive approach are apparent. The emphasis upon independence and the concomitant minimization of institutional intervention are generally beneficial to the client and state. These programs' commitment to short-term intervention often stimulates a rapid mobilization of resources that is in keeping with the urgency of the client's problem. The relatively small caseloads associated with the delivery of intensive forms of social service enable the worker (at least in the short term) to develop the necessary rapport, trust, and relationship with the client. A greater flexibility in the use of method allows for practice choices that are more attuned to the immediate crisis/problems of the client. Additionally, at least one discernible concrete yardstick (minimizing institutional intervention) measures the effectiveness of the worker and program. The highly focused, intense structure of this program clearly provides an array of benefits both to the client and the worker.

Also embedded in the structure of intensive social services is a range of costs. A fundamental question that must be asked is whether limited pragmatic responses to need (such as intensive social services) are sufficient in a period of deepening community and individual crises. A singular focus on the maintenance of intact families potentially misses a whole array of issues that may also be contributing to familial or individual dysfunction. This tendency to miss the broader context of familial or individual crises is further reinforced by other characteristics of the intensive social services model. The short-term focus of the work (driven by both the crisis and cost) forces the worker to address only those aspects of the client's experience associated with the highly specific objective of the agency, without making links to self-help groups and neighborhood associations. Such linkages must occur if family stability is to be achieved for a significant period of time. It is not possible, for example, to maintain a high level of family stability if one's building has crack addicts and the neighborhood lacks a viable economic infrastructure. Only by recognizing such connections are large parts of the client's experience systematically preserved and considered by the practitioner.

The short-term time frames also emphasize rapid resolution of problems. What may remain undiscovered and untouched during, and particularly after, such a process are the more profound problems that persist. Such problems may in the longer run undermine the work of the agency or contribute to other equally compelling client breakdowns. This is especially true in large cities where community infrastructure and supports are already weakened and residents are atomized or socially isolated.

The narrow interventive focus and the restricted timing of such services also affect the opportunity to develop innovative forms of practice. The singular focus on cost and time (as in the industrial sector) inhibits creativity, innovation, and learning. There is little time to discover more fully the complex history of the client, or to consider confusing and contradictory behaviors that emerge from adaptive processes created within the community at large. Instead, such discovery or reflection is put on the back burner. The unexplained or confusing parts of the client's experience, both individually and cumulatively, are systematically ignored in such a context. In an environment of deepening crisis and confusion, however, the client's and worker's ongoing experience and insight must inform the development of practice and policy choices.

This will be particularly critical in the 1990s as we are faced with personal problems and social issues that represent uncharted waters for policymakers. By restricting so dramatically the canvas upon which the worker and client can create, much of the critical opportunity to learn, innovate, and intervene will be lost. Decisions of practice and policy will be made on the basis of a narrowed field of vision and/or insulated expert assumptions. As in the past, this will be at least part of the recipe for modest isolated program successes and a continued decline in the quality of life for individuals, families, and communities.

Intensive, time-limited forms of practice are quite likely to ignore the communal and social context of individual dysfunction, for there is simply little time to consider such variables seriously. This is a crucial omission. In a period of dramatic contraction of resources for poor and working-class communities, any approach that fails continuously to consider the social context of individual problems is seriously deficient. These conditions will influence the client's ability both to engage services and to remain stabilized after the delivery of a service. The lack of employment opportunities, declining health care, and unavailability of housing will, in the short and long run, influence the outcomes associated with intensive forms of social service. The decline of integrating institutions (church, family, school), and the consequent social isolation and violence affecting citizens in an increasing number of poor and working-class communities, also have significant implications for any service strategy. How can citizens regain control over various facets of their lives when daily their communities seem to be slipping more and more out of control?

Although intensive forms of social service are a powerful tool, they represent but one element in an arsenal of interventions that must be developed. The intensive approach is simply not appropriate to many situations facing social service workers and agencies. The needs of individuals and communities are sufficiently complex, persistent, and varied that no single intervention carries the answer. Certainly, a one-dimensional solution to communal and individual breakdown would be more easily digested in the short run by both the public and policymakers—particularly if such a strategy can also assure cost savings. But over time, the appeal of such an approach is likely to fade, particularly given the volatile mix of high expectations and, at best, mixed outcomes. The absence of known solutions to a range of problems, the limits of tinkering around the edges of expansive social problems, and the ineffectiveness of industrial models of practice should stimulate a broader dialogue about the future of social services. It is with this in mind that we will now more generally explore and sketch a number of elemental parts necessary to any service strategy intended to have a positive effect on the quality of life for service workers and citizens.

Formulating a Generative Model of Social Services

The following discussion will identify the elements of an alternative generative approach to social services. This model is structured to encourage growth, learning, and innovation. Generative services are intended to effect change at the level of the individual organization, community, and social order. The following discussion will systematically explore the particular features of generative services at each of these levels of policy/practice.

As has already been noted, cautious responses to the increasingly serious problems of a cross section of communities and social service agencies simply will not suffice. Any strategy that is developed must, by definition, engage in substantial risk-taking. The limits of our present knowledge regarding the effectiveness of interventions and the gravity of community problems demand nothing less.

Social services are at a crossroad. Industrial forms of service are simply incapable of addressing the fundamental communal and personal needs of the 1980s and 1990s. New approaches, such as generative services, must therefore be developed to respond to the particular service needs of the period if we are to have any hope of arresting the range of social problems affecting a cross section of communities. Yet this new formulation is also fraught with dilemmas that will need to be identified and explored. Despite these dilemmas, generative processes remain a particularly compelling direction for social services.

It is important to note that generative social services *do not* represent *the* single clear path to resolving the crisis of social services. As the prior chapters have indicated, the breakdowns of social services are both profound and complex. Consequently, many different questions need to be raised and approaches explored regarding the dysfunction and restructuring of social services. Generative services are but one option to be explored experimentally. We believe that this formulation is particularly responsive to community need and sensitive to the failures of industrial services. However, this model must be tested and, even more critically, joined with other experimental approaches that are struggling to maximize the effectiveness of social services.

Building a Critically Reflective Practice

Given the difficult and confusing situations that daily define the encounters between practitioners and clients, learning must be firmly incorporated into the structure of social service practice. There are no scientific blueprints for the resolution of these difficult and persistent problems, only theories. It is often not immediately apparent to a practitioner why, for instance, a family may be repeatedly falling into a state of homelessness, or particular substance abusers are relapsing. Additionally, a worker may over time see groups of clients that share certain behavioral and historical themes. The meaning of these themes and their impact on presenting problems may be clouded. Available theories, technical approaches, or programmed formats are frequently less than clarifying. They often do not enable the practitioner to make sense of the thematic patterns expressed by people seeking service. As Donald Schön has noted:

> In real world practice, problems do not present themselves to practitioners as givens. They must be constructed from the materials of problematic situations which are puzzling, troubling and uncertain. In order to convert a problematic situation . . . a practitioner must do a certain kind of work. He or she must make sense of uncertain situations that initially make no sense. (Schön 1983, p. 40)

Fundamentally, practitioners must have the opportunity to learn and create if they are to respond most effectively to confusing situations. To a great extent, learning and experimentation must become a core element of social service practice. It is essential that the practitioner's direct line experience be allowed to percolate and perhaps boil over into new perceptions and practice inventions. Such learning space is essential if a sharper understanding of particular client or community need is to be developed. There is no substitute for the client and line practitioner's daily experiences. Only by assembling this data over time can workers develop more appropriate and effective practice approaches. The future growth of the field will thus depend upon the agency's capacity to provide learning space and lend heightened visibility and legitimacy to the inventions of its work force.

Learning and creative opportunity are particularly important in attracting a potentially competent work force. Young workers are frequently attracted to the field because of an idealized sense of possibility associated with the delivery of social services. In the absence of high salaries or benefits, what continues to draw able young people to service work is the desire to make a substantial difference in the lives of vulnerable or needy citizens. Young practitioners come to learn that change is possible only as long as the worker is able to respond flexibly and creatively to client need (see chapter 4 and Lipsky 1980). Once these opportunities disappear, the hope and energy associated with the work of recent recruits will evaporate. This loss of faith will in turn affect the composition of the present and future social service labor force, through burnout, flight from social service work, and greater difficulty recruiting able young workers.

Day in and day out, practitioners in large and small agencies squeezed by various pressures can do little more than rapidly react to presenting problems. They draw intuitively on a variety of experiences and skills first to judge a situation and later to influence it. This *knowing in action* occurs with very little (if any) internal or external dialogue. The assembly of information, practice judgment, and use of skill often occurs in a kind of blur. This process might be likened to a baseball player's plying his craft in a game. When the player is intensely involved in the game, he is forced to react to various situations immediately. The apparently spontaneous reaction to a pitched ball is influenced by its anticipated break, the velocity of the pitch, movement of defensive players, and choices of base runners. Each of these factors must be processed as the hitter is engaged in the active process of attempting to get a base hit. It is not as simple as Roberto Clemente, the late Pittsburgh Pirate, right fielder and Hall of Famer, suggested. When asked what made him such a great hitter, he responded, "I see the ball; I hit the ball." In his day-to-day practice Clemente "made innumerable judgments of quality for which he could not state adequate criteria and displayed skills for which he could not state the rules or procedures." (Schön 1983, p. 50)

Knowing in action is also characteristic of social service work. During encounters with clients, the service worker presses forward in a manner that may appear to be spontaneous and disconnected from any kind of expertise. Like the baseball player, the service worker is engaged in a rapid process of judgment and exercise of skill. Similarly, the worker might have great difficulty explaining the reasons for her choices or the specific nature of the skill that was applied.

Any practice that remains in a kind of fixed state of knowing in action runs at least two risks. The first is that as the practitioner is faced with similar situations over and over again, her responses will become increasingly automatic. To some extent, the practitioner may begin to look for similarity and become desensitized to difference. In this way, the service worker may be able to establish a stable practice. She will begin to develop practice techniques such as the construction of "junk categories" (a blackhole which eliminates new data) to minimize the elements of a situation that may be confusing or surprising (Lipsky 1980). Baseball players engage in such practices when they look for specific pitches they can handle. However, in an environment where the repertoire of pitches is changing rapidly, a hitter who is unwilling to adjust to these new realities by experimenting will become less productive. In time, the player will no longer be able to ply his craft as a professional.

Comparable measures of outcome do not exist for social service workers. More specifically, worker measures of productivity do not emphasize the effectiveness of experimental responses to a volatile environment, but rather the volume of prescribed responses to similar situations. Consequently, the agency retards the service worker's capacity to move her craft from a state of *knowing in action* to *reflection in action*. As Donald Schön (1983, p. 60) has indicated:

> A professional practitioner . . . encounters certain situations again and again. He develops a repertoire of expectations, images and techniques. He learns what to look for and how to respond to what he finds. As long as his practice is stable, in the sense that it brings him the same type of cases, he becomes less and less subject to surprise. His knowing-in-practice tends to become increasingly tacit, spontaneous and automatic. . . .

A second and related risk of such a practice is that surprising or confusing phenomena will not be incorporated into this kind of service work. Perhaps most fundamentally, the practitioner will systematically miss the opportunity to think about what she is doing. A second stage, then, of practice development is *reflection in action*. This is the part of a practice where the line worker critically examines situations that do not fit conventional assumptions or understandings. The critically reflective part of a practice maximizes the creative opportunities associated with confusion. In effect, the practitioner can systematically examine the character of a situation and her tactical use of self in relationship to it (Burghardt 1982).

For the baseball player who has consistently hit a slider but is now awkwardly missing the same pitch again and again, reflection in action is the only way to work his way out of the slump. He must reflect on changes in the pitch, bat speed, or stance. Unlike the ball player who is inwardly focused on change, the service practitioner must look both *inward* (at repertoire of skills, assumptions) and *outward* (at client, community, larger environment) to reflect on change or difference. It is only by struggling to extend the boundaries of present understanding that the practitioner is able to perform the critical function of reinventing her judgment and responses in a volatile environment (Burghardt 1982, chapters 2 and 5).

Reflection in action is not an exact science. Rather, it is often an artful process which demands that the practitioner intuitively reassemble her prior understandings because of new insight or information. It is necessary for the worker to struggle either during (reflection in action) or after such encounters (reflection in relative tranquility) to clarify confusing situations. This intuitive reassembling through the process of critical reflection can bring about new understanding, skill development, and responses (Burghardt 1982). There is, of course, no guarantee that the new actions or insights will be any more accurate or effective than their antecedents. However, through an experimental process of trial and error, or a systematic cataloging of the experience, the opportunities for creating more appropriate interventions will be maximized. It is important that the process and outcomes of such experimentation be shared within and outside the agency. This wider dialogue can more rigorously test the generalizability and/or implications of the practitioner's findings. In the long run, it is expected that this process might contribute to the development of an Action Science.

A number of qualities are clearly essential to the development of a generative practice. To begin with, the worker must be sufficiently committed to the delivery of quality services. This commitment will propel the practitioner's ongoing struggle to examine the constraints and opportunities within her practice situation. In fact, struggle is the hallmark of a critically reflective practice. The worker must be prepared to engage the role strains and dilemmas of the work environment. It is framing tensions within this context that otherwise confusing phenomena become clearer. For instance, a homeless mother in a shelter may repeatedly verbally abuse her child. The automatic response to such a problem might be to attribute such behavior to individual dysfunction or to extreme poverty. In any event, it would be perceived as a parental weakness. However, the repetition of such behavior from this individual or a larger group of residents might stimulate a critically reflective worker to reconsider the situation. The tension between parent and child would be explored. This inquiry should provoke a worker to review case records and speak with other clients or staff. Through this process of data collection, the practitioner might identify and eliminate possible explanations for the behavior. Over time, critical reflection may enable the worker to develop a new understanding of expected behaviors. She may discover that the verbal abuse is triggered by the perception of a situation in a new environment threatening to the child. This behavior may not reflect a weakness or impatience or hostility as much as an impulse to protect. It is then possible to build on this desire to protect as a source of strength. More important than the particular content of this situation is the worker's willingness to engage and act on her confusion. Instead of withdrawing from this dilemma by responding automatically, the practitioner chose to engage in a process of inquiry and critical reflection to understand the situation more fully. The immediate dilemma of the practice situation represents either a stimulant or a repellant for the practitioner. Only by remaining alert to such tensions, developing a sensibility that values critical reflection, and building an array of skills that support the process of inquiry will the worker be able to develop her craft.

The dilemmas and contradictions that spark this process are not exclusively located within the person seeking services. To the contrary, a dilemma may be principally located in the organization. Other points of origin would include the worker, other clients, the neighborhood, or the larger community. The client's dilemma may be sparked and/or reinforced at any one or a number of these points. In a critically reflective process, each of these variables needs to be considered. The worker must be actively engaged in developing the expertise necessary to consider the impact of these factors on the client. Finally, the practitioner's method skills must be sufficiently generic to respond to the varied contexts that conceive and/or feed practice dilemmas. Paolo Friere (1970) has noted:

> Intrinsically these contradictions constitute limit situations, involve themes, and indicate tasks. . . . It is with the apprehension of the complex of contradictions that the second stage of the investigation begins . . . the investigators will select some of these contradictions to be used in the thematic investigation . . . that is the process in which individuals analyzing their own reality become aware of their prior distorted perceptions, and thereby come to have a new perception of that reality. (Pp. 105–6)

Any discussion of a critically reflective practice in social services must also consider the role of the client. Paolo Friere suggests that such inquiry demands that the client enter into this process as a full partner with the practitioner. A climate of mutual trust, he notes, cannot be established in a relationship that is consistently weighted in favor of the worker. While it is clear that the worker brings special skills, accumulated experience and judgment to encounters, the community person also brings experience, and potential creative power to these situations. The worker's dilemma is to decide the extent to which she is prepared to surrender or retain control in the investigative process. In a traditional service relationship, the client is simply a source of information, someone to be acted upon. Yet a monopolization of the learning and inventive process by the worker is fundamentally inorganic. It assumes first that useful learning and effective invention can occur without the creative contribution of the client. (An analogous situation is federal policymakers initiating a variety of programs that will have an impact on localities and severely restricting community input.) How can the practitioner understand confusing situations if the client doesn't have the opportunity to name and explain dilemmas with which he is more familiar? Will inventive and effective responses be formulated principally through a reasoning process that is at least one step removed from such a situation? Does such invention require the creative input of clients who struggle daily and accommodate to these situations? Any critically reflective practice must acknowledge and draw on the special expertise and creative power of community people. The absence of such a dynamic will in all probability result in artificial learning and dysfunctional interventions in the long run.

Another reason for engaging clients in relationships of greater equity, reciprocity, and partnership is the need to develop processes that structurally reinforce anticipated outcomes. If the fundamental objective of social services is to enable clients both to feel greater control over their environments and to achieve a higher level of functioning and problem-solving skill (the two dimensions of empowerment), then a process must be constructed that facilitates movement toward such an objective. This process must engage community people as active learners and teachers. If the community person's principal function is only to learn from the worker, the relationship is likely to breed new forms of dependence. A more dynamic process, which acknowledges the citizen's and worker's areas of mastery, learning, and strength, is more likely to forge a relational bond of mutual respect and trust. Only such a *dialogue* between worker and citizen can stimulate the relational ownership, risk taking, and trust necessary to engage in a struggle for change. Fundamental to this dialogue is a profound respect for the contributions and voice of the citizen.

> The . . . climate and mutual trust . . . leads the dialoguers into ever
> closer partnership in the naming of the world. . . . Trust is contingent on
> the evidence which one party provides the others of his true concrete
> intentions; it cannot exist if the party's words do not coincide with his
> actions. To say one thing and do another—to take one's own words
> lightly—cannot inspire trust. To glorify democracy and to silence the
> people is a farce; to discourse on humanism and to negate man is a lie.
> (Friere 1970, p. 80)

A critically reflective/generative practice defines the worker as a
learner. The method and sources of such learning are varied. Core
dimensions of this practice approach include (a) an engagement of and
attentiveness to work dilemmas; (b) expertise necessary to examine
critically specific areas of dilemma or confusion; and (c) active partnership between worker and client in this investigative process. This
structure essentially envisions generative practice as an ongoing research process. The worker and community person are actively involved in attempting to clarify complex, persistent, and confusing
situations. Finally, the worker and client are actively engaged in the
development of inventive responses to these dilemmas. This dynamic
of reflection and action, which is fueled by an ongoing research process, is substantially different from practice orientations that presently
exist in most social service agencies. Yet this practice approach is
especially appropriate to an era that is producing a number of perplex-
ing dilemmas for social service agencies. Additionally, the very structure of agency-based social services needs to be reconsidered in light
of increasingly ineffective responses to a changing environment.

A New Metaphor for the Service Organization: From Machine to Brain

As has been suggested throughout this analysis, social service organizations are attempting to adapt private-sector manufacturing principles
of production to the enterprise of delivering social services. While new
Japanese innovations suggest that this approach is both deadening and
less effective, old line manufacturing principles remain popular in the
United States, especially in trying to "streamline" social services. This
old approach emphasizes a labor process organized to maximize discrete or quantifiable items of output. While highly alienating, the em-

phasis on quantifying the discrete and concrete nature of outputs (such as units of soda, automobiles, or widgets) allows manufacturers to use "quantity of goods" as the productivity measure to determine profitability. The inventions of Frederic Taylor (principles of scientific management) and Henry Ford (the assembly line) are but a few of the techniques that helped to organize the labor process into a machine-like structure. The process was organized by increasingly centralized decision makers. In general, the primary function of line workers was to repeat the same rote tasks over and over again, often in a rapid process. Their job was not to think, but rather to react to a process that repeatedly recreated their work task, such as stacking soda cases or putting tires on an automobile in an assembly line process.

The machine is, of course, a useful metaphor for visualizing this work process. In any machine, various parts combine to produce certain outcomes, from the repeated rotation of a blade in a fan to flight in an airplane. Each part of the machine has a function that is constantly repeated. Finally, as parts of a machine break down from this process, they are disposed of and replaced. In a sense, the industrial labor process was configured to mirror key active qualities of the product. Put another way, the nature of the product dynamically interacted with and influenced the structure of the labor process.

This merging of outcome and process in the manufacturing sector carries high costs. Human beings cannot function like machines for extended periods of time without certain breakdowns. More specifically, the combination of intense, constant demand and little control over the labor process produces much strain and great resistance (Montgomery 1979). Lately, it has been suggested that there is a critical misfit between modern industrial structures and human physiology (Karasek 1990). A number of studies have suggested that over time such strain will seriously affect the mental and physical health of workers (Karasek 1990). As this stress impairs the workers' health, productivity is likely to be reduced.

Another more subtle cost of the industrial labor process is that the opportunities for learning are minimized. Learning situations require individual psychological energy, challenges, and the exercise of decision-making authority (Karasek 1990). Such opportunities generally do not exist for line workers in industrial settings. The consequent losses in growth (for the individual) and innovation (for the organization) are substantial. Until recently, the growth, inventiveness, and health of line workers have not been valued in the industrial labor process. The production structure, and not the human being, is considered primarily responsible for the maximization of output. Consequently, managerial attention has been focused on the efficiency of the production process, not the quality of work life. This is rapidly changing, however, as the breakdowns of individual workers affect industrial productivity and as new, alternative models of industrial organization have emerged from Japan and elsewhere. Increasingly, private-sector manufacturing firms are perceiving a relationship between the declining productivity of workers (absenteeism, substance abuse, etc.) and the structure of the work environment. Consequently, a number of industries in both Japan and Sweden have taken the lead in restructuring labor processes. These shifts in structure will be more fully discussed later in this section.

For a variety of reasons, the metaphor of the machine is simply inappropriate for organizing the labor process in the social service sector. To begin with, the productivity of social service organizations is not as clearly tied to discernible, measurable units of output. There is no social service analog to a soda bottle, chair, or screw. By using the most apparently quantifiable elements of a service process (clients seen, telephone contacts, etc.) as the principal measures of productivity, the subtle dynamic elements that define quality services are lost. Establishing rapport, trust, or social networks, and the alert processing of information are but a few key elements of social services that are not easily quantified.

Equally important, the service encounter is characteristically marked by uncertainty. Workers face various areas of confusion: unclear or complex client problems, decisions about the use or development of particular interventions, and contradictory goals. As Gareth Morgan (1986) has noted:

> The greater the uncertainty, the more difficult it is to routinize activity . . . uncertainty requires that greater amounts of information be processed between decision makers during task performance. . . . This helps explain why organizations in different *task situations* place different kinds of emphasis on rules, program hierarchy and goal targets as a means of integrating and controlling activity. (P. 82)

The industrial service agency has attempted to gloss over this uncertainty and the less discernible qualities of its outcome by selecting measures of productivity that are appropriate to manufacturing, but not necessarily to service task situations. If social services are to retain (or recapture) their integrity, the metaphor for the labor process (confusion and consequent need for learning) and its outcome (less discernible outcomes or outputs) cannot be machine-like.

The organization—its image and structure—should instead be viewed as a brain. The situations involving relationships, information processing, and learning of tasks in a social service agency have much more in common with the functioning of a brain than that of a machine. The contradiction between the controlled, machine-like industrial structure and the autonomy necessary for learning and craft development in social service work is described below:

> Within highly specialized technically administered systems of control how can professionals think of themselves as autonomous practitioners? How can they strive to achieve standards of . . . excellence, cultivate artistry and concern themselves with the unique features of a case . . . ? These professionals bear more than a superficial resemblance to blue collar workers deskilled by the numbing monotony of the assembly line. (Schön 1983, p. 337)

A social service environment more compatible with task situations and brain-like functions needs to be created. It is logical to assume that in an environment that consistently confronts confusion, a structure must be developed that emphasizes learning and invention. Even more specifically, social service organizations must structurally support the development of craft and a critically reflective practice. The new structure of services must also be monitored in relationship to real outcome (improved health, learning of job skills) as opposed to pseudo-output. Only in this way can the dynamic interplay between practice and organizational structure be assessed on the basis of meeting individual or communal needs. Clearly, this will not be easy. The dilemmas associated with such a process are plentiful and will be spelled out in the next section. Presently, however, it is important to discuss the elements of a redesigned work environment that would support this more dynamic and autonomous form of practice.

The increased centralization of decision-making authority in service organizations is inconsistent with the tasks and demands faced daily by line workers. As has been suggested, the unique and often confusing qualities of personal and communal problems are frequently lost in such a structure. These critical dimensions of a service situation require that workers have greater autonomy and flexibility. Even more specifically, the line worker needs greater discretion in the use of skill and decision-making authority. This would require that the decision-making structure become both more participatory and decentralized. Only in this way can line workers have greater freedom to organize their work life on the programmatic level. It is hoped that over time such change would reverberate through the organization and the community at large.

This more decentralized structure could be organized around relatively autonomous work groups. The heightened independence of these groups would be balanced against countervailing needs of the organizations. A push–pull, however, between line workers (in relation to concrete work life, client, and community experiences) and the distinct survival needs of the organization is necessary if service work is to remain dynamic. In order for such a dialogue to occur, workers must be insulated from areas of direct managerial authority and must have some control over substantial areas of their work life. Otherwise, this process would not facilitate a dialogue, but a managerial monologue.

This more complex and participatory decision-making process might be partially facilitated through the development of agency work groups responsible for addressing distinct task situations. For instance, groups intending to affect the particular service needs of homeless families in a shelter might include housing search specialists, counselors, and recreational staff. Other groups concerned with resource constraints in the community might be comprised of managers and workers. The voice and creative power of homeless residents would need to be thoughtfully incorporated into these processes.

The particular power of these relatively autonomous work groups is twofold. First, the learning that is essential to service work is best facilitated in a dialogue or group. Workers, clients, and administrators can learn from each other's experiences, skills, and insights. This dynamic process is also more likely to contribute to the development of useful techniques. In a sense, the dynamics of a group function as a structural counterpoint to the socially isolated, more uniform quality of work in industrial service agencies.

Second, groups represent a viable mechanism for effecting and preserving decentralized decision making. These benefits are highly interactive inasmuch as learning and dialogue in the generative service agency will greatly depend upon the extent of the line staff's decision-making authority. A number of studies suggest that decentralized decision making in a work group is beneficial to both the worker and the organization (Karasek 1990). The particular utility of autonomous work groups in organizations that must respond innovatively to complex problems is described by Morgan (1986):

> The basic idea is to create a situation where inquiry rather than predesign provides the main driving force. This helps to keep organizations flexible and diversified while capable of evolving a structure sufficient and appropriate to deal with problems that arise. . . .

> learning capacities must be actively encouraged. In an autonomous work group . . . members must . . . value the kinds of learning that allows them to question, challenge and change the design of activity. . . .

> If they use the autonomy to learn how to appropriate levels of connectivity, they can develop a remarkable ability to find novel and increasingly progressive solutions to complex problems. (Pp. 102–3)

The generative service organization will also need to be smaller and, as much as possible, community-based. Like the worker, the agency must have the flexibility to respond to the confusion of daily work life. Such capacity for change is more likely to occur within a smaller organization. The larger bureaucracy is so fragmented, procedure-bound, and centrally controlled that it is often incapable of developing flexible responses to problems. Equally important, if agency innovation or change is to be appropriate, it must maintain a connectedness with the community. Mechanisms and approaches that might more tightly bind the agency and community will be discussed in the next subsection.

The changes in size and decision-making process must support the development of a critically reflective, more generic practice. If the practitioner is to understand more accurately and respond effectively to citizen need, then the blinders of specialization must be minimized. Clearly, workers will preserve and develop specific areas of expertise, but this process must be balanced against the equally compelling need to develop a more holistic understanding of service situations. The problems of clients can no longer be addressed through uni-method approaches. For example, a rehoused family in the South Bronx typically needs access to (a) direct services (concrete emergency assistance and interpersonal skill development); (b) a self-help group such as ACOA (Adult Children of Alcoholics); and (c) processes that build community stability (organizing security patrols, block improvement associations, and political coalitions). The practitioner must be open to learning such skills without preconceived methodological biases that view "need" as just one dimension of practice (individual, group, or community). Remaining alert to the various dimensions of a service situation can be illuminating as it contributes to the development of specific expertise that is consciously understood to be a part of a larger mosaic. In this way, specific pieces of information and expertise can contribute to greater clarity regarding the larger puzzle. The agency's investment in ongoing worker training and competence should reflect these complementary learning needs.

Finally, new measures of outcome need to be developed to reflect the distinctive mission and agenda of social service agencies. Presently available output measures have little utility to a service enterprise focused on learning and the development of effective action. These quantitative measures of output are dependent on: (a) *tangible objects produced* in large repetitive sequences, and (b) situations where *individual contributions* can be *clearly isolated* and quantified. As Karasek (1990) notes, in "today's service economy such measures are not even defensible for 80 percent of the labor force" (Karasek 1990). To the extent that the social service organization is intended to affect learning, growth, and change, new output models need to be developed. Such models must be: (a) process- not product-oriented; (b) inseparably linked to the growth of capability and skill in clients and workers; and (c) focused on the person, not the object (Karasek 1990). The development of such models represents an especially important challenge for social researchers and practitioners.

Lest this formulation read like pie in the sky, it is important to note that an array of organizations internationally is experimenting with this design. In the private sector, multibillion-dollar investments are being made to develop new design plants. Many industries have been persuaded that reduced levels of managerial hierarchy, fewer limits on decision latitude, autonomous work groups, and opportunities for employee growth and development are the best pathways to profitability.

Social service experiments with this organizational model are being conducted in Scandinavia. On a smaller scale, the McConnell–Clark Foundation is experimenting in the United States with a model of intensive case management that combines Homebuilders techniques with the problem-solving and self-help skills developed by Henry Street Settlement's Urban Family Center. The findings from these sectors are quite promising, at least on a preliminary basis. For social service agencies, the promise of the generative model of organization is linked to the nourishment of critically reflective forms of practice (discussed in the prior subsection) and to systematic support of efforts to build community with citizens seeking services.

Reclaiming Community

Traditional community institutions have recently experienced a diminished capacity to meet the basic needs of citizens. Stable employment, adequate housing, quality education, and familial supports are simply less available. A cross section of communities has witnessed increased dropout and illiteracy rates among youngsters attending public schools. The jobs available to high school graduates often offer little more than a minimum wage and boring work in a range of service industries. More and more families are either doubled or tripled up in living quarters or in a more visible state of homelessness. Finally, family and friends are often less able to provide necessary supports to children and young adults, who in alienation and hopelessness turn to gangs, drugs, and violence.

These and other expressions of community breakdown were intensified by the cost-containment policies of the 1980s. Community decay, however, was underway well before the past decade. Migratory patterns of labor in response to the changing geographic distribution of capital, the transformation of the economy from manufacturing to services, the de facto segregationist development of suburbs, urban renewal, and racism are but a few of the economic and social externalities of the past fifty years that have undermined the fabric of urban communities. Each of these variables has affected the breakdown or weakening of community structures such as the family, church, and schools. The capacity of these institutions to establish and enforce a range of communal norms, however, was further undermined by the budget cutting of the 1980s. The increasingly fragile resource base of traditional institutions has affected their ability to meet concrete needs and to maintain personal community norms. This in turn has helped to set the stage for the ascendance of alternative groups, such as youth or drug gangs. The norms (violence, drug abuse), resources (money), and social supports of youth gangs have proven particularly attractive to the growing number of socially isolated and angry youngsters who have fewer life options.

It is important that the historical role of traditional community institutions not be romanticized. These structures have often assimilated many of their constituents to intolerable community norms and to a labor market that did not advance their class interests. These institutions, however, have also performed critical functions around which community life cohered. At no time in recent memory have traditional community institutions performing basic social reproduction functions been so weak or had so little legitimacy. Conversely, community structures that are hostile to prevailing norms and institutions are growing in size and strength. These tensions and dysfunctions have left most community residents with few options but to withdraw and, to the extent possible, fend for themselves in an environment that is increasingly hostile.

Any attempt to create generative forms of service must acknowledge and respond to the shifting definitions and breakdowns of the community. The origins of public and not-for-profit social service agencies can be traced to such communal breaks. The economic and social forces promoting this decay have left many social problems in their wake. For instance, the destabilization of families as they were dislocated from rural to urban areas, or from one part of the country to another, diminished the capacity of communities (and families) to care informally for the elderly, young preschool children, widows, single women with children, and other needy groups.

In the past, these needs were at least partially addressed by extended families and more formal communal structures (such as the Grange or the Black church). As extended families and communities were weakened because of rapid unregulated change within and outside of the marketplace, their historical capacity to meet an array of personal needs was also diminished. In their place, social service agencies were organized to meet the *employment* (chopping wood in return for an hourly wage, public works programs, unemployment insurance), *nurturing* (elderly, preschool children), *health* (clinics, hospitals), and other human needs of citizens. Over time, economic and social change shifted the locus of responsibility for these services from small, often informal community institutions to larger, more formal agencies.

As the locus for service provision shifted, so did the nature of service. Once a service was offered within a principally institutional rather than communal context, the critical connection between service and community was frequently lost. So although certain basic individual needs were met through the formal institutional provision of service, the exchange was no longer a gesture of community (there were exceptions to this tendency, for instance, some settlement houses). The ongoing dynamic interplay between the evolution of community ties and service evaporated. The profound connection between individual and communal growth was sacrificed in this exchange. Ironically, by altering the character of service to clients, service agencies have further weakened a fundamental underpinning of community and thus contributed to an expanding need for service.

The expansion of the welfare state between 1930 and the mid-1970s did represent a modest statement of obligation to address certain aspects of communal and personal breakdown associated with rapid change. Despite the structural limitations of this response, it does represent an ongoing statement of collective or social responsibility. More recently, the state has encouraged a *reprivatization* of social and personal problems. In effect, families and local communities are increasingly being asked to assume nineteenth-century service functions. Unfortunately, their capacity to provide such services independently has long since faded, as informal communal networks have either wilted through increased dependence on welfare state institutions, or disappeared due to economic dispersion of community members and destruction of supports. This is a crucial contradiction of contemporary social policy. How, for instance, can a daughter care for her aging mother, given the often prohibitively expensive costs of nursing care, when: (1) other members of her family are spread about the country; (2) she is working a full-time job; or (3) the performance of such functions may be a technical mystery? Alternatively, who can a homeless woman and her children turn to when they are essentially disconnected from family, friends, or institutional affiliation? Clearly, turning back the clock to an essentially nineteenth-century configuration of services and responsibility will not work.

There is at least one dimension of nineteenth-century services, however, that is highly pertinent to present service and community dilemmas. Given the increasingly critical relationship between personal need and communal breakdown, agency services now must be structured to support a process of community building. For example, how else can a counseling agency meet the emotional needs of citizens who are otherwise socially isolated, a school address the learning deficits of students without parental involvement, or a shelter assume that families, once housed, will remain stable without a natural support network?

In the absence of community, the increasingly profound problems of more isolated citizens cannot be addressed seriously. The immediate impact of a service will soon fade if it is not reinforced through communal supports and processes. In a period that has witnessed an expansion of problems and diminution of resources, the availability of communal supports is particularly critical. *Generative services must be organized to promote the development of community.* As has been suggested, the structure of social services must respond simultaneously to both the communal and personal needs of citizens. Conversely, the counterproductive tendency of agencies to sever services from a process of community building would be corrected by this reconfiguration.

Can social service agencies engage in a process of rebuilding with citizens what has been systematically lost? For this to occur, most agencies will have to extend beyond their historical limits to create the structure of a community-building process. It might be useful, for instance, to look at the experience of such institutions as churches to learn how feelings of community are created. Ultimately, however, steps must be taken to develop processes that are more specific to the agency–service experience.

Fundamental to initiating a process of community building is some shared connection (faith, need, etc.) between members. A church or synagogue, for instance, begins with a presumption of shared faith. It is through such sharing that the *public affirmation of self* can be created. In this way, citizens may find the inner resources (self-esteem, pride, competence) necessary to promote the development of personal strengths and collective action.

Emergent definitions of community in this discussion must be consistent with the generative structure of services outlined in prior subsections. The emphasis of this discussion upon reciprocity, partnership, learning, and growth is consistent with an intention to build community between agency and citizens. Equally important, the multifaceted content of generative services and its emphasis upon struggle are essential to any process that has to connect dynamically the work of service agencies to the life of the community. In effect, these practice and organizational processes consciously contribute to an integration of agency and community by socially reproducing individual and collective expectations of greater worth and responsibility that heretofore have been lost.

This third dimension of service provision needs to be developed simultaneously within a generative model if one of the agency's *primary functions* is to address the communal needs of citizens. Such a primary process is necessary if the service agency's responsibility is not only to engage more fully the surrounding community, but also to recreate the organic connection between service provision and the building of community. Only by responding to more concrete problems while building community can the agency realistically hope to coherently affect client need. Equally important, this approach offers a potential trajectory to broader change.

It is important to keep in mind that any effort intended to create a sense of community will require a multilayered, sequential process that provokes an intensifying and flowering sense of connection between the client and the agency. The process should be systematically organized to: (1) open the individual to the possibilities of communal participation; (2) support greater participation or inclusion in decision making; (3) build a feeling of membership; and (4) focus attention on the needs of the larger community. In this way, agency process mirrors social reality as personal needs are organically connected to rebuilding community. These phases of the community-building process represent natural benchmarks in a reconstructed process of service provision.

Any effort to rebuild community through the structure of agency work will be riddled with dilemmas. By definition, this process will be initiated and to some extent structured by the agency. A danger exists that the community's unique voice will be engulfed and muted by an independent organizational agenda. This tension is, of course, critical because it would poison any effort that is intended to use organizational structure to regenerate community. This is part of the struggle faced by schools experimenting with shared decision making.

Equally important, how can social service agencies function as the tissue for communal regeneration in a climate of cost containment and budget cutting? These and other dilemmas associated with the development of generative services will be more specifically addressed in the next section. It is important at this point in the analysis to acknowledge that a host of troubling dilemmas will accompany any process that is devoted to the implementation of generative services. Dilemma and contradiction, however, are not unique to generative services. To the contrary, as was suggested earlier, a range of contradictions also affects industrial services. Specific political, economic, and social realities will always be in tension with any social service structure. Thus, different structures will provoke distinctive areas of struggle. *The issue, then, is not so much the existence of dilemma, but the extent to which dilemma (and choice of structure) affects struggles that are potentially beneficial to individuals in need, workers, and communities.* One litmus test of any service structure must be the quality and nature of the struggle it promotes.

The ongoing process of community building that will be sketched is not an abstract blueprint. Rather, it represents a distillation of successful community-building experiments in school systems, settlement houses, homeless shelters, and agencies for the mentally disabled. For each of these agencies, an initial task has been to engage citizens in new ways. Often, client encounters with social service agencies are less than pleasant. Any first step in the process of community building must be to develop a new message.

The agency must find ways to welcome the client and develop a more open and hospitable environment. In a sense, the agency must replicate conditions that any one of us would expect in less formal settings. Clearly, our sense of connection or affiliation at a local block party is heightened if residents are warm and receptive. This kind of attentiveness is likely to kindle (at the very least) a preliminary connection between individuals and the association. It also begins a process of public affirmation.

Thus, agencies and line workers who systematically welcome citizens are more likely to pass through initial barriers of distrust and establish forms of connection and relationship with the client. Welcoming may include as concrete an act as painting areas or shelter units in bright colors and hanging attractive pictures on the walls. A more subtle expression of hospitality might involve the worker's moving out from behind her desk to greet and engage clients. What the agency must consider if it is involved in a serious process of community building is how it can structure new forms of greeting or hospitality into its daily work life.

Once the client has been welcomed to the agency, he or she should be engaged in an ongoing process of affirmed participation. Many of the qualities of this experience were presented in the earlier discussion on critically reflective practice. It is important to reiterate that what is fundamental to a process of critical reflection is a structure of partnership between client and worker. The learning process must be informed by client perception and experience. In effect, the person seeking service must be able to function as a teacher and learner. Only in this way can the cumulative expertise and creative power of the citizen be affirmed in ongoing encounters with workers. Such affirmation cannot occur predictably or represent a rote, agency-suggested response to specific situations. Instead, the worker must be trained to understand and remain alert to learning opportunities that originate with the client. Only through learning from the client in this more dynamic manner can the process retain its authenticity and ring true.

An affirming participatory process should also structurally enable citizens to participate in agencywide forums. Discussions with decision makers that address critical facets of agency life need to be encouraged. In shelters, these forums might raise questions of safety or housing location. At a settlement house, the declining quality of child care or senior meals might be raised. It is critical that these forums have the feeling of a town meeting. *Citizens must have an opportunity to participate in contexts other than those that are focused on their problems or with individual workers.* Only in this way can public affirmation of self begin developing within the agency.

This second stage of community building must establish more varied and intense bonds between client and agency. *In general, a process must be facilitated that heightens the client's connection both to the particular service experience and to the larger agency.* Again, it is not enough for clients simply to participate in these agency meetings. Their comments and proposals, when appropriate, must be affirmed. Equally important, verbal affirmation is not enough. Workers and administrators must struggle to find ways to act on client insights or proposals. To the extent possible, a representative group of clients should participate in such an ongoing process of change.

Finally, affirmed participation also requires general acknowledg-

ment of the client's struggles and victories. A mentally disabled client who is struggling and failing in a new job, or a homeless woman in a shelter who has recently located housing both need to be acknowledged by workers. Aspects of a client's life that may fall outside their more formal relationship with the agency, but are pertinent, should be commented upon when possible. For instance, a worker may have learned that an unemployed community person using the latchkey program for her children has located a job. Although this information may have little bearing on the formal relationship between client and worker, acknowledgment and affirmation of this victory could contribute to a more generic connection between the worker and client. Ultimately, it is this movement from specific and functional to more generic relationships that marks part of the transition to community membership.

Only when clients begin to feel they are an essential part of the life of an agency can ties of communal affiliation begin to develop. In a sense, the first two stages of the process of community building are intended to provide the foundation necessary to build this fuller commitment. To a great extent, the transition from a feeling of mutual respect and concern to community involves a depth of bonding that is both more varied and risky. To begin with, citizens must be given the opportunity to participate as equals in certain agency decision-making structures. In this way, client groups can begin to define themselves as full *members of a community.* As in other circumstances, people that are locked out of all decision making are little more than disenfranchised, second-class citizens. Such disenfranchisement is the antithesis of community.

Quite clearly, all citizens will not be able to participate in all decision making. Additionally, final agency authority for various decisions will continue to reside with particular administrators or staff. Despite these constraints, however, a number of areas of agency decision making can be opened to more democratic processes with clients. For instance, a number of governance structures such as boards of directors or advisory groups exist in every agency. Identifying or creating such bodies is relatively easy. What is difficult for both administrators and staff is either to tolerate or to define the parameters of such participation.

The participation of citizens in agencywide decision making requires competence. It is counterproductive if a citizen's presence in decision-making circles is symbolic or insubstantial. Often, citizens have neither the training nor the experience to influence such a process or make informed judgments. Consequently, if the agency is serious about involving citizens in decision making, it must invest in training in certain circumstances. This point is underscored by the quality of parental involvement in the New Haven school experiment:

> workers at both schools met with parents to try and identify and respond to factors limiting parental participation. . . . Parents pointed out they wanted to participate in program policy issues but they could not do so unless they had some way to learn and understand school operations. . . . Curricula and extracurricular activities were sponsored . . . to enable them to learn about children and schools . . . and plan and implement programs. (Comer 1980, p. 132)

Feelings of communal affiliation can be deepened through various forms of celebration. When celebrations are created through a process of rituals (monthly, birthdays, award ceremonies, etc.) that build a sense of tradition, they allow the client and worker to behave in new ways and consistently recreate their perceptions of each other. People can shed or step out of their formal roles. New areas of competence may become evident—dancing, singing, playing the guitar, or acting. As old roles and perceptions are thrown into flux, opportunities to develop more complex and multifaceted relationships emerge. In a sense, celebration and ritual can stimulate richer understanding and connection between worker and citizen. These events can also function as a consistent and effective reminder of the joys associated with agency life. Finally, to the extent that celebration acknowledges special moments in the life of a client or worker, it makes yet another contribution to the formation of community.

The clients' budding attachments must, however, extend beyond the agency. Some attention in this process must be paid to issues affecting the broader community. It is expected that to some extent, the aforementioned processes will prepare citizens individually and collectively *to engage a number of the problems in the larger community.* Equally important, the agency must extend communal support (resources, etc.) to the broader struggles its members initiate or join. The refocusing of attention to the larger community may be specifically intended to build new communal structures or strengthen existent but weakened institutions. The particular substantive focus might vary, but the general commitment would be to improve the quality of community life. Forays into the larger community might therefore involve the agency and its members in efforts to build more housing, reduce crime, or improve access to services. The particular substantive or tactical focus is less important than the agency and its members looking outward to create links with other sectors of the community. This last step in the community-building process recognizes environmental dynamics that daily affect the life of the agency and its members and demands activism to alter these conditions.

The processes outlined in this section are equally applicable to agency staff. The increased isolation of the worker mirrors the circumstance of the client. Worker alienation will be greatly reduced by the *direct practice* and *organizational changes* described in earlier sections. However, the particular qualitative shift in consciousness and experience that stimulates a *sense of community membership* is not specifically or systematically structured into these dimensions of generative service. A shared emphasis in each of these strains of generative service, for instance, on more inclusive decision making, may reduce worker or citizen alienation, but will not independently contribute to a greater feeling of communal affiliation. It is important to reiterate that although these processes are complementary and at times overlapping, they cannot be substituted for each other. The generative experience is not as linear as manufacturing a product or producing an industrial service. Instead, a number of dynamically interactive yet critically independent processes must be initiated simultaneously to stimulate growth and innovation. Consequently, a community-building process consistent with the principle discussed in this section must also be structured to respond to the specific circumstances and needs of workers. Any process that fails to address the communal needs of both citizens and workers independently is doomed to fail.

Imbuing Daily Work with a Social Vision

The potential to affect the circumstance of workers or citizens positively is greatly influenced by the larger environment. The unavailability of essential items like housing, food, or health care profoundly affects the functioning and potential growth of clients. The impact is felt by the agency and its workers not only through the present pool of citizens who are homeless, sick, or hungry, but also in the rapid reproduction of such problems and the consequently expanding ranks of desperately needy clients. Diminished access to basic resources is a primary trend that has affected the lives of poor and working-class people across the nation. Other tendencies within the larger social environment such as racism, sexism, and homophobia also daily destabilize the lives both of citizens seeking services and of workers. These often less visible roadblocks will consistently limit the potential of any generative service experience if workers and clients do not engage in an ongoing dialogue to address them. The development and constant actualization of a social vision must be an elemental part of this process.

To begin with, any long-term social goal must at least be approximately envisioned. Clearly, this ultimate objective is not fixed and, depending on personal or social change, will be reconfigured over time. The goal will be greatly influenced by societal values that define areas of fundamental entitlement for workers and clients. There should be an awareness that such goals will be achieved only in the very longest time frames. It marks a general direction for the larger change process, and it is an idealization against which concrete objectives can be set and incremental progress evaluated. For example, the availability of a variety of medicines may be an interim step in the longer-term fight to eradicate and prevent AIDS.

The second stage in this process is the development of a social map. The citizen and worker must be able to understand more fully how movement toward this vision will be affected by present conditions or roadblocks. An ongoing analysis of the problem must be developed on this basis. For example, factors that perpetuate or reproduce problems such as illiteracy must be understood. Equally important, obstacles that prevent movement must be discerned. Short- and mid-term goals must be identified. These choices will in turn greatly influence the kinds of resources, tactics, and strategies that will be identified as necessary to move forward. For instance, different tactics and strategies are needed to address racist attacks on blacks in white communities, other than the conservative dismantling of Civil Rights legislation.

Finally, an effort must be made to build a vehicle for movement to specific objectives. This mechanism must function to channel and build a collective energy for change. At the local level, coalitions and grass-roots associations have proven to be effective instruments in such a process. Over time and when appropriate, larger vehicles will also be developed. It is important to note that national or regional movement structures are almost without exception created and sustained by local groups. In effect, these local groups' analysis of specific problems can affect a decision to develop more ambitious coalition structures.

Workers, clients, and agencies struggling to develop generative services must attach themselves to this fundamentally broader struggle. This dimension of generative services is critical, precisely because it acknowledges and struggles to act upon broader forces that inhibit personal and communal growth. Consistent with the generative service process, it sees the connections between the dynamics of social reproduction (client and worker) and broader struggles that potentially affect the accumulation functions of the state. Each of these elements, when combined, represents an organic dynamic whole. These strains are most effective when they simultaneously and interactively attempt both to address personal need and effect social change. If a dimension of the experience is ignored or neglected, however, it will influence every other part of the generative service experience. For example, an agency's unwillingness to address racist attacks in its community will affect the capacity and willingness of citizens to engage in the personal and communal processes outlined earlier. Similar illustrations could be developed in the areas of crime, homelessness, substance abuse, or education.

Although this formulation of generative services contains many contradictions, it may be most affected by the dilemmas associated with relatively broad efforts to effect change. This is understandable, given the agency's and worker's greater control over their own internal operation and lesser influence over any part of the social environment. The broader struggle is more difficult and often involves greater risk taking. Consequently, the agency must be realistic in its aspirations and assess its fiscal exposure in a climate increasingly hostile to social services. These caveats are touchstones that must be consistently returned to as the agency, client, and worker struggle to fashion responses to broader problems.

In a sense, this discussion has presented a vision of generative social services. It is an idealization that will in all probability not be fully implemented in the short run. However, the development and restructuring of social service work can be measured against this general standard. It is clear that any effort to implement a generative service plan will be accompanied by a number of dilemmas, for dilemmas are a natural by-product of any service approach. What will vary is the content of the dilemmas provoked by different service structures. For the purposes of this discussion, it is necessary to discuss briefly the dilemmas that are most apparently associated with a generative model of social services.

The Dilemmas of Generative Social Services

Any substantially different approach to the delivery and structure of social service work will provoke questions and doubt. One of the most critical tests of any service structure's health is the extent to which it honestly raises and struggles with tensions that affect its daily functioning. Such a process is critical to the ongoing learning that must occur within service agencies. How can complex problems be more fully understood or new interventions created in an environment that fails systematically to raise and address such dilemmas? In effect, dilemma is the necessary grist for practice/agency learning and innovation.

The industrial model of services by temperament and structure deflects attention away from certain dilemmas. It is only interested in those tensions that impair the productivity of the organization or worker. Questions of quality, context, or ongoing dysfunctions are rarely raised or considered. In a sense, industrial services are structurally tied to the axiom that only phenomena that can be measured exist. Consequently, the more profound, subtle dilemmas that riddle this model of services are rarely raised.

In contrast, the character of generative social services is defined by struggle, growth, and invention. Concomitantly, generative service structures and processes are organized to focus attention on dilemmas. Greater value is not assigned to problems that lend themselves to quantitative definition or resolution. To the contrary, qualitative, more subtle areas of tension are recognized as being of at least equal importance in understanding and affecting problems.

A number of tensions are built into the structure of generative social services. For reasons already noted, it is important to raise and briefly discuss these areas of tension. It will not be the purpose of this discussion to resolve these tensions; in many instances that would in fact be both artificial and impossible. Instead, consistent with the intention of generative services, this initial stage of dilemma posing is intended to provoke dialogue, learning, and invention. The following discussion will address some of the tensions experienced by (a) the worker/client,

(b) the organization, (c) the community, and (d) larger change processes.

The generative service process requires a labor force that is committed to learning and growth. By definition, consistently higher levels of creative energy, connection to clients, and resolve will be required of generative service workers as compared to their industrial counterparts. As Michael Lipsky has noted, new workers are more likely to have such qualities. However, even in the most supportive, learning-centered environment, new workers will be sapped by the demands and restrictions of service work. A critical frustration that will be repeatedly experienced by workers is the relative modesty of their interventions. The nature of client need, as has been noted repeatedly, is increasingly complex and persistent. Equally important, the scope of crises is growing. No service structure will be insulated from the dynamic of rising need and diminished resources. These conditions, however, will tend to overwhelm, frustrate, and alienate workers. How can the generative service agency develop and retain critically engaged and reflective practitioners in an increasingly threatening environment? Clearly, generative agencies will develop training, structural, and process supports that acknowledge and modestly respond to this turbulence. However, the limited possibilities for immediate change will be an ongoing source of tension for generative service workers.

The very process of learning and growth will also be affected by the more profound problems and urgent needs of citizens. The kind of trust, patience, verbal skills, and emotional margin necessary to such an experience may be less available. For instance, the concrete housing or sheltering needs of homeless people will sharply focus their encounters with workers. Equally important, citizens who have repeatedly had unsatisfactory experiences with service agencies, or are struggling with a long history of difficult problems, will be more difficult to engage in a dialogue. Yet the more persistent, urgent, and difficult circumstance is characteristic of the emergent client profile. The dilemma for the worker is not simply whether such citizens can be engaged in dialogue. The greater tension is in breaching the chasm of ever widening difference in experience and determining when and how to initiate such a process. Historically, clients have been socialized to expect workers to play the principal and dominating role in service encounters. The perception of the worker as the primary or perhaps even single repository of expertise is challenged by the very structure of generative services.

Definitions of skill, process, role, and expectations are dramatically restructured. The changed experience of workers and citizens within this new service structure will be threatening. The more dynamic and less rigidly bounded relationship will require various forms of resocialization. This resocialization to an ethos of uncertainty, partnership, and struggle will be in consistent tension with the impulse to predetermine problems, dominate through formal expertise, and respond automatically.

Daily, powerful socioeconomic forces are driving more and more citizens into increasingly desperate situations. Nevertheless, it is more difficult for workers even to consider social currents in a service environment that is characterized by expansive personal crises. Consequently, discussions have come to focus on visible personal expressions of breakdown in individual behavior. Conversely, the less visible yet more powerful social forces associated with individual behavior have been increasingly ignored.

This process of blaming the victim has been intensified by the widening mismatch between available resources and growing problems. These tendencies are especially destructive to a service process that is expected to be learning-focused and responsive to the complex factors that influence citizen and communal behavior. It is especially critical, then, that generative service workers remain alert to the powerful undertow of each service encounter that pulls workers and citizens to isolate individual dysfunction from social context. Clearly, consequent losses in learning, growth, and invention are substantial.

Many of the elements of the generative paradigm of service are also in tension with the impulses of bureaucracy. Bureaucracies have historically tended to establish a hierarchy of workers. This mechanism has enabled the organization, through its managers, to maximize control over decision making and the labor process. Likewise, the hierarchical vertical structure of bureaucracies has helped increase the specialization and fragmentation of social service workers' functions.

Alternatively, the process of generative service emphasizes more generic expertise, horizontal decision making, and decentralization of authority. At the same time, certain areas of decision making must be handled by a central authority (for example, daily budgetary requirements, personnel procedures, and the like). Such issues cannot logistically involve everyone at all times in the decision-making process. How can a structure be created that grants administrative decision makers a degree of autonomy and authority without sacrificing the integrity or potential of the generative service process? Clearly, the balancing of these interests represents a particularly important challenge in the development of a generative service structure. In general, as organizations become established, they are less and less likely to engage in risk taking or to acknowledge confusion. The agency's primary interest is in stabilizing and controlling to the extent possible its internal and external environment. These objectives are supported by projecting certainty (expertise) and accomplishment (performance measures). By definition, however, generative service organizations encourage risk taking and an ongoing acknowledgment of confusion. The tension between organizational impulses to survive or expand and a mission that demands risk taking and learning is substantial. This tension is more easily resolved in environments where cutting-edge technologies are being developed.

To some extent, the organization's survival is dependent on its capacity to innovate. Consequently, its structure is organized to facilitate such an outcome. Unfortunately, similar incentives do not exist in the domain of social services. Perhaps, however, in this period of mounting personal and social crises, a similar structure of incentive needs to be created. In order to effect such change, measures of performance will have to be reconstituted to encourage more open-ended processes of learning and innovation. Relatedly, the greater confusion associated with these concepts and outcomes will have to be tolerated. The effort to capture dimensions of processes as elusive as learning, growth, or innovation represents a particularly compelling challenge for social researchers.

In any social service agency the demand for quality services will be infinite and the supply finite. This gap between supply and demand will be especially troubling for generative service agencies that wish to maintain standards of quality without curbing or closing off intake. To some extent, this dilemma has been intensifying because of diminished government support for social services. This aspect of the problem will be discussed later in the section. However, even in the most ideal economic circumstances, there will be a gap between available resources and demand. Any effort to close this gap must draw upon the resources of citizens seeking service in the surrounding community. Social service organizations also need to utilize more fully available software technology. The technical expertise and hardware necessary to free administrators from the more detached (and onerous) forms of accountability that now dominate their work lives are presently available. Yet the more general dilemma of supply and demand will not disappear and represents a particular threat to the development of easily accessible generative social services.

The development of generative social services will also be in tension with certain community currents. To the extent that the agency is perceived as being removed from the community, trusting relationships will be more difficult to establish. Differences of class, race, and other social factors represent an ongoing area of struggle. Workers are more likely to be white and/or middle-class than citizens seeking services. An array of obstacles preventing engagement and understanding is likely to emerge. This represents a particularly fertile area for growth and innovation.

Growth and innovation can only occur, however, if such tensions are recognized and addressed. Efforts to engage the community must originate with the agency. If the racial makeup of the agency's labor force is substantially different from that of the surrounding community, efforts must be made to reduce the difference. Recruitment efforts must emphasize the hiring of African-American and Hispanic workers. Equally important, a certain flexibility must be incorporated into the hiring practices of generative social service agencies so that poor, relatively uneducated members of the community (often former clients) can be hired for certain jobs. The contributions of such staff to reframing perceptions of experience, establishing new connections to the community, and heightening the level of practitioner commitment can be substantial. However, the gaps in the expertise of community people will also be substantial. A particular dilemma for the agency is the extent to which it can hire uncredentialed community people without trading off expertise that is critical to the generative service experience. This tension can be addressed partially in the short-run and more comprehensively over the longer haul through various kinds of training.

An agency's relationship to the community is also influenced by its decision-making structure. The surrounding community will be disconnected from an agency that unilaterally determines operational or policy directions. In general, the greater its participation in such decision making, the more likely the community will feel a part of the agency. The agency, however, frequently may need or want to minimize such participation in situations that are either particularly critical or require rapid response. For the agency, the dilemma is how to retain a capacity for certain independent decision making while working with the community to establish significant areas of participation. The demarcation, however, between exclusively agency and shared areas of decision making will not always be clear and consequently represents an ongoing area of tension that will require constant monitoring.

It is equally important not to romanticize the communities in which agencies work. Long-term disenfranchisement, ancient power struggles over turf, and the personal political ambitions of various individuals are no less common in poor communities than elsewhere. The dilemma associated with remaining open to positive expressions of community input yet necessarily resistant to anyone's attempt to dominate and control decision making is of critical importance to generative service agencies.

The larger social order has also been an especially important incubator for dilemmas faced by social service agencies. Clearly, the distribution of scarce resources has profoundly influenced agency development. The impact of budget decisions on the content of social services has never been more apparent than during the past two decades. The ascent of industrial social services has been propelled by resource deficit. The deepening fiscal crisis of the state has especially troubling implications for the development of generative social services. The generative service structure's emphasis on learning, growth, and innovation will, for instance, require lower case loads. This reduction can only be implemented by some combination of more limited citizen access to services and/or increased staff. Diminished access to service, however, will erode a generative service agency's capacity to engage in a process of community building. Alternatively, in a period of deepening deficit government is not likely to increase the cohort of staff available to social service agencies. Equally important, the destabilizing effect of resource contraction on poor communities may compel generative service agencies to take greater risks in challenging the allocation decisions of government. By engaging in such struggle, however, the agency heightens its risk of losing critical sources of revenue. In effect, the central community-building function of generative social services may (particularly in a period of resource deficit) undermine its longer-term prospects for survival. The tension between resource scarcity or deficit and the wide-scale implementation of a generative approach to social services will not abate.

In fact, as the present fiscal crisis deepens, at least one substantial current within society will demand more industrialized and cheaper forms of social service. More specifically, in a climate of reaction dominated by the Right, experimentation and reform are likely to be limited to the mechanization and privatization of various features of the welfare state.

A countervailing tendency also has the potential to emerge in this climate. Ineffective industrial responses to intensifying social problems may contribute to the formation of a new social movement. The movement's principal intention to redistribute surplus value (to build more housing, provide additional health care, etc.) will intensify class tensions. These tensions will be particularly taut in a period of resource deficit. Only in the context of such ferment and dialogue will generative approaches to social services be considered. The struggle for quality services must originate with groups that most immediately stand to benefit from such a commitment. Clearly, the initial nucleus of such a struggle must include citizens of poorer communities and service providers.

The danger, however, is that movement pressure will be exclusively directed at the most concrete and visible expressions of need (such as housing). This tendency is understandable. It is also historically consistent. Such a focus would continue to neglect the more subtle, qualitative dimensions of need being experienced by both poor communities and individuals. This reflexive response would ultimately be self-defeating.

Generative approaches to social service are in tension with at least the following tendencies in the larger social order: (a) deepening deficit; (b) ideological, often class-based commitment to cheaper, more industrialized forms of service; and (c) a social movement's initial, often exclusive, attention to the most concrete areas of communal or individual need. Clearly, any effort to implement more generative or qualitative forms of service will face substantial dilemmas and struggle. However, struggle toward such a formulation is not automatic. If countervailing forces within poorer communities, service agencies, social movements, and other sectors of the social order do not perceive the importance of such a structure, this focused struggle is unlikely to occur. The choice to further develop industrial models of service or to experiment with alternative generative forms of service is a critical policy decision. Embedded in this choice are distinctive assumptions about the future of poorer communities and the larger social order. A tacit commitment to either approach involves certain inherent trade-offs. A more specific discussion of the policy trade-offs associated with industrial or generative forms of service follows.

What Is at Stake

Dilemma and struggle are central to the development and provision of all social services. Consequently, it is not the existence of struggle that is at stake in a choice between generative and industrial forms of social services, but its direction. In general, a choice must be made between the maintenance of an increasingly dysfunctional, relatively inexpensive structure that over time contributes to spiraling social costs (industrial services), and the development of more experimental, initially expensive, approaches that have the potential to invent long-term cost-effective responses to individual and communal need.

The industrial service structure has very limited potential. It is principally organized to move more and more citizens through the service process at ever-increasing speed. The intensifying press for movement is propelled by cost-containment policies (resource scarcity) and an increased emphasis on concrete, discrete indices of output to measure productivity. Over time, within this industrial structure, the processing of agency needs more frequently displaces a conflicting intention or objective to meet citizen need. This displacement assures a certain failure of social services. As social services are restructured to meet industrial requirements, they are less likely to address basic generative needs of workers and citizens. As its basic functioning and quality of life deteriorates, the agency increasingly withdraws to an ever more narrow and controllable definition of social services. This structural shift carries an illusion of control through concrete measures and an emphasis upon aggregated output as well as worker productivity. The result is a devaluation of the complex and often overwhelming realities of community need and strength.

This apparent organizational breakdown, however, is part of a broader social dynamic and set of contradictions. Only through this wider lens can the trade-offs associated with industrial forms of service be understood. The industrial service organization's narrow quantitative response to communal and individual need is driven by a particular set of social priorities. It is one of the more subtle, yet particularly powerful instruments expected to produce short-term savings for the welfare state. More intensified industrial forms of social services, budget cutting, and heightened access costs for clients are but a few of the cost-saving devices that became increasingly popular in the 1980s. The fiscal crisis has provoked an increasingly unbalanced policy response. The short-term savings gained by cost-cutting and containment strategies have marginally supported short-term capital accumulation in the larger economy. Theoretically, these savings can be used more productively in the private sector. Equally important, the redirection of such capital in the early 1980s was expected to bolster an unstable economy.

The costs of these policies, however, have not received as much attention as the short-term benefits. An initially hidden, but increasingly visible, consequence of social policies primarily intended to cut or contain budgets is that substantial numbers of working-class and poor people are being defined as expendable. The mounting emotional and concrete problems of poor and working-class people can in part be traced to such policy making. These conditions are further reinforced by the service agency's systematic neglect of the intensifying breakdowns among poor and working-class citizens. Fundamentally, service agencies are sacrificing both their legitimacy and social reproduction functions for short-term savings. This is a profound trade-off because in the absence of other interventions, it must be expected that the social costs associated with this choice will spiral upward. The social order, for instance, will either directly or indirectly have to absorb the costs of undereducated youngsters unprepared to enter the labor market, homeless families living in shelters for years, and the many isolated families engaged in various kinds of abusive behavior. Increased community violence, expansive prison populations, and labor market shortages represent only a part of the price tag of such neglect.

Most fundamentally, a policy principally attending to budget containment is in rapid retreat from persistent and complex social problems. Such a choice accepts as a given that poorer communities will be increasingly unstable and detached from the labor market. Efforts will be made to placate and control, but not to seriously address needs. Such an approach assumes that the increased frequency of breakdown in these communities can be isolated and controlled. This strain of social epidemic, however, will not be so easily contained. Over time it will diminish the quality of life in larger numbers of communities. The costs of short-term savings and long-term surrender will be high. More to the point, such a choice is in fundamental tension with the long-term health and survival of the social order.

There is another choice. A strategy with the potential to address the generative and concrete needs of poor communities can be developed. Such an initiative, however, demands a certain level of systemwide social tension. Historically, the interests of poorer communities have only been advanced through welfare state reform when strong social movements aggressively advocated for change. The social reforms of the 1930s and 1960s, for instance, can be traced to the strength of social movements representing the interests of working-class and disenfranchised citizens. The emergence of such movements is especially important if resources are to be redirected to meet human needs in a period of intensifying budget deficit. Another predicate to such change is that policymakers incorporate longer-term calculations of social or economic benefits and costs into their policy decisions. Only in this way can the relative strengths and weaknesses of generative and industrial social service strategies be assessed.

A second choice is for the social order to invest in the generative potential of poor and working-class communities. A certain tolerance must be cultivated for this less precise service process steeped in confusion, learning, and invention. Such a climate is essential if social services are to have any hope of addressing the generative needs of citizens and workers. Only through such a reconstituted process and struggle can the service agency help to advance the interests of poor and working-class people. The personal, communal, and social dimensions of need are incorporated into this approach. The latter variable is especially important because it stimulates the agency to support the broader reform movement's efforts to confront the social context of communal breakdown. More specifically, this dimension of generative services recognizes and responds to the critical impact of scarce resources on the quality of community life.

At its core, the generative service experience is intended to support the struggle of workers and citizens to improve the quality of their lives. To a great extent, such support for struggle and change has always represented the best hope of social services. It is apparent that service agencies cannot independently address the many needs of poor citizens and their communities. Clearly, such an effort will need to be more broad based and draw on other social resources such as churches, social movements, and kinship networks. However, service agencies must be key participants in any overarching strategy intended to attend to growing social need.

Generative social service has the potential to make citizens and workers stakeholders in a change process. This kind of investment is critically associated with opportunities to honestly name problems and struggle to effect change. The potential of this process also rests with the opportunity for service workers and citizens seeking services to take greater control of their lives by initiating and not simply reacting to change. It is through such engagement at the practice level (to processes of social reproduction) that the client, worker, and agency begin to make connections to larger struggles within the welfare state. As new tensions emerge and expanded possibilities for collaborative relationships are established, the ability of workers and clients to affect the accumulation–legitimation functions of the welfare state increases. This process is guided by the interaction among worker–client relations, agency need, and coalitional efforts. These conditions tightly fasten the "politics of social services" to daily work experiences.

Clearly, neither industrial nor generative services are likely to be implemented in a pure form. These approaches are archetypes that reflect broader currents within the welfare state. This is not a question of purity, but of emphasis. The increased dominance of industrial approaches must be corrected if service agencies are to have any hope of arresting the erosion of their legitimacy and abating community decline. A profound shift must be made, then, from industrial to generative forms of service. Only in this way can services have the potential to address and resolve the difficult social problems we face at the dawn of the twenty-first century.

References

Burghardt, Steve. *The Other Side of Organizing.* Cambridge, MA: Schenkman, 1982.

Comer, James. *School Power.* New York: The Free Press, 1980.

Fabricant, Michael. "The Industrialization of Social Work Practice." *Social Work* (September 1985).

Fisher, Jacob. *The Response of Social Work to the Depression.* Cambridge, MA: Schenkman, 1980.

Friere, Paolo. *Pedagogy of the Oppressed.* New York: Herder & Herder, 1970.

Karasek, Robert, and Tores Theorell. *Healthy Work: Stress, Productivity and the Reconstruction of Working Life.* New York: Basic Books, 1990.

Kinney, Jill. "Questions Commonly Asked about the Homebuilders Program." Unpublished paper. Washington, DC, 1988.

Kinney, Jill, David Haapala, Charlotte Booth, and Sidney Levitt. "The Homebuilders' Model." In James Whittaker, Jill Kinney, Elizabeth Tracy, and Charlotte Booth, eds., *Reaching High Risk Families.* New York: Aldine deGruyter, 1990.

Lipsky, Michael. *Street-Level Bureaucracy: Dilemmas of the Individual in Public Services.* New York: Russell Sage, 1980.

Lubove, Roy. *The Professional Altruist.* New York: Athenum, 1973.

Montgomery, David. *Worker Control in America: Studies in the History of Work Technology and Labor Struggles.* New York: Cambridge University Press, 1979.

Morgan, Gareth. *Images of Organization.* Beverly Hills, CA: Sage, 1986.

Riccio, James, Barbara Goldman, Gayle Hamilton, Karin Martinson, and Alan Orenstein. *GAIN: Early Implementation Experiences and Lessons.* New York: M.D.R.C., 1989.

Schön, Donald. *The Reflective Practitioner: How Professionals Think in Action.* New York: Basic Books, 1983.

Schorr, Lisbeth B., and Daniel Schorr. *Within Our Reach: Breaking the Cycle of Disadvantage.* New York: Anchor, 1989.

Wood, Gale Goldberg, and Ruth Middleman. *The Structural Approach to Direct Practice in Social Work.* New York: Columbia University Press, 1989.

Index